The People of
Three Mile Island

Middletown, July 19, 1979

The People of
Three Mile Island

Interviews and photographs by
Robert Del Tredici

Sierra Club Books   San Francisco

The Sierra Club, founded in 1892 by John Muir, has devoted itself to the study and protection of the earth's scenic and ecological resources—mountains, wetlands, woodlands, wild shores and rivers, deserts and plains. The publishing program of the Sierra Club offers books to the public as a nonprofit educational service in the hope that they may enlarge the public's understanding of the Club's basic concerns. The point of view expressed in each book, however, does not necessarily represent that of the Club. The Sierra Club has some fifty chapters coast to coast, in Canada, Hawaii, and Alaska. For information about how you may participate in its programs to preserve wilderness and the quality of life, please address inquiries to:

Sierra Club
530 Bush Street
San Francisco, California 94108.

Printed in the United States of America

10 9 8 7 6 5 4 3 2 1

For Leslie, who kept the fires crackling at critical points

Most especially to Al Higbee for technical assistance in tape recording the majority of the interviews and for his invaluable companionship throughout. To Sidney Peterson, who crystallized my inspiration; and to Danny Moses, who guided the project to a safe conclusion. To Carl Oblinger for helping me, early, to arrive at an overview; to Martha Lester, who gave me a lot of good leads; and to the Bretz family for putting me up and driving me around. To Mary Ann Yensan, Miriam Silverman, and Susan Barley for their timely help and encouragement; and to David Rahn, who made most of the photographic prints for this edition.

Library of Congress Cataloging in Publication Data

Del Tredici, Robert.
  The people of Three Mile Island.
  1. Three Mile Island Nuclear Power Plant, Pa. 2. Atomic power-plants—Pennsylvania—Harrisburg—Accidents.
I. Title.
TK1345.H37D44   974.8'18   80-13558
ISBN 0-87156-237-5

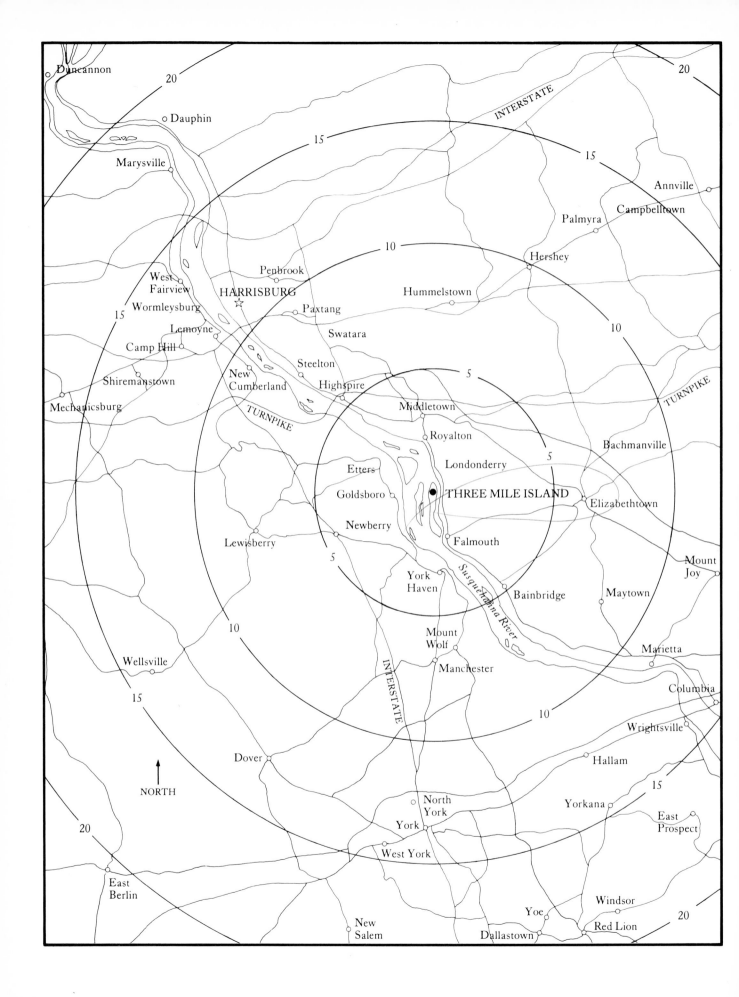

The Interviews

The Accident: A Chronology

The accident generated everything in this book. Setting down at this point what happened, why it happened, how it played itself out, and the repercussions it had in the surrounding communities will clarify references made in interviews to follow. This particular chronology was culled from a dozen local, state, and national news treatments of the event, as well as from Metropolitan Edison logs, NRC documents, testimony before the President's commission on Three Mile Island, and from off-the-record conversations with plant personnel.

Three Mile Island Unit Two began commercial operation—that is, its core supported a controlled chain reaction for the first time—on March 28, 1978. Unit Two (like Unit One) is a pressurized water reactor that produces electricity by boiling water into steam that propels the blades of a turbine generator. The source of heat for turning water to steam is the chain-reaction fissioning of uranium fuel in the reactor core (1). The core, immersed in water, is enclosed in a pressure vessel forty feet tall with eight-inch-thick steel walls. The water surrounding, or covering, the core is called "primary coolant." It is radioactive and is meant never to leave its closed system of pipes (called the "primary loop," and shaded in the diagram) where intense pressure is maintained so that the water can become ultra-hot (575° F.) without boiling. Pressure is regulated in this system by means of a cushion of steam in a pressurizer vessel which is above and beside the reactor vessel (4); the steam cushion equalizes the varying pressures in the primary loop. Heat from the fissioning fuel is removed by the primary coolant as it is rapidly pumped from the core through the primary loop to the steam generator (2) in the boiler region. There the primary coolant transfers some of its heat (but none of its liquid) to "clean," cooler water that circulates in a secondary system. This secondary water is not under such high pressure, and it quickly turns to steam that propels the blades of a turbine (5), which drives an electrical generator.

Next the steam in the secondary system is cooled in a condenser, becomes water again, and is pumped back into the boiler region, where it once more draws heat away from the primary coolant and turns to steam. The secondary loop of pipes, which feeds the cool water back into the boiler region is called the "feedwater" circuit (6); it is here that the troubles began.

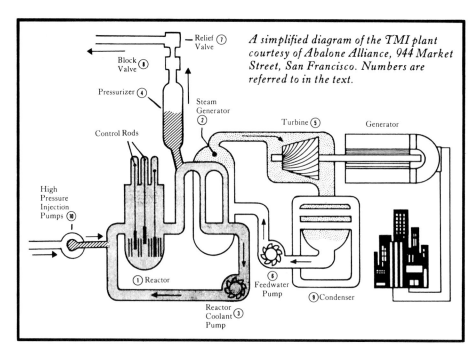

A simplified diagram of the TMI plant courtesy of Abalone Alliance, 944 Market Street, San Francisco. Numbers are referred to in the text.

Day 1: Wednesday, March 28, 1979

4:00:37 A.M. The plant is operating at 97 percent maximum power. Two pumps that feed water through the secondary loop back to the steam generator in the boiler region shut down because a water leak into an air line causes valves to close (2). Water in the secondary cooling system stops flowing.

4:00:41 A.M. The steam turbine that generates electricity (5) shuts down automatically, releasing its steam into the outside atmosphere with a loud roar. This steam is not radioactive. Immediately the secondary pipes in contact with the primary loop boiler start to boil dry. This prevents the primary coolant from transferring its intense heat away from the core. The primary coolant begins to come to a boil, dangerously increasing pressure in the primary loop and in the reactor vessel. A safety valve in the primary loop—the pressurizer relief valve (7)—automatically pops open, releasing radioactive steam and water. Pressure in the primary loop is thus kept from reaching a level that will rupture its pipes in a deadly primary coolant steam explosion. The radioactive steam and water escaping through the relief valve collect safely in the reactor-coolant drain tank designed for this purpose. This relief valve should close after thirteen seconds. Instead it will stick and remain open for more than two hours without anyone knowing—with awesome consequences. Right now, because of continued overheating, pressure is still on the rise.

4:00:47 A.M. Control rods automatically descend into the core, meshing with the fuel bundles to halt the fission chain reaction.

Unstable atomic fragments in the core unavoidably generate an intense "decay heat" that cannot be shut off. This is normal. But if this heat is not removed it can cause a core meltdown.

4:01:17 A.M. Three emergency back-up feedwater pumps (6) automatically kick on to supply new water to the secondary cooling loop so that the now hot and dry pipes around the boiler vessel will fill with coolant. The pumps are running, and operators assume they are moving water. But the water the pumps are meant to move has been cut off from the boiler region because two "block valves" have been manually shut. Red tags that no one notices on the control-room console indicate that these valves have been closed for testing and maintenance procedures for the past two weeks. One of the strictest directives of the NRC requires that a nuclear plant be shut down if even one of these valves is closed for more than 72 hours.

4:02:47 A.M. The emergency core coolant system automatically activates to pump new water at the rate of 1,000 gallons a minute into the increasingly hot reactor core. However, operators think the core is already full of water. The truth is, the core is undergoing a loss-of-coolant accident never described in the operator manuals: loss of coolant through the pressurizer above and beside the reactor vessel. Operators assume the relief valve is closed because the light on the control panel tells them electrical power to the relief valve solenoid has been cut off. The actual position of the valve is not programmed to be indicated on the control console. It will be two hours and twenty minutes before operators realize the difference between what the light implies and what the valve is doing. There are also other warning systems that could have told operators the valve was stuck open—alarms on temperature and pressure gauges in the reactor-coolant drain tank. One such alarm is visual, a set of lights that goes unnoticed because it is situated on a panel far from the main console and faces away from the operator, so it can not be seen from the central console. There is also an audible alarm for the drain tank; this alarm activates, but its audio signal sounds like many of the other alarms and is not singled out from among

While the valve sticks open, the plant will be experiencing, without operators knowing it, an uncovered core (whose temperature climbs 40° F. per second towards the 5000° F. meltdown point), severe fuel damage, hydrogen gas generation, a vapor-bound coolant system, and a quarter of a million gallons of radioactive primary coolant on the reactor-building floor.

4:06:37 A.M. Control-room operators see from their indicators that pressure is high in the primary loop. To them, this means the system is filling completely with water— "going solid"—a state to be avoided at all costs. They know that if they lose the steam cushion in the pressurizer, further increases in pressure (from more heat) could rupture the primary-coolant pipes. So they override the emergency core-coolant system and shut off first one pump, then, at 4:12:30 A.M., half the power of another. The override deprives the reactor of a crucial defense against overheating. What operators have not realized is that the high pressure readings are from the pressurizer, not the reactor vessel; the primary loop's boiling coolant has created steam pockets that are now forcing the primary coolant up into the pressurizer. In this reactor—as in nearly all American reactors—there is no instrument designed to measure directly the depth of water around the fuel rods. (The Crystal River nuclear plant in Florida installed such an instrument as a result of this accident.

4:08:30 A.M. An operator sees red tags on valve controls and realizes that for the past eight minutes no feedwater has reached the boiler region. These valves are opened; the secondary-loop pipes in the boiler fill with coolant and begin drawing heat from the primary loop.

4:14 A.M. The stuck-open pressurizer relief valve has been releasing primary-coolant steam and water into the reactor drain tank at the rate of 220 gallons per minute. Now a rupture disc on the drain tank bursts, and radioactive primary coolant starts spilling onto the floor of the containment building. When this water reaches a depth of two feet, the reactor sump pump automatically kicks on, moving primary coolant into the auxiliary building.

4:38 A.M. Auxiliary-building operators report that radioactive water is being pumped into the building. About 8,000 gallons of this primary coolant are in the auxiliary-building sump tank. Operators terminate the transfer of primary coolant. Radioactive steam and gases from this water pass into the atmosphere through the auxiliary building vent stack.

4:55 A.M. Indicators continue to show an increasing average count-rate of neutron activity in the core, with increasing amplitudes of oscillation. This indicates either that the chain reaction is restarting in the core—but the control rods are fully in place to prevent any chain reaction—or that the core is boiling dry—but operators still think the core is covered with water.

5:13 A.M. Severe vibrations are noted in two sets of reactor cooling pumps that control the flow of water around the core (3). No one understands that these vibrations are caused by pockets of steam—from the boiling primary coolant—that are caught in the pumps. Operators shut off one set of pumps to save them.

5:41 A.M. The last set of reactor-coolant pumps is shut down, to save them. Some steam pockets merge to form a vapor lock in the pipes that blocks the normal circulation of coolant through the system. The reactor's entire cooling system has thus been brought to a standstill, and it is now—between 5:14 and 6:18—that severe core damage occurs. The twelve-foot fuel bundles are more than half uncovered. Zirconium fuel cladding around the uranium pellets disintegrates in the intense heat, and the rupture spills fission products into the primary coolant, which is itself spilling onto the floor. Potentially explosive, noncondensible hydrogen gas begins to form above the fuel rods. Parts of the core sag. Radioactive gases from the coolant, along with hydrogen gas, exit from the stuck-open relief valve and begin collecting, undetected, inside the huge containment building. Temperature-reading devices at the top of the core register as high as 750° F.; then the computer starts printing out rows of question marks instead of numbers, which it will continue to do for the next eight hours. Operators still think the core is covered with water.

6:18 A.M. Brian Mehler concludes that the pressurizer relief valve must be stuck open and orders the emergency block valve (8) below it to be closed. Had this valve stayed open another 30 to 60 minutes, "an eventual core meltdown probably would have occurred," according to the NRC's Rogovin Report. In the report, the consequences of this valve's having stayed open for two hours and twenty minutes, the loss-of-coolant accident, are not taken into account.

6:35 A.M. The reactor building's high-range gamma-monitor alert alarm goes off. It is unnoticed.

6:40 A.M. Technicians obtain a primary-coolant sample from the drain line that leads from the containment building to the auxiliary building; the sample shows 350 times greater radioactivity than normal. This indicates severe core damage. The coolant has begun coming up out of the floor drains in the auxiliary building via the containment let-down system. Gases from it escape to the atmosphere through the ventilation system in the auxiliary building.

6:48:08 A.M. The control room's Utility Typer, which has been printing out alarm-status data, is now running an hour and three-quarters behind. An operator actuates the "alarm suppress function," dumping print-out memory for the period from 5:13:39 to 6:48:08 in order to start current alarm print-out. Data from dumped alarm-status memory is not retrievable.

6:50 A.M. The high-pitched alarm of the radiation monitoring system goes off in the containment building and in the auxiliary building. A "site emergency" is declared. Calculation of the radiation exposure in nearby Goldsboro is initiated.

7:02 A.M. The Pennsylvania Emergency Management Agency and the Dauphin County Civil Defense are notified.

7:10 A.M. The calculation of radiation exposure in Goldsboro is completed, projecting a whole-body exposure rate of 40 millirems per hour.

7:24 A.M. After looking at a containment-dome monitor reading of more than 8 rems per hour of high-range gamma radiation, the station manager declares a "general emergency"—for the first time in the history of commercial nuclear power. This designation heralds danger owing to off-site radiation. The governor's office is notified.

7:30–7:40 A.M. A unit vent gas monitor indicates releases more than 100 times greater than the normal release limit.

7:45 A.M. A central portion of the core collapses. This goes unnoticed.

7:50 A.M. Communication is first established with NRC headquarters.

8:00 A.M. A roving traffic reporter picks up on his CB radio a state-police call referring to the emergency. He calls in the tip to his station, WKBO Radio Harrisburg, which scoops the story in a bulletin on the 8:25 newsbreak.

8:00–8:30 A.M. Ivan Porter, an engineer, takes a series of fifty-one temperature readings, nine of which indicate that spots within the core are hotter than 2000° F.

8:43 A.M. A sample of primary coolant is collected—without the appropriate precautions. Because the sample is brought into the primary chemistry laboratory, airborne radioactivity levels there rise dramatically, and it is evacuated. These levels also disable the Unit One counting room, which contains the only instrument on the site capable of performing gamma isotopic analysis.

8:45 A.M. Mayor Reid of Middletown is notified of the accident by a local official.

9:00 A.M. The NRC notifies the White House situations room. President Carter finds out fifteen minutes later.

9:02 A.M. An Associated Press bulletin reports that a general emergency has been declared, but that radiation has not been released to the environment.

9:30 A.M. Metropolitan Edison information officers release a statement to the press that "No off-site radiation has been found and we do not expect any." The press release contains no reference to the fact that a general emergency has been declared.

10:00 A.M. Met Ed says that radiation levels inside the reactor have been found to be ten times the normal level; the NRC says the levels are one thousand times higher than normal.

10:17 A.M. An air sample indicates high gross beta radioactivity; control-room personnel wear respirator masks for the next 6 hours.

10:38 A.M. The highest official off-site radiation reading of the day is recorded: 13 millirems per hour, near Kunkel School, 5.56 miles north-northwest of TMI.

11:10 A.M. Nonessential personnel are evacuated from the TMI site.

11:30 A.M. Operators have been having great difficulty transferring heat away from the core because noncondensible hydrogen gas voids (of which they are not yet aware) and steam voids in the lines are blocking the flow of water. For nearly three hours heat has been removed chiefly by opening and shutting the block valve beneath the pressurizer relief valve, which vents radioactive steam and gases into the containment building. This raises temperatures and pressures inside the structure and the gases are pushed into the auxiliary building through valves that should have automatically sealed shut, but did not. Result: more releases to the atmosphere.

1:51:21 P.M. A rapid rise and sudden decrease in the pressure within the containment building occurs. This results from a six- to eight-second burn of hydrogen gas that has been collecting in the building. The sudden high pressure triggers the building's sprinkler system, which unloads half its capacity before being shut off. A spike on a graph records the sudden high pressure. Operators, not realizing the core has become hot enough to generate hydrogen gas, decide the pressure spike is the result of malfunctioning instrumentation.

7:50 P.M. The high-pressure injection pumps (10) are restarted in spite of problems with steam and gas pockets. The reactor is put into a "forced cooling mode," and the first major phase of the accident comes to an end.

11:25 P.M. The highest recorded on-site reading outside the plant during the period of March 28 to 30 is measured at 365 millirems per hour, 1,000 feet northwest of the Unit Two station vent.

Day 2: Thursday, March 29, 1979

4:35 A.M. All during the night, coolant water has been injected into the core under high pressure, but temperatures in the reactor have failed to go down. The failure is due to gas and (still unrecognized) hydrogen pockets in the system. Operators decide to initiate a series of "burps" of this gas into waste-gas hold-up tanks in the auxiliary building. This is done through a pipe that leaks; thus radioactivity escapes, as before, into the auxiliary building exhaust system, and so into the atmosphere.

6:00 A.M. Thirty millirems of radiation per hour is measured in Goldsboro. Bursts of radiation keep coming from the plant; they are expected to continue.

10:00 A.M. Met Ed holds its first press conference, in the Aztec Room of the Hershey Motor Lodge. President Walter Kreitz says the radiation released has not been out of the "ordinary realm," and Vice President Jack Herbein tells the 120 reporters that

The NRC's five commissioners are briefed in Washington, D.C., by NRC staff from TMI, who say their knowledge of what happened is very limited, and that the accident appears to be over. The possibility of the core's having become uncovered is not brought up. After the meeting, NRC Chairman Joseph Hendrie briefs members of Congress, saying the accident is about over.

In the afternoon, the Pennsylvania Secretary of Health, Dr. MacLeod, receives a call from Dr. Robbins of HEW recommending evacuation of the area. MacLeod consults Henderson (Pennsylvania Emergency Management Agency), Gerusky (Bureau of Radiological Protection), and other state officials. Their consensus: Radiation levels do not warrant evacuation.

2:10 P.M. A helicopter measures 3,000 millirems of radiation per hour, 15 feet above the plant venting stack. Little progress has been made all day in cooling the reactor. Airborne radiation has made respirators a requirement on site.

4:15 P.M. A 100-milliliter sample of primary coolant gives off a dose rate of 1,000 rems per hour. Ten percent of the radioactive contents of the core is estimated to have been released into the coolant.

6:00 P.M. Met Ed is ordered to stop discharging low-level waste water into the Susquehanna (40,000 gallons have been released so far). Met Ed considers the discharge necessary to prevent an overflow of waste-water storage tanks. Later in the day permission is given to resume discharges.

10:30 P.M. NRC officials inform the governor that about 50 percent of the core is damaged. In the control room, some of the crew realize that a noncondensible hydrogen gas bubble has been forming.

Day 3: Friday, March 30, 1979

Because of extensive core damage, primary-coolant water now has in it radioactivity that is several orders of magnitude greater than normal, and this water has continued to circulate throughout the system. Radioactive gases held within the coolant water by the pressure in the primary loop are released when the water passes into the auxiliary building's makeup and purification tanks, which are at lower pressures. As these gases then collect in the makeup tank they create pressures that make it necessary for the gas to be transferred into waste-gas decay tanks for storage. In the transfer, the gases travel through a vent header that leaks. The auxiliary building exhaust system sends radioactive material into the environment. Operators know this is happening and cannot prevent it.

7:00 A.M. Rising pressure in the makeup tank leads operators to open its vent valve, as before; this time they decide to *leave* it open until the pressure is down to normal. This results in a large, continuous, "planned but uncontrolled" release.

8:01 A.M. A helicopter measures 1,200 millirems per hour in the plume 130 feet above the Unit Two vent stack.

8:34 A.M. The operator who authorized the release, fearing that the vent, when ordered closed, may fail to do so, calls the Pennsylvania Emergency Management Agency to alert it that an evacuation downwind from the plant *may* be necessary because of an "uncontrolled release." A PEMA official relays this message to its director Oran Henderson; he informs the lieutenant governor, who relays the message and the 1,200-millirem-per-hour reading to the governor.

8:45 A.M. Lake Barrett, whose job on the NRC technical staff is to assess radiological information, receives a message from NRC regional headquarters that the waste-gas storage tanks are full, and any additional gases will be released to the environment. The report is incorrect, but Barrett cannot know it at this time. Alarmed, he calculates that an off-site dose rate to an individual as a result of such releases would be about 1,200 millirems per hour.

9:00 A.M. Barrett briefs the NRC Executive Management Team. (Harold Denton is a member.) He tells them of his projected dose rate, and within fifteen seconds a call comes from the governor's office reporting a reading of "1,200 millirems per hour from one of the cooling towers." Panic ensues. No one realizes that the plume reading is different from the off-site dose projection. Denton tells a PEMA official to notify the state of Pennsylvania and recommend evacuation.

Henderson calls the lieutenant governor and also Kevin Molloy of Emergency Preparedness for Dauphin County, telling Molloy to expect an evacuation order from the governor within five minutes. Molloy immediately notifies all the fire departments within a ten-mile radius, and Civil Defense in the cities of York and Lancaster. He also calls emergency radio station WHB, which announces that there may be an evacuation.

10:00 A.M. A Harrisburg city employee sets off the Civil Defense air raid siren. It sounds for six minutes. The city panics.

10:10 A.M. Governor Thornburgh phones Commissioner Hendrie to find out if an evacuation is necessary. Hendrie says it is not, but recommends that people within a five-mile radius stay indoors, as there will be continuing emissions. Thornburgh asks Hendrie to send an NRC expert. The Pennsylvania National Guard is put on standby for a possible evacuation.

10:25 A.M. Over WHB, the governor's advice is that evacuation is not necessary, but that people within a ten-mile radius should stay indoors, close their windows, and turn off their air conditioning.

10:45 A.M. President Carter calls Hendrie for an update and asks him to recommend a senior official to send to TMI. Hendrie recommends Harold Denton.

11:00 A.M. Another release of radioactive gases is announced.

11:40 A.M. Hendrie calls Thornburgh and suggests that pregnant women and small children be evacuated.

11:45 A.M. Word of Wednesday's hydrogen burn in the containment building reaches NRC headquarters.

12:30 P.M. The governor announces at a press conference that pregnant women and preschool children should evacuate the area within a five-mile radius of the plant. He orders 23 schools in the area closed. Some 75,000 citizens begin to flee the area.

1:30 P.M. In the White House situations room, a briefing takes place about Hendrie's concern over the large hydrogen bubble in the reactor vessel.

2:00 P.M. Denton arrives at TMI with a staff of NRC experts. The hydrogen bubble is 1,000 cubic feet and growing larger, they are told, and may self-ignite in five to eight days. The bubble may also force coolant water away from the core, keeping it uncovered. That afternoon the NRC opens a new press center in Bethesda to give the media access to NRC briefings. During one such briefing, Dudley Thompson says the bubble

has made meltdown a possibility. News media seize upon the word, and deep panic breaks out everywhere the word spreads.

8:30 P.M. Denton briefs the governor on the extensive fuel damage and the hydrogen bubble. He tells him wholesale evacuation is not yet necessary.

9:30 P.M. Hendrie becomes increasingly concerned over the possibility of the hydrogen bubble's exploding as a result of oxygen forming in the system. He urges his staff to study radiolysis, the freeing of oxygen from water by intense radioactivity.

Day 4: Saturday, March 31, 1979

HEW, concerned about releases of radioactive iodine, has begun a search for large quantities of potassium iodide, which, though not an antidote, when taken internally prevents radioactive iodine from lodging in the thyroid gland.

3:05 A.M. A chemical company in St. Louis, a pharmaceutical company in Detroit, and a bottle-dropper manufacturer in New Jersey agree to work around the clock to provide a quarter of a million half-ounce bottles of potassium iodide.

4:00 A.M. Radiation continues to be released from the plant. The NRC forms a "Bubble Squad," which surmises that the ratio of hydrogen and oxygen is slowly approaching the flammability and detonation point. For the moment, precautionary wholesale evacuation has been ruled out. The Bubble Squad decides to siphon the hydrogen into a recombining chamber, where it is turned into water. But the recombiner is in the auxiliary building, now an area of high radiation. Workmen must isolate it and build a wall around it with lead bricks, seventy tons of which have been flown in for this purpose.

11:00 A.M. Met Ed holds its last press conference. Denton will now take charge of giving information on plant status. Herbein states that the bubble has decreased by two-thirds its size overnight. He says he feels the crisis is over.

12:00 noon. Denton disagrees with Herbein, saying the crisis is not yet over. He later tells the governor that the bubble is growing, as is its oxygen content.

2:45 P.M. Hendrie, in a Bethesda press conference, says that forcing the hydrogen out of the reactor might cause it to explode; he advises a precautionary evacuation of the area 10 to 20 miles downwind of the plant. Many more people begin to flee. Thornburgh phones Hendrie; they discuss the impact of Hendrie's pronouncement. Thornburgh announces that he does not believe a mass evacuation is warranted.

8:27 P.M. The Associated Press runs an "urgent" story on its wire: The bubble may explode at any minute.

10:10 P.M. Denton briefs Thornburgh in his office, telling of a 10 percent decrease in bubble size. Their conversation is interrupted by a call from the White House: President Carter will visit the area Sunday.

11:00 P.M. Denton and Thornburgh hold a press conference. Thornburgh says "there is no imminent catastrophic event foreseeable," and he asks Pennsylvanians to "display an appropriate degree of calm and resolve and patience." By late Saturday, thirty of the nation's experts on nuclear technology have arrived in the area, forming an Industry Advisory Group to tackle the crisis. Ninety percent of Goldsboro's population is now gone; reporters outnumber inhabitants. Hendrie's radiolysis group announces its conclusions: The bubble could be as much as 5 percent oxygen before being flammable and as much as 11 percent oxygen before detonating. A "worst case" assessment is that oxygen is being produced at the rate of 1 percent per day and that the oxygen concentration has already reached the 5 percent flammability limit. The bubble could become explosive in 6 to 7 days. The NRC group does not agree with these conclusions. The two groups are not sure what to tell the president.

Sunday, April 1, 1979

1:00 P.M. The president arrives and is briefed in Middletown by Denton and Stello on the bubble's potential for explosion and the conflicting conclusions about it.

1:45 P.M. The president, Mrs. Carter, Denton, and Thornburgh spend ten minutes in the Unit Two control room. They wear protective boots.

2:00 P.M. Carter and Thornburgh address the people of Middletown. Carter says the reactor is stable but that the governor may ask for a precautionary evacuation. If he does, Carter asks that people carry out instructions "calmly and exactly." He promises a presidential-commission inquiry into the accident.

3:00 P.M. The NRC's radiolysis group concludes that the bubble is "not going to boom." By midafternoon the bubble begins to disappear, and Hendrie is convinced there will be no explosion. It is learned that oxygen is not evolved by radiolysis in a hydrogen-rich environment. Met Ed's efforts to degas the system are meeting with success.

Wednesday, April 4, 1979

Governor Thornburgh appears on the "Today Show" and declares an end to the threat of immediate catastrophe.

Monday, April 9, 1979

The NRC commissioners vote to recommend lifting all advisories. The governor does so.

1.

William Whittock, retired civil engineer, the first eyewitness to the accident. Goldsboro, July 3, 1979

What happened? Well, I was sleeping about four o'clock in the morning, the twenty-eighth of March. And the thing erupted. It was dark. But they have the area floodlighted over there, all night. Floodlighted all the time every night. Power means nothing to them at all, I'll tell you that.

I sat up in bed, and I went to the window. I could see it spurting up. The steam was escaping and rolling and going up in the air —not from the towers, but from the containment room of Unit Two. It went up as far as the towers. It was a jet of steam. It went up like a plume. It was narrow when it started, and when it went up it expanded until it was half the width of the towers as it went out over the top. And roaring. That was a terrible roar. It sounded like a big jet taking off. It was built right into the thing. It'd done that several times before, maybe half a dozen. I thought, well, this is just another time Old Limpy's gone off over there again! I went back to bed.

But five minutes later it popped off again! Only this time it was for a long time, it kept blowing almost five minutes. Gradually it decreased, and then it stopped. I went back to sleep.

In the morning, about seven o'clock, the local broadcaster said on the radio that there had been a release of radioactivity.

About nine o'clock I went up to get the mail, and I noticed a metallic taste in my mouth. I stopped in at the George Marina and I asked Mr. George if he noticed any taste in his mouth. And he said, yes, he did. Then there was a young fellow on a tractor, and he also noticed this metallic taste. Then someone came running over and said there was a helicopter landing up here on the other side of the railroad. I thought it was the state police. I went up there, and it was an NBC-TV crew. They asked me how to get to where they could see the towers, and I took them down in my bus. I told them I'd seen it go off, and they asked for an interview. Later on I was on national TV all over the country.

I guess I was the first witness of it, though I'm sure others must have heard it go off, but the first eyewitness, at least from this side of the river.

We definitely have some effects. And we mostly notice it in the trees.

Crisis: Official Confusion

These transcripts are taken and edited from tapes of the Friday morning, March 30, 1979, closed meeting in Washington, D.C., of the NRC commissioners, who met in continuous session for the duration of the Three Mile Island accident. These transcripts do not represent formal commission statements on the matters discussed herein, nor have they been reviewed or edited by the commission.

Mr. Fouchard: This is Joe, Mr. Chairman, I just had a call from my guy in the governor's office, and he says the governor says the information he is getting from the plant is ambiguous, that he needs some recommendations from the NRC.

Mr. Denton: It is really difficult to get the data. We seem to get it after the fact. They opened the valves this morning, or the letdown, and were releasing at a 6-curie per second rate before anyone knew about it. By the time we got fully up to speed, apparently they had stopped, there was a possible release on the order of an hour or an hour and a half—

Commissioner Gilinsky: This is from the containment.

Mr. Denton: Well, it was coolant from the containment, apparently it got released into the radwaste or the auxiliary building and was vented out through the normal release point. We calculate doses of 170 millirems per hour at one mile, about half that at two miles and at five miles about 17. Apparently it's stopped now, though I'd say there is a puff-release cloud going in the northeast direction, and we'll just have to see. We did advise the state police to evacuate out to five miles, but whether that has really gotten pulled off, we'll just have to—

Chairman Hendrie: For a puff release, what you have got is an oblong plume headed out. Harold, where is it now, would you guess, if we go ahead and suggest to the governor that the evacuation in that direction out to five miles be carried out, is it going to be after the fact of the passage of the cloud?

Mr. Denton: Well, if they haven't gotten it cranked up, it might well be after passage. There are people living fairly close to the northeast direction. I guess the plume has already passed there.

Commissioner Gilinsky: What is the wind speed, do you have any idea?

Mr. Denton: We are trying to establish that.

Commissioner Gilinsky: And when was the puff released?

Mr. Denton: Within the last two hours.

Commissioner Gilinsky: Last couple of hours?

Chairman Hendrie: Presumably it has just terminated recently then.

Mr. Denton: We don't know how long, but if it was a continuous release over a period of an hour or an hour and a half which, from what I understand, is a kind of a lot of puff.

Commissioner Gilinsky: So even with a modest wind.

Chairman Hendrie: A couple of knot wind and the damned thing—the head edge of it is already past the five-mile line.

Commissioner Kennedy: Harold, has anybody checked the rest of the meteorology? It seems to me the weather map suggests that if it isn't already, it is going to be raining there shortly.

Mr. Denton: I don't have the weather report handy.

Commissioner Kennedy: Somebody ought to go get it.

Mr. Denton: Yes, I think the important thing for evacuation is to get ahead of the plume, to get a start, rather than sitting here waiting to decide. Even if we can't minimize the individual dose, there might still be a chance to limit the population dose.

. . .

Mr. Denton: But the people at the site are much better prepared to direct and run emergency plans than we are, and I would hope the plant people and our own people are really monitoring what is going on in there and acting on it from moment to moment. Our number really was a factor of 60 ratio and from some limited plant data. It just seems like we are always second-, third-hand, second guessing them. We almost ought to consider the chairman talking to the owner of the shop up there and get somebody from the company who is going to inform us about these things in advance if he can and then what he is doing about it if he can't. We seem not to have that contact.

Commissioner Gilinsky: It seems to me we better think about getting better data.

Mr. Fouchard: Well, the governor is waiting on it, and, Mr. Chairman, I think you should call Governor Thornburgh and tell him what we know. I don't know whether you are prepared at the present time to make a commission recommendation or not. The civil defense people up there say that our state programs people have advised evacuation out to five miles in the direction of the plume.

Commissioner Gilinsky: Well, one thing we have got to do is get better data. Get a link established with that helicopter to make sure that from now on we get reasonable data quickly.

Mr. Fouchard: But it does seem to me you have to make a judgment promptly.

Commissioner Gilinsky: Well, that's right, but it also doesn't look like this thing is going to be over with that judgment call.

Mr. Denton: It just seems to be we are going to have to operate on the basis that primary coolant has very high dissolved gas levels; it's a five-day half-life, and it is going to persist like this for a long time until they really get to a situation where they don't have to get any of the primary coolants out of the containment area. I sure wish I had better data.

Chairman Hendrie: Yes. Your current link out to the site is just not operating, or what is the situation? Who are you talking to out there, and is there an open line out there?

Mr. Denton: I'm not sure. Let me ask. What is our line on the site?

We talk to our guy in the control room who bends over and asks the questions while we are talking to him and gets back on the phone. So do we have our people in the control room who search out the answers. But with regard to any actual or hard numbers for release rate, curies, quantities, doses off-site, that process seems to take hours.

Mr. Fouchard: Don't you think as a precautionary measure there should be some evacuation?

. . .

Chairman Hendrie: It would certainly be helpful if Vollmer could find the senior company officer present and stay fairly close to him and then report regularly back to us. They could have advance notice of the steps that they take from time to time, so we don't go through yesterday's flap on the sewerage; and, furthermore, so if we are going to have to have another transfer of water out of the primary for some reason that we (a) understand that it is necessary, and (b) can go ahead and get the people out of the way in advance.

Mr. Denton: Well, people who go up there fall into a morass, it seems like they are never heard from. It seems like you might want to consider having something like rotating shifts through senior people there in the control room or in a room off the control room that we could communicate with about these kinds of things directly. I would be happy to volunteer and see how things go along for a while.

Chairman Hendrie: You decide whether you ought to be one, Harold, but it seems to me that we ought to back Vollmer up with coverage as this could go around the clock for the next couple of days. I don't know what you can do to improve the communication situation, but it is certainly lousy.

Now, Joe, it seems to me that I have got to call the governor—

Mr. Fouchard: I do. I think you have got to talk to him immediately.

Chairman Hendrie: —to do it immediately. We are operating almost totally in the blind, his information is ambiguous, mine is non-existent and—I don't know, it's like a couple of blind men staggering around making decisions.

. . .

Mr. Fouchard: Is there anybody who disagrees that we ought to advise the governor on what to do?

Mr. Denton: I don't. Just on the basis of what we know. It's a good first step.

Chairman Hendrie: Go ahead with the evacuation?

Mr. Fouchard: I think you and the other commissioners should get on the line with the governor, sir.

Commissioner Ahearne: Harold and Ed, what are you recommending though?

Chairman Hendrie: I can't hear the background muttering. Is there a consensus there that we ought to recommend to the governor he move people out within the five-mile quadrant?

Mr. Denton: I certainly recommended we do it when we first got the word, Commissioner. Since the rains have stopped and the plume is going—I would still recommend a precautionary evacuation in front and under. And if it turns out to have been too conservative—

Mr. Grimes: My view is that it might have been useful right near the site, but now it is down below the Environmental Protection Agency particulate level, so probably the most that should be done, in my view, is to tell people to stay inside this morning.

. . .

Commissioner Ahearne: I was just going to ask about pregnant women and children?

Commissioner Gilinsky: Brian says a factor of 10 can be gained by staying indoors.

Anyway, I just think it is worth getting that half hour to find out. You are alerting people that they are going to have to do something, and they are not going to be able to do something in a half hour anyway.

Commissioner Ahearne: I'd alert the state police though.

Commissioner Gilinsky: Got to be ready for the possibility.

Commissioner Bradford: How much low-level—nobody knows, right?

. . .

Ms. Shuttleworth: He's on now.

Voice: Just one moment.

Governor Thornburgh: Chairman Hendrie?

Chairman Hendrie: Governor Thornburgh, glad to get in touch with you at last. I am here with the commissioners. I must say that the state of our information is not much better than I understand yours is. It appears to us that it would be desirable to suggest that people out in that northeast quadrant within five miles of the plant stay indoors for the next half hour.

We have got one of those monitoring aircraft up and seem to have an open line to it, and we ought to be able to get some information in the next ten to fifteen minutes. They can tell us whether it would be prudent to go ahead and start an evacuation out in that direction.

Governor Thornburgh: So your immediate recommendation would be for people to stay indoors?

Chairman Hendrie: Yes, out in the northeast direction from the plant.

Governor Thornburgh: The northeast direction from the plant to a distance of?

Chairman Hendrie: To a distance of about five miles.

. . .

Chairman Hendrie: Okay, let's compare numbers.

Governor Thornburgh: Hope they are the same.

Chairman Hendrie: I have got a reading. During one of these burst releases several hours ago, up over the plant it was about 1200 millirems per hour. By the time the plume comes to the ground where people would get it, it is still below EPA evacuation trigger levels; on the other hand, it certainly is a pretty husky dose rate to be having off-site. However, I'm afraid that we are behind the event, so that that dose rate is no longer being experienced since it is probably over an hour ago—

2.

*Robert Reid, mayor of Middletown.
June 6, 1979*

What were some of the more difficult moments during the crisis?

Well, every moment was a difficult moment, because we didn't know what was going on half the time. Everything was confusing and contradictory. For example, I was notified of the accident at 8:45 A.M. the first day. I left my job at the high school and came to my office, and from that time until 11:00 A.M. we didn't know what was going on. The information that we were getting was information that was being given out on TV. And as we changed from channel to channel, we got different information. At eleven o'clock I decided to call down to the Island. They didn't have any information. They told me to call Met Ed's office in Reading. So I called there. The man I was supposed to talk to was in a meeting and I was told he'd call me back later in the after-

noon. He never did call me back, but another man did, and he said, "Mayor, I want to assure you that no radioactive particles escaped and no one was injured." I said, "Well, that's great!" I went out to my car, turned on the radio, and there it was as big as you please: the announcer came on saying there were radioactive particles that had escaped. I said, "Here we are, my God, we're going to be lost." I didn't know what to believe. And it went that way the entire day.

People say that you were very well organized during the crisis; can you explain how that came to be?

Well, all along I'd felt something had to be done. We didn't have a plan in the area. During my first three months in office I tried to get the communities in the area to come together to draw up a disaster plan. I was thinking of everything. I was thinking of chemical spills on the turnpike, Route 283. We have a chemical plant right here in town. The Amtrak line's going through town, and they're in bad shape. The Harrisburg International Airport, a possible crash. And TMI. All these things. Well, we had two meetings, with representatives from

Steelton, Highspire, Lower Swatara, Londonberry, and Royalton. Third meeting: nothing. So I was in a bind. I said, "Well, if they're not interested, let me get something together for Middletown." I was working at it and had gotten bits and pieces of it together, but it wasn't complete when this whole thing blew up. Then I knew exactly what I wanted to do because it was in my mind, I'd been working on it, so everything sort of clicked and went together. That's why it wasn't too difficult to do some of the things that I did.

The one main thing I tried to do was not let people see that I was upset. I talked to a lot of citizens, and I couldn't allow them to see me upset, because I knew they would be upset. And I've had people tell me, "Bob, every time we saw you, you had a smile on your face, and it just made us feel pretty good too. And we weren't as concerned as we would've been if you'd walked around with a sour puss."

Did you stay in Middletown the whole time?

Oh, yes. No question in my mind about leaving, never even thought about that. Sort of like going down with the ship.

3.

*Ken Meyers, mayor of Goldsboro,
Memorial Day, May 28, 1979*

How long have you been mayor?

This is my second year. I was elected in November of 1977, took office in January 1978, and it's a four-year term.

How were you notified of the accident?

Well, as the mayor I wasn't notified by any officials. I got a phone call from my mother at work at ten o'clock Wednesday, that's how I found out.

What did you feel was your duty as mayor?

I felt as mayor I should come home and find out what was going on. So that was exactly what I did.

What did you find when you got here?

I found a quiet town, and I couldn't understand exactly why. Before I left to come home one of the employees sitting near me who had a radio on said to me, "Hey, aren't you from Goldsboro?" I said, "Yes." And she said, "They are evacuating your town." I said, "What?" "Yes," she said, "Something happened over at Three Mile Island, and they are asking the people to leave town." I told my boss that I was going home and got in my car and left. I thought I would be passing people on the road, and I didn't see anyone, didn't pass a car on the road or anything. I got home and said, "What is going on?" My mother said that they came around with a truck and loud-speaker and said to forget about the evacuation, but that everyone was to stay indoors and keep their doors and windows locked. That's why I didn't see anyone on the street.

What do you think personally when somebody tells you there is a radiation leak and you should keep your doors and windows shut?

What goes through my head is this: I don't think shutting the doors and windows will keep it out.

What do you think of their telling you to keep your windows shut?

I really don't know. I can't understand what the reasoning is behind that. Maybe to make people feel a little bit better.

Did you stay during the accident, or did you leave?

I stayed the whole time. I went to work in Harrisburg on Thursday and worked all day. Then Friday morning they had another leak of radiation, then I came home again at noon on Friday, and then I stayed home all the next week.

Were the people who stayed in the minority?

Yes, on Saturday we took a head count and we had, I guess, around sixty to sixty-five people. There are about six hundred people in the town, so everybody had left. In fact, I think what helped the situation was that on Wednesday night I got ahold of the president of the Town Council and told him that I thought we should have a council meeting; there are seven councilmen. He said he would get ahold of them and he did and we had a meeting at the hall at seven thirty. We discussed things we had heard on the radio and had seen on TV and read in the newspapers. Everything was so confusing we didn't know who to believe, and so finally we decided that we would set up a plan of our own to evacuate the town, *if* we had to leave.

What was that plan?

We were going to go west from here, out to Gettysburg, around fifty or sixty miles from here.

Did you have some kind of signal for leaving?

Yes, our signal was to set off the fire sirens.

Did you do that?

No, we didn't because there was no word from the state or county to evacuate, but had the governor or somebody like that ordered evacuation, we would have.

Did you find people turning to you for consolation or some kind of advice or support?

No, I don't think so. Everybody was just on their own or helter skelter. Our people didn't get panicky or anything else like that. After our council meeting we knocked on doors and told people what we knew so far and about our evacuation plans should we have to leave. People asked if they should leave now, and we said, "Well, it's your prerogative; do what you want to do; we can't force you out of your home." A lot of them with young children left when the governor made the announcement about preschool children and pregnant women. We only had one lady in town that was pregnant, and she had already left before the governor said anything.

How does the population break down in terms of young people?

We have a slew of children.

What's happening right now? Does it seem to be over?

Oh, I don't know. I believe some people are still concerned about it, but I think most people think it's over.

How do you feel? Are things back to normal?

I feel that things are back to normal. People are still concerned about the waste water that is in there. They don't know what to do with it. They're trying to purify it. I don't really know too much about that.

Are people concerned about radiation falling on the land and working into the food chain and milk?

Some of them are. I think the majority of the people aren't too concerned about it because a lot of people are starting their gardens and claim they are going to eat their vegetables.

How would you describe the psychological impact of the event on the people here?

I think the older people aren't too excited. They aren't worried about the fact that we read in the papers that thirty years from now you'll feel the impact, they feel thirty years from now they'll be dead. That's why it doesn't worry me. I can see younger people are still a little bit shaky about it yet. If you go and knock on doors and talk to the younger ones, you'll probably get some good remarks from them. The older people aren't really too concerned, I think.

What are your feelings about it?

Well, I feel like this. We need the electric and we have to have the electric somehow and if we don't have it that way, we need to find other sources. And right now the way everything is everybody wants electric. Everything's electric, this house here is all total electric. And my theory is this: what would teach these people a good lesson, who want to close this down, is that if the electric would be scarce this summer and we'd have two or three days of total no electric, then I think they would open their eyes.

Did the people of Goldsboro and Middletown and the other towns get together at any time during the accident?

No, we never did and haven't as yet. I haven't even spoken to the mayor of Middletown.

What's your feeling about getting together?

They are on that side of the river and we're on this side. We have no other connections. In fact, we're closer to Three Mile Island than they are. We're three-quarters of a mile away; they're three miles away.

4.

John Garver. salesman. Middletown, June 20, 1979 and January 4, 1980

If our forefathers could ever see this country today, they'd probably have heart attacks right on the spot. We have become the laziest people. We just throw things away. Somebody'd be a millionaire in another country with what we throw away in a year in metal alone.

John, you have had a reputation as a leading antinuclear activist in the Middletown community for a while now. Did that begin with the accident?

I've had that reputation ever since they first broke ground over there. I was against that plant then, as I am against it now. When they first came around trying to sell us on the idea of how wonderful nuclear power would be for us, I told them that I didn't believe them and that we didn't really need it and that I didn't want to see them build the plant there on the island and in that river. It's like anything else; when something threatens you, you don't want it. That's the way I felt about it.

Were you in the minority of those who felt threatened?

Oh yes. I probably wasn't the *only* one, but I was the only one who *said* so. For what reasons other people didn't voice their opinions, I don't know. Now everybody's upset.

Has the Unit Two reactor arrived at a cold shutdown yet?

Oh, my God, no. Nowhere near that.

Is there a possibility of trouble?

Absolutely. That plant is down there operating on its own, and man doesn't have control over it right now. It's sitting down there in some places with 300 to 400 degrees in spots in the core where it melted down and water can't get through to cool it. They can't open it up, and the amount of contaminated water from the primary loop is increasing every day. So far we have 750,000 gallons of it in the building. Right now they're building something to take that water out of there, but they're going to have a hell of a time doing that because every day the level of that contaminated water in the containment building rises 1 inch. That building was not designed to hold water.

I've never heard in the media about the level of primary coolant water rising an inch a day in the containment building!

Well, they kind of downplay it. The news? I don't know where the hell the news media

is, but no questions are being asked about what they're doing down there and what's happening and why this water is leaking like that. Well, I can tell you why it's leaking; the damn thing blew up! They had a couple of "pressure spikes" in their monitoring system, and they probably had pipes rupture. And this is where the leak's coming from. They can't stop it because, of course, no human being can go into it. You can't open the doors because it's so highly radioactive. I don't even know if they can get the core out. There's 37,500 fuel rods in there, and the damage that was done prevents them from being able to turn it off or remove it. It's operating at about 2 megawatts right now; before the accident it was about 100 megawatts. All of the fuel is still in there, and water cannot pass between the rods to cool that core and get it to what they call a "cold shutdown," below boiling temperature. On its own it can feed itself indefinitely. And now the core looks like an inverted bell. Normally it's a cube. But the accident made it cave in around the middle. I still think we're going to have to leave this area in the future for a while because they don't know what's going to happen when they open that door! I know that when they do I would like to be entirely out of the area.

Here we have the richest farmland in the world today, Lancaster County. And one power plant can wipe Lancaster County off the map—the ground, the people, cannot be used for hundreds of thousands of years. There's just *got* to be a better source of energy.

Did you know that during normal operations each nuclear power plant produces 400 pounds of plutonium every year? That half-life is what? Maybe 100,000 years, 250,000? An ungodly amount of time before it would ever decay. Yet the containers they store it in last only 40 years. And one billionth of an ounce of plutonium will kill you. There's no question; it will kill you, just one billionth of an ounce. And there's 400 pounds of that stuff every year. If you ask me, they just don't know what the hell they're doing over there.

I know one thing; they waste a hell of a lot of money. Hopefully they'll go down the tubes, meaning bankruptcy, so we won't have to listen to them anymore. Maybe they'll close the whole damn thing down.

Is there a real possibility that will happen?

If we lose it here, I don't think anybody will ever shut one down anywhere. We have the best shot at it ever. If we do close it down, there are two feelings I would have about that. One is it would be a victory for the people of Middletown and its surrounding area. But then again, when I really look at it hard, from a politician's viewpoint, say if I were the president of the United States or the five commissioners of the NRC, I would say that they can go ahead and feed Met Ed to the wolves to placate the antinuclear

forces. "Look, you guys made a mistake, you gotta pay for it, and you're not going to be a nuclear entity anymore."

What sort of things do you tell people who want to do something about nuclear plants where they live but who don't know how to go about it?

Those people are going to have to rise up and voice their opinions, but you can't do anything alone. When you're fighting the NRC and the nuclear industry itself, plus all the politicians and the policies that have been laid down by past presidents and so forth, it's a hell of a fight. So you should organize into local groups, the way it's come about in the townships throughout this area; and you start working with your town supervisors, the mayor, the councilmen, and from there go right on up the line.

One other very important thing I can say is if you know there's going to be a plant built, don't wait until it's built; by then it's too late. As soon as they put the first shovel in the ground, it's going to be a plant. I don't give a damn how many hearings you have later on down the line. There's only one way to stop them: stop them before they're built, before the groundbreaking takes place. Because you'll never stop them after that. That's been proven too many times. Did you know that they don't get a license until the plant's been built? So who's going to build a billion-dollar plant and then not get a twenty-five-dollar license to operate it? That's what the license costs, twenty-five dollars! Nobody invests a billion dollars and then doesn't get a license. Nobody. There are seventy-two operating plants in the United States, and not one plant has ever been denied a license or been shut down.

Let's talk about the Susquehanna River. You've been dubbed "the river rat" around here. I guess you and the river go back a long way.

Everybody's a river rat around here! My father goes back to 1900—he was born in 1906. And, well, all his people have always been on the river. My place, where my cabin's located on the river, that's called Sawmill Chute, and there used to be a sawmill in there. It's now called Hill Island. They used to bring their rafts of logs in and tie 'em up and cut 'em up and sell the lumber off the island. In fact, when I built my summer place over there, I found coins that dated back 157 years, even an old American half-dime. There were once three farms out there. The Shelleys farmed an island (called Shelley's Island now) and left goats on it that went wild. Hunters would go over there and shoot them. My uncle and I got the last set of horns from the last of those wild goats. They used to build eel dams out there too, and catch the eels and sell them. And they had coal flats, too. They'd dredge the coal dirt that the mines sent down the river and sell it to Met Ed, when Met Ed ran the old coal-fired plant in Middletown.

Is the river good fishing?

Yeah, we have the bass and the rock bass, sunfish, carp, suckers, what we call the Susquehanna salmon—that's the pickerel—and shad used to run. When they put the dam in, of course, the shad never made it up the river anymore because of the 3 hydro-electric plants on the river. We've been trying to get them to build fish dams, and we almost had the fish dams passed in the Senate, but I guess big money got to us again and they were forgotten.

As long as I've been on that river, we have never had anything affect the river and its environment as much as Three Mile Island. The prime purpose of building a recreational home and the reason that you go to a river or a national park is to get away from what you have to deal with when you go to work all the time. The traffic. The noise. The sirens. Doesn't matter what it is, that's what you want to get away from. Go over to the river now and you hear Met Ed leave off steam over there and it almost knocks you off your chair. Or you hear the loudspeakers, "Joe Doe, you're wanted on 391." It's a loudspeaker that you can hear for three miles around.

Do you mean that literally?

Yes, absolutely. It's just ruined the whole environment of the river. The lights of the place, and the steam all the time—you go across the river on a sunny day and you feel the water dropping on you and you wonder what the hell is going on, and here it's the steam falling out of the air from the towers. These kinds of things. So, really, they have ruined it. For as long as I can remember Three Mile Island has been a sanctuary or a stopping-off place for geese and ducks by the tens of thousands. We don't see them

anymore. When we go out duck hunting, we're lucky if we shoot two ducks in two weeks of hunting. The ducks just aren't around anymore.

What about those unusual shellfish you came across that you'd never seen on the river before?

I saw them for the first time in large numbers last December. That would be ten months after the accident, after they shut down both reactors. In forty years of being on the river and taking notice of everything in it, that's the first time I have ever seen them. There were thousands of them churning up the water by the shoreline—tiny things. They're called freshwater shrimp, or scuds, or side-swimmers. I finally got back the report on them from the Fish Ministry, today as a matter of fact. I like this little statement they put in at the bottom of the page. It says "Water temperatures in the vicinity of the TMI facility should be somewhat lower now than they were when the facility was open, thus creating conditions more or less favorable to certain species of animals inhabiting the river there." I don't know what they mean by "more or less favorable"—they don't elaborate on it.

Have you seen these side-swimmers before, but less abundantly?

No. I never saw those creatures before. I don't know what that means. It says right here that "They occur in a wide variety of unpolluted lakes, ponds, streams, brooks, and springs." Of course our river has been cleaned up. If it weren't for TMI, it would probably be the cleanest river in the eastern part of the United States.

Another thing—this really kills me—they had the guts to name that lake backed up by the dam Lake Frederick. Mr. Arnold referenced that one night. I could have choked him to death, the son of a bitch.

"Lake Frederick!" I don't know who the hell Frederick is or was. I don't know if he was someone in Met Ed or the president of GPU or what the hell he was but, really, it disgusts me so much it makes me ill in my stomach.

Is that lake now part of the island?

No, it's just the water backed up the river, you know, to feed the generating plant and they have the audacity to call that son of a bitch Lake Frederick. And they were gonna build such great facilities down there for everybody. You know, they were gonna put in boat ramps and they were gonna do this and they were gonna do that.

And they didn't?

No, not one bit of it. They'll never do it now. They probably don't have the money. It's the old flimflam man coming into town, trying to sell you something, saying we're gonna do this for you, we're gonna do that for you. And after they get what they want, then to hell with everybody else. And that's what it amounts to. Mr. Arnold and the rest of them. Flimflam men, that's what they are. So they got burnt. I hope they go down the tubes, meaning bankruptcy.

You know, it's unbelievable. What they did to this area can never be put back the same, because it will always be there—whether they open it again or they don't. And if we do close it down, it will be a lot safer here. But it will always be there and that's the sad part about it. There's still the health effects that have yet to come in.

I'll probably be dead and gone before we ever really find out the facts. It's unbelievable. Why Middletown? and Londonderry? and Goldsboro? Lancaster is the richest farmland in the United States of America. In fact, the world. And they damn near wiped it out with their machine. The big machine.

Londonderry Township, June 20, 1979

5.

Jane Lee manages a dairy farm in Etters, 3½ miles west of Three Mile Island. She made this report. February 20, 1980.

We have noticed defoliation in the trees. By late March and early April, shortly after the accident, we began to notice defoliation along the tips, on the extreme edges of the trees. The trees then got progressively worse. It was a slow thing, but by August the damage was severe, and by the end of August some of the trees were totally defoliated. It really looked funny seeing all those trees bare that early. We had a botanist over here, and he said that there was definitely something coming from the at-mosphere. They didn't know what it was that was damaging the trees, but it was not disease. There is some web worm, but I have never seen a tree defoliated from web worm the way they were this year. There wasn't a leaf left on them, and we know it wasn't gypsy moth.

Fruit trees were hit the hardest. Some of the trees were defoliated on only one side; others had it up the center. And one tree down at Charlie Conley's had a hole about 15 by 15 feet smack through the middle of it. Damnedest thing I ever saw. Just like some-body had taken a blowtorch and gone right around the edge of that hole, right through the middle of the tree. As the summer pro-gressed, there was more deterioration around the center and it got ragged. Also, by September a number of the affected trees began showing several growing seasons at once: spring, autumn, and winter all to-gether. Another thing, in August down by Bill Whittock's place, we noticed a lot of sap coming off the trees, just pouring off the leaves. The sap runs in the springtime nat-urally, but it's never run at this time of year before, and never so much of it, like this. The Japanese scientists were very interested in all of this. Mitsuru, a teacher and writer, and Ogino, a nuclear physicist, came here for several weeks in August and September and found many things that needed further explanation. They took hundreds of sam-ples back to Japan with them.

There was also something with the birds. They disappeared for months following the accident. In fact, we saw only one robin all last summer [1979]. No bluejays, humming-birds, finches, cardinals, or red-winged blackbirds; and I saw only six swallows. And the starlings, which have always plagued the area by the hundreds of thou-sands, never showed up at all. Just before winter of this year [1980] a handful of star-lings and sparrows appeared. It is our hope that they will return in the spring.

23

6.

Chauncey Kepford, Ph.D., a radiation chemist who is the legal representative for the Environmental Coalition on Nuclear Power. This interview was done after a day of radon hearings. Harrisburg, February 24, 1980.

There are so many unusual things about that accident, it's not really funny. I had always thought when the first one happened, it'd be in somebody else's backyard. So when it happened to the one power plant I had been litigating against for five years—which in my opinion had shown overwhelmingly at the licensing stage that it shouldn't have been operating—it was a shock. Then the way it took place, with the releases

coming out continuously over a period of days and then weeks—nobody ever expected a reactor accident like that. I think most people figured you'll know whether or not you're going to lose the eastern United States in a few hours and if you don't lose it then, you're home free. Well, this one turned out to be quite a bit different. One thing people are beginning to realize in this area is that the accident sure as hell ain't over with, and will not be over with for quite some time. If they didn't learn enough last spring when it happened, they're learning it now.

It may be more beneficial that they're learning it now. For example, they only found out very recently that krypton is coming out of that thing at the rate of a curie or 2 a day, and has been for months. That got everybody all upset because they had thought that it was all over with. Now, in fact, those levels are quite a bit smaller than would be coming out during normal operation. Normal operation releases from 10 to

30 curies of krypton a day. But people were interested only in the absolute amount coming out now, after the accident, and even the 1 or 2 curies a day bothers them. So along come the people from Met Ed and the NRC and tell them, expecting to comfort them, "Look, what's coming out is less than would be during normal operations." And people are starting to think: You mean it puts out *more* during normal operation? I don't want this coming out now, and that means I don't want normal operation.

What kind of radioactivity was released from the plant during the accident?

The vast majority of stuff was xenon 133. In the early hours Wednesday, as I recall, nothing came out of the plant until around one or two o'clock. Then it started coming up, and by midnight it was pouring out at a horrendous rate, on the order of tens of curies per second. Per second! And it *stayed* that way for a day, for twenty-four hours. So when people talk about the 1200-milli-

24

rem-per-hour dose-rate that everybody was ranting and raving about Friday, that was nothing compared to what came out Wednesday night.

Tens of curies per second: how many curies are considered an acceptable dose per year?

From 5,000 to 8,000 curies per year is considered acceptable in the safety analysis report for that plant. So they were dumping a year's worth in less than an hour Wednesday night.

Where have you gotten your data on how much has been released? One hears so many conflicting reports.

Two main sources. A memorandum, dated April 12, 1979, from a gentleman in the NRC by the name of Lake Barrett. In it he talks about 13 million curies of xenon. I think his estimate at that time was 1.4 curies of iodine, but that estimate was only for the March 28 through April 7 period. A *lot* of iodine kept coming out of that plant for about a month after the accident, so he missed a lot of it.

How do you know that?

Oh, that's in this other report, the second source, TDR-TMI-116, which you can get by writing to Dr. Frank Congel of the NRC and asking for it by number. It was put out by Pickard, Lowe, and Garrick, who was employed as a contractor by Met Ed to study the airplane issue. That company also did a study of the releases from the accident. They came up with a figure of about 8 or 10 million curies of xenon 133. There is a lot of very interesting stuff in that contractor study. They have an hour-by-hour estimation and isotopic breakdown of the kinds of materials that they estimate were coming out of the plant.

Why do you say "estimate"?

Because nobody knows. It's as simple as that.

Why don't they know?

Because their instruments went off scale. They went "click!" when the needle went all the way over, and they stayed there.

All the instruments went off scale?

Everything went off scale, everything that was measuring for those parts of the plant where radioactive materials were going out. In principle, they *were* monitoring, but they couldn't monitor, because all the instruments were off scale, every single one, and they stayed off for a few days.

Has Met Ed owned up to this fact?

Oh, yes, that's not secret information, although everybody was awfully quiet about it for the first month after. I think it was June before I found out about that, and I'd been as close as I could to the situation here.

When we talk about the amounts of radio-

activity, it really depends on what the elements are, does it not?

Absolutely.

How would you describe what xenon 133 can do to organic life?

First, it's a member, like all the gases that were released except iodine, of a family of chemicals called "noble gases." Back in the early days of chemistry, in the eighteenth and nineteenth centuries, a couple of members of this family were known, but nobody could make them react chemically with anything; because of their perceived purity, they were called "noble gases." If you had to release a large amount of radio-active materials and you had your choice and wanted to minimize damage, you would release the noble gases because of their chemical inertness. They do not incorporate themselves, like carbon or strontium or cesium, in biological tissues. They simply go where the air goes. The physical quantity that we are talking about here, the 13 million curies of xenon 133, would fit into a fairly small container, something on the order of a box about 10 inches on its side. When you consider that box, when that's released over a period of a week, you're really not talking about a large physical quantity. But as far as radioactivity goes, it's a fairly large amount. I guess in a way you would have to say that everybody was lucky, but that's really a damnation with faint praise because it shouldn't have happened in the first place. Dumping 13 million curies of xenon in the kind of weather conditions that were around, at least off and on, during that accident had the potential of creating some pretty hefty doses.

What were the weather conditions during the accident?

For most hours during the weeks after the accident, the weather conditions were pretty awful. For two nights during that time the weather conditions were among the 5 percent worst that we could have had. During those times, a very narrow, defined plume should have been delivered—had there been detectors out in the right places—fairly high levels of doses. But there were so sufficiently few detectors out that that kind of a phenomenon was completely missed.

The cumulative phenomenon?

No, more like a "spike" dose. When the wind is blowing in a particular direction and the meteorological conditions are such that the plume is not scattering out, it's staying a very narrow plume, and as a result the ex-posures are not scattered over a wide area. They are confined to a very narrow area, so the doses would be much higher. Unless that kind of plume blows essentially directly over a detector, you don't see anything.

Where did the plume go?

It went in every single direction from that

plant. At times during that accident the wind would blow from the north to the east to the southeast to the south. Virtually, in a matter of five or six hours, it would go in a complete circle.

Does a plume of radioactive gas behave like any other plume of gas or smoke?

Sure, and it will disperse like any other gas, which it did. Have you ever actually watched a smoke plume? When you start watching the damn things, you can see them make some pretty surprising moves; they can come out of a stack and go almost in a circular route down to the ground and effec-tively bounce, or they can come out and go straight, or on a nice, sunny day they just go straight up and funnel out and disappear. The kind of meteorological conditions that are really nasty are usually at night when there is a temperature inversion and the wind blows very steadily at a low speed from one direction and stays there. That's nasty because if you're releasing something in the air, it might go up only 100 or 200 feet off the ground, then it'll hit the bottom of the inversion layer and not rise any higher. And the length of travel of the gamma rays might be 200 to 500 feet, depending on the energy, so if the inversion layer's got it locked down and the wind is blowing steady in one direc-tion, slowly, *somebody's going to get a lot.* Somebody gets a really focused dose, and most everybody else gets nothing. That kind of condition was going on for two nights right after the accident—during the 5 percent least probable and most damaging weather conditions. When you put that plume problem together with the fact that there are some other unusual meteorological conditions that pertain to this area of the United States, the potential is for things to get pretty bad. One of the worst in my opin-ion is when the stuff goes up the river or slightly west over into the hills. On the west side of the Susquehanna, with the ridges of low mountains that close that area in, some funny things can happen, and it's no secret that funny things in that kind of a situation *do* happen.

Was there a lot of iodine released?

In terms of millions of curies, no. In terms of possible biological damage there was prob-ably quite a bit. The estimates I've seen run between 10 and 20 curies total. The differ-ence between the noble gases and things like iodine 131 is that about the only exposure you can get from the noble gases is this cloud passage. Once the cloud comes out of the plant, there are really no physical forces that will concentrate it more than what it is; in fact, there are processes that will tend to dilute it. But with the iodines and the stron-tium 90s and virtually all the others, there are biological processes that can concentrate these things, and the concentration factors are sufficiently high for iodine. It could very well be that the exposure from iodine from

that accident caused more of a population dosage than the xenon. I don't know. I don't know if *anybody* knows.

There's this business with the thyroid, the fact that there has been just within the last week or so a reasonably high incidence of hypothyroidism reported in Lancaster County. I think there were six cases in Lancaster where there should have been only one, and thirteen cases in three other counties where there were normally only three cases. These were kids that would have been fetuses at the time of the accident. It's a normal time lapse. I think it is somewhere around five to six months when the fetal thyroid starts becoming active. Prior to that it's not really an active gland, but when it starts becoming active it can soak up radioiodine. And, of course, it's a growing gland at that time, and probably on the order of fifty or one hundred times more sensitive than your thyroid or mine would be. When you throw on top of that the normal biological variability of human

beings, there is probably that fringe out there of fetuses for which a dose of 10 or 15 millirems might act like 1 or 2 or 5 rems for other fetuses. This is what we're talking about. Those sensitive people need protection, too, and they don't get it from radiation standards.

What else came out of the plant?

I don't think any of the nasty stuff came out. By nasty stuff, I mean strontium 90.

What about that rule that was passed in the summer that the plants are no longer required to measure strontium 90 releases?

That doesn't surprise me. It's about what I would expect from the NRC. Because, you see, Ernest Sternglass really blasted them with his report on Millstone [nuclear plant in Connecticut] in October 1977. Using the utility's data he showed that for the farms where they gathered milk, and they were quite close to the plant, they had strontium 90 levels that were two, three, four, even

five times higher than they were fifteen or twenty miles further away, and about the same number of times higher than strontium 90 levels for the major cities across most of the rest of the country. And, as you get farther from the plant in virtually every direction, the concentration of strontium 90 in the milk will drop markedly down to this level of 4 or 5 picocuries per liter, which is a fairly constant level of strontium 90 in the milk in the United States now. They were getting up to 20 and 25 picocuries per liter around the plant.

Is that 4 or 5 picocuries per liter from the nuclear fuel cycle?

No, it's fallout, from fifteen to twenty years ago. Now the difference between what Ernest was getting right around the plant and what he was getting fifteen or twenty miles away from it he attributed to the plant itself. He found it first around Millstone, and he found it around the Connecticut Yankee Plant, and he also found something pretty surprising in Windsor Locks, Connecticut. That really puzzled him until it dawned on him that Combustion Engineering is at Windsor Locks, that's where their test reactor is. So Ernest presented this information and he calculated some doses of this for kids, and he said, "All right, suppose a kid drinks this milk for five years: what kind of a dose is he going to get?" A liter a day or whatever they assume. He used the NRC's computational models; he used their dose-conversion factors, and he got kids getting doses, after a few years, between 200 and 400 millirems a year. A year! They're not supposed to get more than 15 to any organ. And the NRC guys said, "Oh, it's fallout." Well, fine. If you want to accept that proposition, then you've got to accept the proposition that nuclear plants attract fallout. On the other hand, there might be *other* possibilities. The NRC denied it. Their response, rather than factually checking it out, rather than protecting the health and safety of the public like they're required to by law, was to simply delete the requirement that the utilities monitor for strontium 90. So that's it.

Is strontium 90 the most lethal element?

Strontium 90 is the most lethal one that's not an alpha-particle emitter—like plutonium, uranium, radon. That's what the radon sweat is all about. It and its daughters are alpha-particle emitters. Strontium 90 is, by a reasonable margin, the most toxic element that's not an alpha-particle emitter. Now these thunderheads from Met Ed are probably going to get into that plant and start scraping down the walls where that hot water has been soaking for eleven months. There's a lot of strontium 90 in that water, and it'll absorb into the walls, and the only way they can make those walls safe is to go in there and scrub, grind, or whatever they have to do to get that strontium 90 out. What worries me is, if that dust starts getting out, it won't take much of that dust before they'll have to evacuate. That dust will be *damned* toxic. Then you're talking about the real problem of a nuclear accident: land contamination, inhalation of intensely radioactive dust and so on—the internal disposition of strontium 90.

So the big danger is yet to come?

Yes, and what really hurts is that in the TMI One restart proceedings, the licensing board is treating Met Ed like they would any other applicant for a license. They're treating them very kindly, very gently, with kid gloves, and the intervenors are being treated like shit, like they are treated in every other proceeding. It's just business as usual.

Is it possible they don't understand the magnitude of what's going on?

They know damn well what happened. Their job, as I see it, is to cover it up, to license that plant now. I was told that the word apparently went through to the workers at the plant, early in January, that they had already gotten their okay that their jobs were secure: TMI One would go back into operation. That word came down in early January from some Met Ed official. The commissioners, in their order for a hearing, had said that Met Ed has to do this, this, this, and this, to demonstrate short-term compliance with certain orders, and so on. And the staff report, I think it was on January 11 or something like that, said, "Well, they haven't met all the requirements yet, but we expect they will." Which means that Unit One will start up again unless something different happens, such as an honest, fair hearing before a fair tribunal, using one set of rules which applies equally to all parties. There has never been that set of conditions at any licensing proceeding for any nuclear power plant in the United States.

What makes you think it might happen this time?

Well, I guess I'm optimistic. For very little reason, though, having dealt with them.

Met Ed is having a lot of trouble getting people to feel okay about the release of the krypton 85. What do you make of their statements to the public that they simply have to start releasing it soon, because the seals and valves will soon start to give out, and then we'll be in real trouble?

That's a wonderfully educational thing. Because, you see, a lot of people have had this belief that if a core does melt down, with its massive containment structure, they can contain it. Now if they're having problems with the little tiny accident that they did have, if their seals are going, they'd better rethink that idea of being able to contain a core meltdown. Because, if they had a molten core in the basement of that plant right now, the ambient radiation levels would be hundreds to thousands of times higher, if not much higher yet; and their seals would have long since gone; and strontium 90 would be oozing out of that plant on a continuous basis, along with a lot of the other goodies. So when they talk about containing a core meltdown, take it with a grain of salt; if the seals are failing now, with 200,000 pounds of uranium oxide glowing white hot on the floor and cooking all this crap out of it, their seals would have long since gone.

You said "little tiny accident"?

Compared to a molten core in the basement, this is a little tiny accident.

If a molten core in the basement is 100, how would you rate this?

Point one.

Point one? They just barely scratched the surface?

That's right. There were 150 million curies of xenon 133 in that core when it shut down. Maybe 10 percent got out. A thousandth of the amount of the radioactive iodine, and nothing else. No strontium 90, no cesium, no plutonium, no technicium, no barium. I don't know if all of that would get out, but there are a lot of mechanisms for a lot of them to get out, and if it had melted down, there would probably have to have been a permanent evacuation. People could go back in, in dribs and drabs, and get their stuff and get the hell out. But you would not want to live within ten or twenty miles of that plant, because you would never know when there might be a sudden failure of something that lets a lot more out. And to talk about repairing it is really ludicrous. They're talking through their hats quite a bit about their plans, since they don't really know what they're going to get into with that thing. I don't think the most inventive and creative minds in the country have been studying the accident and what really happened. There are areas of that plant which are still too hot for people to go into, and I don't really know what can be done with those things other than to sit and let it cool off over a long period of time. I wouldn't want to be the person who says, "All right, you go in there." Nor would I volunteer to go in there myself. If I want to kill myself, I'll choose my own way to do it, and radiation will not be it. And, at the present time, I do not want to kill myself.

[*Chauncey Kepford has been admitted by the NRC as an intervenor, a full participant, in the agency's licensing proceedings for the Susquehanna, Fulton, and Peach Bottom nuclear plants and for Three Mile Island Units One and Two. He is the only intervenor in the still-incomplete licensing proceedings for TMI Two.*]

7.

Clair Hoover runs a dairy farm in Bainbridge, 5½ miles from the Three Mile Island plant. He hit the news when his cattle started aborting and dying one week after the accident. In all, he lost seven cows and thirteen calves. June 28, 1979

I'm not proud of the fact that our milk is being sold. We have quite a few people backing us up saying today that our milk should not be sold. I feel the only reason it has been sold throughout this whole period is that if they wouldn't take our milk it would be admitting there's something wrong in the area. And there's enough people who don't want to admit that there is anything wrong here.

Did an independent agency examine the dead cattle?

The state laboratory, and then we hired the New Bolton Center Laboratory. But the state paid the fees and got the returns. I'm not happy with the arrangement. We hired them, and we figured on paying the bill and getting the answers. We neither paid the bill nor got the answers.

At what point did the state move in and decide to pay the bill?

We didn't know that they'd paid the bill until we did not get our reports, and we inquired, and then we read in the newspaper that the Department of Agriculture had paid the bill because they said that we were all learning together. They seemed to be very anxious to point the finger at me and say that it could have been management problems or things weren't done right on the farm, but I really questioned when they paid the laboratory—the bills and things like that. They're not doing that for me. If it was my problem, I'd be stuck with the bills. It would all go back to me and the way my operation was managed and things like that; they wouldn't have been out paying my bills.

I'm definitely not satisfied with their reports. I'm hoping that it can be blamed on something other than Three Mile Island, because if our cattle are hurt from Three Mile Island, so are a lot of other things in the area. I feel the cattle are just a forerunner of other problems that are going to come. Dr. Sternglass really backed me up on that point last night. He definitely said the cattle got the first effects.

Is that because they are more sensitive?

Well, they're out in the open. They're eating the grass. They're out in the air day and night. I had no problems with the cattle in the barn, it was just the cattle out in the back. If it had been infections and things like that, it definitely would have reached further into the herd than it did.

And we know of four other dairy farmers right close here who have lost cattle in the last month, probably more than we lost. We also have reports of other people I know who have problems with other types of animals, like pets, cats, rabbits, ducks, geese, chickens, and goats—you name it.

What are the problems they are experiencing?

Dying. Abortions. Sterility. And even birth defects.

I thought it took a few years before things like that—

Well, we've been experiencing problems for the last four years in this area, ever since Number One started up. Dr. Sternglass, last night at the meeting, stood up front and said in no uncertain terms that he knows what killed my cattle, and so does NRC, and so does Metropolitan Edison, and so do a lot of other people in the area. He did not deny that they may have viral infections, uterus infections, and be weak in the back legs, but what is causing all these problems? There's definitely a bigger problem in the area that weakens the cows so that they go down with all these things. Normally these things wouldn't kill them.

Did they check out the viral situation?

Yes and no. As far as we know our cattle don't have the viral infection, but four weeks later the state came and said we do have the viral infection. But when they said we had the viral infection, we had more problems with our cattle. Our cattle are okay now. And if we had that viral problem, it wouldn't have gone away on its own.

If something were to happen again would you have them examined in the same way?

Like I say, we definitely were not happy with the results that came back. I guess some people read in the newspapers that everything's solved. But it's far from over, far from over. We'd have to go out of state if anything happened again. Our veterinarian is very disturbed. He says it's the first time that he ever experienced not being able to put full confidence in the laboratories in our area. He's always been able to go to them to get the help that he needs, but this is one time that he feels they really let him down hard.

I guess this is one spring we really marvelled when we saw things turning green. It seemed like an extra blessing.

. . .

Unit Two had problems from the very beginning. Nobody was ever told. You think about this whole mess from beginning to end: how many farmers, like, say, a chicken farmer who has too much odor from manure, which isn't going to kill anybody, would have been put out of business overnight? Yet something like *this* they have got away with it over and over again.

You know what they say? They say that the only people who are stirred up by this are people that have had emotional problems before. And that the only people that are upset are the people that would get upset if it would rain heavy one day. That was in the Lancaster evening paper, on the front page. They also say that real estate has not been hurt in the area. They also said there's a lot of people in the area that are still proud of the towers. I'd like to challenge that guy to go to Bainbridge and find ten people that are proud of them towers.

I challenged somebody not long ago to go into Bainbridge and see how many of the people would sell if they were offered a price for their property. You don't see half the houses with "For Sale" signs in front, no, but a lot of people would go if they'd know they could sell their houses. And just last night again somebody said, "Well, why don't you move out of the area?" I sure can't say it hasn't crossed my mind, but it's not easy. How easy is it for me to pack up and go, you know? I'd much rather see this plant shut down.

The farm was here before the plant was. It's like the white man and the Indians. Over at Goldsboro there were a couple of hot discussions at one meeting we were at. The one man said that when his grandfather moved into the area, he said he had problems with the red man. But he said that the problems he has with white men are a whole lot worse than the problems his grandfather had with red men!

We're not just fighting Met Ed or Three Mile Island. We're fighting every nuclear plant in America and even the world. They're all concerned to see what the outcome is. Everybody's just waiting to see what happens here. Like I say, we're not proud of our story, in no way. And we're not making money giving our story, I'll let you know that 100 percent.

At this point I wish I knew who to go to for answers. We've been saying for weeks we hope answers come. There for a while we woke up every day hoping that we'd get answers, but we just finally learned to live without answers. Learning to live without answers, that's the name of the game.

Sternglass was the first man that in a public meeting stood up with no doubts in his mind and said that he knows what killed my cattle, Met Ed knows what killed our cattle, NRC knows what killed our cattle. It's just our job to prove to them that we know. And it's not an easy thing to prove.

The only reason I'm telling my story is to try and prevent this from happening to anybody else, so they won't have to go through what we went through; and I feel we're talking for a thousand people that should be talking, but aren't.

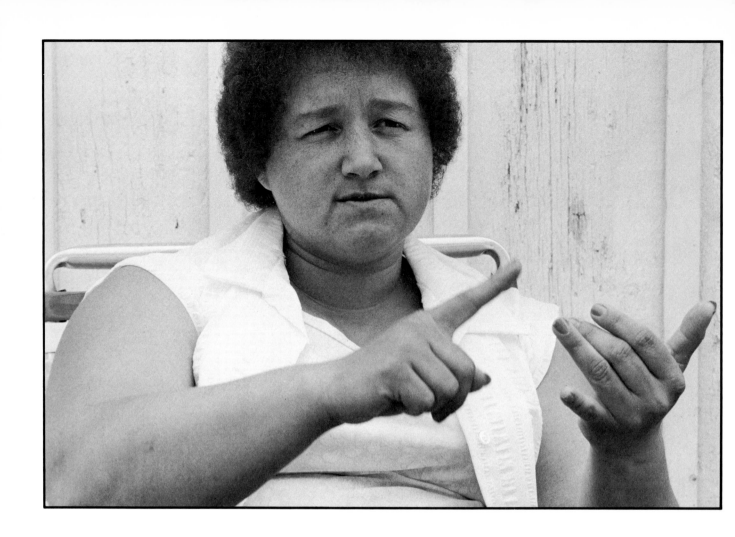

8.

Ruth Hoover runs a dairy farm in Bainbridge with her husband, Clair. June 28, 1979

Met Ed will tell you, you can't see it, Number 1, right? Okay, we've seen the white fallout.

Number 2: they say you can never taste radiation. Okay, that's true, but you sure can taste the iodine. We had the bitter taste in our mouths, which we were told by medical doctors that it was the iodine. Dr. Schoff from Hershey Medical Center told us, if you have that taste for more than an hour in your mouth at a time, look out, because that iodine is, well—

And Number 3: they say you can't smell it. When the air comes from the island, the days that the air normally comes down our way, you can smell it. It smells like somebody's cookin' hot mush. Which means you're getting the steam. It comes in this direction, so whatever else comes, comes this way too. The three things that they tell you you can't, we've seen 'em all, and that's what really gets me, you know? And what can you do?

Did you say "white fallout"? I've never heard about that before.

Oh, yes. We saw it right here. And go to Goldsboro. People there will tell you they've seen it.

Well, what does it look like? How thick is it?

Okay. When you burn trash, and afterwards when it's blowing away little particles —it looked like fine snow, real tiny, but it was white enough for me to know it was white or grayish, kind of. But it was very fine, and it came down. I don't know how long it continued because we were fleeing at the time I saw it.

Was it moving like rain?

It came more straight down. But they told me last night, whatever you do, don't let anybody tell you that you didn't see it, because a lot of other people have seen it too. And Dr. Sternglass is a very firm believer that it's up in the air and it comes down with rain. All I wanted to do was get out of there. But I know that I've seen it. I probably wouldn't have seen it against the house, but I saw it against the red pickup. "Look at the snow on Daddy's pickup," I said. We all now wish we wouldn't have seen it. I guess it's okay to tell you this, but we went to a motel that night, and we had little red spots on our arms. The next morning they were gone. The next morning they said on TV that if you thought you had fallout on your body, take a shower immediately. But we didn't. We were so exhausted we went straight to bed. I didn't realize what we'd seen until about a week later. And then I was petrified. I was watching on channel 33, it showed the people in Nevada when they had the bomb tests. It showed this woman, she said, "I was out in my garden pulling onions and I thought, my it's a late snow!" And do you know, the chills just went all over my body, and I said, "My God, I know what we have seen now." I asked a doctor, "What does this mean, the little prickly spots on the arms, can you tell me anything for my future?" He said they really can't, no. But he said if you have seen the fallout, definitely you've got a lot of chemicals.

People outside the state, or outside the twenty-mile or fifty-mile radius, they don't understand. It's easy for them to forget. We wish we could. But there's some people that have the guts to call us and say, "Hey, where's your faith? Don't you have any faith in the Lord?" People would say that to us when we were leaving. Just stay there, and pray! Hey! If we have a fire in our homes, so we're to say to the kids, "Just sit tight, stay right in there and pray because we're Christians and the Lord's going to take care of us?" When the floods came, the [hurricane] Agnes, and the river came up, just sit by the river? And I said, "Hold it." Just because they couldn't see this thing, you were supposed to sit and pray? That's pathetic! I'd like to know just how much longer can nuclear power plants use the people in their five- and ten-mile radius for their guinea pigs? How much longer can it go on?

People have really been awakened to nuclear power. They know now things they never used to know. But if they would have put it in the papers and educated the people, Three Mile Island or any nuclear reactor would never have been built in the whole United States. I don't believe they could have got away with it. But the people were led like sheep to the slaughter. They were never told from the very beginning.

31

9.

David Fisher lives with his family on the same farm as his aunt, Jane Lee, who made this report. Etters, July 3, 1979

David is eight years old. During the accident we had to evacuate him and his mother. When David returned, he developed severe psychological problems and regressed to the stage of a three year old psychologically. He clung to his mother, and when we sent him back to school, he had to call home as high as twice a day to be reassured that everything was all right. Two questions that stood out: Is everything still alive? and Is everybody all right? He would break out into uncontrollable sobbing in school, and finally they gave him a little corner all his own; it was called David's corner. He could take anything that he could relate to from home, and he could take any schoolmate in the classroom with him into the corner until he was able to overcome his fears. And he did pretty well up until school closed.

Then last night we had a very traumatic experience with him. It was late, around ten o'clock, and he was playing with his friend in the barn. I went upstairs to help his grandmother shell some peas, and I was still in the house. I came out and I thought, well, he won't come to the house; I'm going out for a minute. And, of course, he did. He came to the house, and the house was empty. Well, I'll tell you, we had a terrible time with him. He just cried and cried and sobbed and sobbed his heart out because he's so afraid that something's going to happen to us. It's very difficult to deal with. We talk to him, and he's in reality, fortunately, which is more than a lot of the kids are. A lot of the kids are not in reality with this at all. They have nightmares about it.

Now, interestingly enough, David dreamt two weeks before the accident that the towers blew up. Two weeks before it happened. Isn't that something?

33

10.

Oran Henderson, director of Pennsylvania Emergency Management Agency. Harrisburg, January 31, 1980

Everybody knows that there was a great deal of confusion in terms of the possibility of the complete evacuation working out. Did it catch you by surprise, the whole thing?

No, well, I wouldn't say totally by surprise, but the TMI kind of an accident we had here was one that we really hadn't planned on. The assumption was that the level of safety attained by the nuclear power plants was more than adequate to meet the needs. So they never spent too much time on it. As

far as our priorities of planning were concerned, we were more concerned with flash floods, tornadoes, chemical spills. So we had not devoted the degree of attention to a nuclear power plant that the lessons of TMI had pointed out we should have. And not only the state government but the federal government and the local governments were all caught, I won't say napping, but we were caught short.

A lot of people, especially the local people, feel that something could still go wrong with the Three Mile Island operation. Do you think there is a chance for something to go haywire?

Well, as long as we have the radiation that we have at Three Mile Island, there is always that potential. Of course, each day that radiation is decreasing in intensity, and the possibilities of a precautionary evacuation, or other protective action, are necessarily decreasing. It's still a threat. And the

term "risk" is almost like a dirty four-letter word. People have taken for granted for years that they are generally greater and since the invention of the wheel, we have generated greater and greater risk, and the public for the most part has accepted this risk. The public has been willing to accept that on a long weekend we're going to have 600 auto accident deaths, nationwide. This is accepted because it happens regularly. We hear of one person that's killed, one or two here, or two there, and they've gotten accustomed to this. But when something new and startling develops like a nuclear power plant, suddenly the public seems to perceive that they want a risk-free kind of society as it pertains to a nuclear power plant, and there's no way of getting it. You can't have a complete 100 percent risk-free environment around a nuclear power plant. You can put in all the safety devices that you can develop scientifically and technically, but there is always a possibility of

34

something occurring. And we're trying to balance off what is tolerable. And I can't even identify what *is* tolerable now, what *is* acceptable, as opposed to what is the risk involved, and so we have to plan as if nothing is acceptable.

In other words, you're planning for the worst?

We're planning for the worst kind of emergency with the intent that it's never going to happen, but if we have to execute any part of it, we're a hell of a lot better off than we would have been if we had taken any middle-of-the-road ground. Now that makes planning much more difficult when you have to plan for the bottom line.

Before this accident most people didn't even know what a meltdown was, and now it's a household word.

Right. And they still don't know what a meltdown is. And it's still a household word.

I understand that in the event of some similar accident in the near future, you're planning to rely on volunteer fire departments and local people to help facilitate the evacuation plan.

Well, this is correct. These are our emergency forces. Civil defense or emergency management has no forces of its own. What we basically have is an organization. We have a state organization, we have county organizations, we have local government organizations. But usually they're designated personnel; many of them have other duties and jobs and responsibilities. But for our forces we are heavily dependent on volunteers, the Red Cross, the Mennonites, the Salvation Army, those kinds of groups, plus the fire departments and the police departments. And also on our state police and National Guard, if time is available to activate them. The National Guard is our primary resource to augment local government. But the primary responsibility for evacuation or any other protective action taken, whether it be a nuclear accident or any other kind of a natural disaster, rests with the local units of government.

Do you feel that you need more funding? Or do you feel that the shifting of personnel and a change of emphasis is sufficient for now?

Well, it's only an interim stopgap measure. If we're going to do the job and continue to do the job as it should be done, we're going to need increased federal funding to do that kind of planning. And the federal government, to be perfectly frank with you, hasn't got its act entirely together.

The federal government is putting out the guidance, and a considerable amount of that guidance is uncoordinated. Now we understand that the Federal Emergency Management Agency has, as of January 1980, been charged by the president to assume full

responsibility for the off-site consequences of a Three Mile Island kind of accident. We have had no guidance yet from the Federal Emergency Management Agency as to what their role is or what they expect from us.

So you have not heard from them?

That's correct.

What do you need to be the most efficient you could be?

Well, the first thing we need from the federal government—I don't know how we could get it elsewhere—is a specific site assessment of each one of our nuclear power plants, to provide us with the concrete parameters of the problem. Right now the federal government is going with ten miles, or some further distance, from the nuclear power plant for which we should have emergency plans for evacuation or other protective actions, out to a range of fifty miles. I personally don't like to work with just a ten-mile parameter. I think considering the geography, the population densities, and atmospheric considerations around our power plants, that you could not toss down just an arbitrary ten-mile figure. I would rather see a site-specific survey that tells me at Peach Bottom, because of the terrain, because of the atmospheric conditions that exist there, that you ought to plan for three miles or six miles, something based on specifics and not just something brought out of the air. During the Three Mile incident we were informed on Friday night, the thirtieth of March, that it would be prudent on our part to have plans out to twenty miles. So we developed such twenty-mile plans. It's going to be extremely difficult for us to plan for anything less than twenty miles around Three Mile Island for a conceivable period of time.

For example?

The perception of the public who live within twenty miles is that if you had an incident that affected a two-mile radius and you had to evacuate for that, then you'd have a great number of these people out to twenty miles wanting to be evacuated also. So I think we're going to have to accept for some time the need for a twenty-mile plan around Three Mile Island.

I heard the figure 4.8 miles as the minimum parameter in evacuation. Is that accurate?

Well, prior to Three Mile Island 2.2 miles was the population zone around Three Mile Island for which NRC suggested the state should have evacuation plans. Peach Bottom was 4.6 miles and Beaver was 3.5 miles. So to standardize it within the state we arbitrarily picked a figure of 5 miles and told our people in these areas that they should plan out to 5 miles. So, we in effect had a 5-mile plan for evacuation at the time of the Three Mile Island accident.

But now that has changed?

That *has* changed and now NRC says ten miles; although I read in the paper over the weekend that there's another element of NRC, or at least an independent study that is being contracted by NRC, that's suggesting that thirty miles is the proper, more appropriate range.

So those earlier estimates seem extremely low and probably are not so adequate in the light of the potential risks involved.

Yes. And until we have a site-specific survey, I think that we're just always going to be confronted with this problem of justifying why we're planning for ten miles, or any other range.

But you mentioned that you didn't see how you could get that. In other words, that type of survey isn't even possible for you to do.

Well, it's not within our capability. We requested this in April of last year from the federal government, and we haven't received any response as of this time. Now I would hope that the federal government, when it gets its act together, will include that in its—

It would seem to be one of the first things that they should do.

Anytime you start tackling a problem, at least you want to know what the problem is, and the parameters of the problem. It seems to be extremely difficult for us to get that kind of information.

Now as far as evacuation is concerned, we don't need a great number of firemen or a great number of policemen to actually man the roadblocks if we can properly educate the public that this is the route they're going to take. You're going to head north, or east, or south, whichever the direction is, you continue along that route until you come to X turnoff and there you will be prepared for.

In our current planning we are requiring that the counties publish this plan in the local newspapers twice a year, because we recognize that people move, that people don't always save the instructions or warnings. We think that by updating this every six months that at least people who are concerned will either save the document or can make reference to it.

I think I've seen that already.

Well, yes, it was published during the Three Mile Island incident. We did publish it very, very hurriedly. We based it on our own evaluation here of the best routes, so that people could get out. We subsequently have refined that evacuation route, and it's now out and in the hands of our county personnel.

At the height of the actual emergency, were you simply terrified for your life or for the lives of people you knew? Or did you find your own computer, so to speak, going

Well, yes, I think this is true of any disaster we go through. We try to draw as we go along, or I do. I try to make notes to myself of what went wrong, so that we can correct it in the future. And one of the greatest things that went wrong was the lack of an automatic flow of information. When this incident first happened on Wednesday, the twenty-eighth of March, this agency was misled into feeling that the incident was something that had occurred and now it was basically *over*. Clear through Friday morning, up until six or seven o'clock that morning, we were receiving reports to the effect that it'll be in a cold shutdown, the plant will be in a cold shutdown mode in thirty minutes. Earlier that morning they said, "Well, it's run into a snag, but maybe two hours from now—" We were *never* informed properly of whether they were controlled or accidental emissions. We learned many, many hours later that things were happening that we should have been notified of at the time or even before they happened. So we didn't have either the eyeball contact or the kind of communications rapport with either our Bureau of Radiation Protection or with the plant that gave us any confidence that the kind of information we were getting we could work with.

So this was a very serious detraction from our ability to keep our counties informed of what was going on in a timely manner. We spent a great amount of time putting out fires, rumors would get started and published, and we found that we were spending an *inordinate* amount of our time trying to research and run back on these so-called rumors or reports to find out who said what to whom, and whether it was in fact true or false.

And so, because of these kinds of things, we've got to do a better job of informing the public in a more timely manner of what is occurring and what the public should be prepared to face.

And then on the other hand, besides all that kind of contradictory misleading information, there came the directive from Washington to evacuate.

Yes, the NRC made a strong recommendation to us at 9:15 Friday morning, the thirtieth of March, that we should evacuate out to a range of ten miles. This was rescinded about forty-five minutes to an hour later, and that's when the governor issued an advisory for people to stay indoors. And at noon that day to evacuate pregnant women and preschool-age children from the five-mile area. The NRC at that time were stumbling as to what was going on. They didn't have a handle on it; and if they didn't have a handle on it, we certainly couldn't be expected to have a handle on it.

11.

Matt and Suzanne Magda. Matt works for the Pennsylvania Historical Museum Commission in Harrisburg; Suzanne teaches juniors and seniors at Bishop McDevitt High School, nine miles north of Three Mile Island. Harrisburg, January 10, 1980

Matt: When I first came home at the end of Wednesday, the twenty-eighth of March, Suzanne was already there; she had returned from school and she had heard nothing of the accident; so I told her about it. I said, "Quick, let's put on the radio." We always listen to National Public Radio, especially "All Things Considered." The first item on the news was about the accident that morning. Suzanne didn't even know

about it, and I remember her first statement was, "Those bastards! Good for them." I said, "Wait a minute, what are you saying? That's a highly dangerous reactor." I think she was just reacting because she doesn't like nuclear power at all. She was sort of glad that they were caught, and everything was going to be fine; in other words, these guys were going to pay for that, and it was going to come to light.

Everything quieted down and on Thursday, as a matter of fact, it had pretty much left my mind. Although Thursday night I watched the McNeil-Lehrer show, which was a follow-up on the accident, and that created some more doubts in my mind. Professor Kendall, who was from the Union of Concerned Scientists, was on that show, and he knew that what had happened was a portent of some incompetence and of dangers that could exist out of the plant. I think he understood that. On that same show was William Scranton III, the lieutenant governor, who said that he had gone down to look at the plant for the governor and had seen the reactor, supposedly, where

there was a spillage of water that had leaked into the containment building. He said, "Well, it's like your basement when it gets flooded and you throw plastic over it." He said, "Yes, they had plastic over it." When I heard that I was highly suspicious, knowing from my readings about reactors there was no way, if they had a leakage there, that he was going to see plastic there. It made no sense to me whatsoever. It meant that there was something very unusual, and I was unhappy about that. A PR man from the Atomic Industrial Forum was also on the show; he was saying that the incident on that day, Thursday, the twenty-ninth of March, was a victory for nuclear power because nothing major had happened; they had contained the radiation. All the safety systems had operated properly, and the men on the spot had had good reactions.

Well, the following morning you know what happened. At nine o'clock on the radio I heard at work that there was an uncontrolled release of radiation. When I heard that, my whole body just had a tingle through it and I got very nervous. I was trying to control myself because I had been suspicious all along and now I was sure something major was going on, that they weren't telling the complete truth and that I'd better consider getting out of there. It wasn't completely thought out. We were listening for more news, and the more I heard the more dangerous it sounded, because the next item I heard was that they were considering an evacuation of a four-county area. I remember I ran down to a colleague's office to tell him about this. He was on the phone and was trying to wave me off. I had been telling him about the accident earlier, that it was very dangerous, and I knew this was very important. I had to get through to him because he might have to clear out very quickly, so I grabbed a piece of paper and I just wrote down a note, "They have a serious problem at the nuclear plant, and we may have to evacuate," and I put at the bottom, "No joke." When he saw it he was just shocked, and he turned around and started telling the person on the phone what I had written. Then I had to leave the room because I wanted to get on the phone and call Suzanne, who was at school. When I called her I was aware that I would have to control myself because being at school she'd probably heard nothing about it.

Suzanne: I was called to the phone, the nearest phone was in the library.

Matt: When I got on the phone my emotions were running wild. But I was trying to act calm for her sake and for those students. The first thing I asked her was, "Are you in a classroom?" and she said, "Yes." I said, "I am about to tell you something very bad, but I want you to be calm for the students. I have heard that they had an uncontrolled release of radiation. Did you hear about it?" She said, "No, nothing about it at all." I said I thought it was a good idea that we clear out as soon as possible. There could be a major panic. I had no idea what was going to be occurring. I told her if she had to clear out of the school that I would meet her at the house, that I was going to be heading for there immediately. I would get suitcases together and other items that we would need, and I would assume that she would get there; if not, she would arrive at the end of the day, and we should take off.

Suzanne: When I got the phone call I was surprised that something had come up, but I immediately knew this was just a further unfolding of what had already been occurring, and as I answered the phone my reactions were very limited, very monosyllabic: yes, no, okay, fine. I just stood perfectly still, and I was very careful. There was a sister, the librarian, standing right next to me and she was watching my face. I swear I did not react and when I hung up the phone, I just stood for a moment saying, "Okay, where do we go from here?" She

turned to me and said, "It's TMI, isn't it?" I said, "Yes." "Is it bad?" I said, "Oh yes, very bad." And she immediately, being a sister, said, "Oh, dear God, we've got to start praying," and immediately she launched into praying. Her first prayer was, "Oh God, think about the unborn."

Then I left. When I went back to my classroom, one of the students came to me and said, "There are state police all over the office. Do you know why?" This was very early in the morning, about nine o'clock. I proceeded to teach—I was not totally effective—but I taught nevertheless. It was Greek mythology and I took up where I left off. I was teaching Cassandra, the Trojan War, and Cassandra's dire warnings of what would happen if they let the horse into the walls, which is actually interesting, isn't it? I'm sure Aeschylus would have loved it.

Then an announcement from the principal, Father Gotwald, came over the loudspeaker, and unfortunately what he said did not lend itself to calm in the building. He said, "All right, everybody get calm. Everybody stay quiet." Well, you don't tell a thousand highly emotional adolescents to be calm. He said, "What we're going to do is do whatever the state police and the government tell us." He said, with no explanation at all of what was going on, "First of all, shut your windows," and there was a resounding crash throughout the whole building—SLAM. Every window came down. Everybody knew immediately. The reaction on every student's face was, oh, my God, please tell us, please tell us; somebody tell us, we've got to know. They said, "What is it? We know it's down there, isn't it? It's the plant, isn't it?" They had heard it Wednesday, and they were aware; it was something in the back of their minds. Immediately all the horror rushed to the surface. That's when I decided they should know. It's worse to function without knowledge. So I said, "Everybody sit down and be very quiet and I will tell you what I know." I told them what I had heard from Matthew. And they were very grateful for the information, desperately grateful, and immediately went up and down the halls and told everybody so the whole school quickly knew.

From that point on we were dealing with a whole different emotional scheme in the school. The rule was laid down that no student was allowed to leave the school unless his or her parent came for him, because the parents would not know where their children were going. Families were being desperately gathered together and the streets were crazy. There were accidents in front of the school. Hysterical parents coming to pick up their children were smashing into one another, going through stop signs and red lights, really a panic situation. When the students left, there was an incredible sense among them that they would probably not see one another again.

They were leaving for Washington, New York, Ohio, Pittsburgh, some were leaving for Florida, some were going to Canada, there was a great sense of flight. The ranks thinned gradually during the day and as the day wore on, some students became more and more hysterical; it was their first intimation of mortality, and they thought they were going to blow up. They didn't know what was going on; they didn't understand it. Students who for one reason or another stayed started crying, breaking down, being held, being calmed. But there was another reaction too: "Well, I'll never have to x-ray my teeth again, I'll just glow in the dark from now on," and "Oh well, I'll never have to buy batteries for my watch anymore, I'll just put it on my arm and it'll run." There were blacker ones about the kinds of children one might have. Soon they started being not quite so funny any more. People became more and more serious about the whole situation. We decided to look around and see what was going on. Two of my accelerated physics students remembered that there were Geiger counters and got them out of the physics lab. Fifty is background radiation, and at two o'clock in the afternoon we were at 250 in the building and over 350 outside. It was extremely high. The scale goes from 50 to 500. We were nine miles directly north of the island, so we would be right smack in the path of the plume. The students were just incredibly traumatized by the experience. There was chaos, there was a great deal of fear, a great deal of hysteria, something that I would not ever want to experience again. The intensity of it I could never really communicate to anyone, the horror of it. Eventually the children left, and I stayed—it was my responsibility—desperately as I wanted to get home. Every minute I wanted to get home more and more. I stayed until they left. Finally I left and went home to find not only Matthew there, but my sister, who was then a senior in high school. Being a little more independent minded, she had walked out of her school saying, "See you later," and went right out the door. She called Matthew, and he picked her up on the way home.

. . .

It's amazing. I was aware that I could not do anything in my given situation; I was aware that I had made this commitment to care for these young people until their parents could get them, and that it was not just babysitting, but also a psychological caring for. I realized that I couldn't react. There was no space, no time; I didn't have the leisure to react. So I just turned everything off. I did not want to be there. I did not want to be within a million miles of the place, or at least 500 miles. I knew what was going on, I was very aware of the dangers, the horrors; I was constantly aware of the fact that any second now it could blow. We were all just being very quiet, very calm. And after a time period when the jokes and the hysteria passed, there was a very unemotional calm that came over everybody, a resignation of, "Well, we're here. We're just going to sit here and we're not going to think and we're not going to react, because it's too enormous." The enormity of the emotional reaction overcame just about everyone. We were just all very, very quiet.

Matt: It was very quiet and very hot, abnormally hot that day. My hands were sweating profusely. After I finished calling Suzanne my one thought was I've got to get out of here. I was picturing what downtown Harrisburg would be like in the middle of an evacuation, and I wanted to avoid being caught in that at all costs. My emotions were still running wild, and I was trying to keep my mind together. As I was driving out of town, I was listening to the radio, and the conflicting tales started. All over the radio they were saying, "Although we still may have to evacuate, it now appears that this was a controlled emission of radiation." So they weren't sure whether it was controlled or uncontrolled! I finally got back to the place I live. I turned on the TV and turned on the radio so I could get all sources of information, and I started packing. But as I was doing that I was almost traumatized by the fact that I didn't know if I was being victimized right now, if it was all over to begin with, or if I had a chance and should leave now, you know, go, run, get her, and leave because I had no idea of what was happening. I did not know if I was wasting time. I felt like an idiot staying there, trying to calmly pack bags, waiting to leave simply because you're conditioned, and leaving when her work is over. Is this a stupid idea?

No one really knew what was going on. When Thornburgh came on the TV and they started questioning him, he didn't seem to understand what was happening at all. There seemed to be a very tense, antagonistic relationship between any spokesman —the governor, the lieutenant governor, any official from Met Ed, other people whom they were bringing in as spokesmen —and the reporters, who seemed to be having a hell of a time trying to get information from these folks. As I listened, more and more I was beginning to feel worse; my suspicions were growing and growing. I thought, you've got to either stay and wait for her or you've got to go and get her. Then I got a phone call from Suzanne's sister, and she was asking me to come and get her; the school she was calling from was not that far from our place, and she would not walk the

2/3 of a mile to our house. She was ready to leave, but she would not go outside. So I drove up to the school. When I got there, it was a madhouse. There were cars whipping around corners, coming up to their kids out in front of the school. Many of them were screaming and crying.

When I picked her up, a friend of hers was with her and she said, "If you're going to leave, I'm going to go with you," and I said, "That's fine." But her friend completely lost control of herself. She was sitting in the back seat as I was driving, and she started crying and screaming because she didn't know where her folks were. I said, "Don't worry, I'm sure your folks are trying to get in touch with you, and they will, and when I get you home you should pack and also pack for your parents, and just get yourself mentally prepared to leave, that's all. Don't worry about anything else." I dropped her off and came back home, and an hour later Suzanne came home.

Suzanne: I noticed on the way home that all the gas stations had long lines of cars filling up with gas, with people desperately running, being very demanding, screaming, and filling their cars with gas. The thing was you didn't want to be out of your car, so they were running out, filling up, and jumping back into the car; and everybody's in a kind of hunched-over position, like there's something going on outside. I saw people outside their houses with all their car doors open, just pitching food and clothing and household goods, just throwing them into their cars. All around, in houses all over. Clothes being thrown in, not packed, just thrown in, thrown in trunks, trunks slammed shut. Just incredible. Quick, throw everything you can into the car and run.

I got home and we immediately started throwing things into our car and took those things that were the most valuable. That's a very strange experience too; all of a sudden, oh, good heavens, what do I save? We took Matt's dissertation and the dogs and my sister, and we ended up with room for a little bit of clothes and that was it. We turned everything off and locked the house and got in the car and left, not knowing if we'd ever come back and see our home again.

It was definitely a historical evacuation. There were long lines of cars on the roads, and you could see clothes filling the windows—that's what ours was like too. The mood was very panicky, but not to take it out on somebody else; there wasn't any

fighting or honking of horns, just a lot of pressure to get moving. It was like everything was too precious at that moment, too precious. You just sat and you just contained yourself. You only had a few things on your mind: to get out, that was it. You couldn't afford emotional outbursts. The last news item we got was that the bubble had appeared. And a news cable had come from Washington announcing that that portended a possible explosion. When we heard that we thought, well, we're leaving even faster. We just leapt in the car and took off, we must have left around four o'clock. My parents did not leave. And it was very emotional, particularly because we were taking my sister, the youngest child, and would they ever see her again. It's not clear in my mind why they stayed.

Matt: My instincts were to grab them, to compel them to go, but I knew that was impossible. We got to my mother's and my uncle's place in Derby, Connecticut, a town about 10 miles west of New Haven, early Saturday morning. It's about 260 miles away. I wanted to go somewhere quite far, and I wanted to go somewhere we could stay for a while, because we didn't have cash, we didn't get time to go to the bank. But at the same moment I thought there was a good possibility I would have to go further. I knew even that wasn't safe. We ended up going to Boston, staying with friends because we felt even more comfortable farther away.

What do you know about distances? What's the kill-zone?

We know what Helen Caldecott said when she came down here. She said as soon as she heard that there was a potential meltdown because of a hydrogen bubble, she bought plane tickets for her children who were in Boston, to get out, to fly up to San Francisco. Boston is about 340 miles from here. My idea was that it was a 300-mile area around the plant, and you had to be out of that area.

What have you learned since?

Well, the exact statements from NRC studies, or AEC studies, or the Berkhaven report said that an area the size of Pennsylvania would be devastated if you had a meltdown. If you took Pennsylvania and superimposed it over our area, it would cover Baltimore, Washington, Trenton, Philadelphia, New York City. We're talking about 300 to 350 miles; that's the length of Pennsylvania.

12.

Janice Schlappig runs the Twin Oaks Nursing Home in Campbell-town, thirteen miles northeast of Three Mile Island. January 4, 1980

You have to have something of an evacuation plan in mind, there's a state regulation. You must have a disaster plan. But usually you just have them because you have to have them, and they are on paper.

But you did more than that?

The night before, when we knew this was imminent, we stayed up the whole night. I was right in this seat devising the whole thing. The first murmurs we heard were on Friday morning. We didn't know anything before that. There was a little thing in the paper. And it was nothing. Friday morning a man started calling me because his girl friend works here. Also the students from the campus at Middletown had been sent home, and my maintenance man's wife, who is a student there, came in and sat here on my couch saying, "What are we going to do?" These were the first real contacts we had that indicated there was a real problem. Then we put all the radios on and started calling people.

Did you get any kind of official notification that there was something you should be doing?

We got nothing until Sunday when I called our local fire company, and they came in here on Sunday afternoon and said they were on their way to a civil defense meeting, I guess in Harrisburg, and that they would get back to me. That was the first of anything, and I called them initially. And when they walked out of here one of them said, "Let me give you a little advice, S.Y.A.F.—Save Your Ass First," and left. So that gave us a whole lot of confidence. That was Sunday. Sunday evening at home at about eleven or eleven thirty they called and said that the local fire department and civil defense had finalized plans for evacuation to the Lebanon Good Samaritan Hospital for Monday morning at eight o'clock.

How many miles away is that?

About fifteen miles northeast of here.

So another fifteen miles would put you twenty-five miles outside of TMI?

So we started planning. I started planning in my mind on Friday, just thinking. On Sunday at noon I met with the owner and my director of nursing. Then we felt even if no one told us to evacuate, we wanted to be ready in case. At that time I had the staff tell the patients as much as they could understand, that something might be up. We have skilled-care patients here, and a lot of them comprehend very little. They need almost total care. They range probably from slightly incompetent to totally incompetent. They need to be bathed, they need to have help to be fed. So that Sunday afternoon, I told my staff to put armbands on the residents' arms.

What do the armbands say?

Their name, doctor, any allergies, name of the nursing home—because I didn't know where they'd be. I also told each charge nurse on each shift to keep a very complete, up-to-date list of anyone calling off or leaving the area, where they're going, when they're leaving, when it's possible they are expected back. Do not talk anyone into staying. As it turned out, only about five people out of close to forty left. But no one on staff was talked into staying. I just laid out the orders, bang, bang, bang. Not one person, not one family, not one agency questioned anything I said, which I couldn't believe.

Once you got moving, how long did it take?

We completely evacuated forty residents fifteen miles away in 1½ hours. Completely, in their beds. No incidents. No upsets. No screaming. No problem.

In their beds?

In their beds, in their rooms completely quiet, from this home to the Good Samaritan Hospital. Forty patients in an hour and a half.

How did you do that?

Well there were, as I recall, eight or ten ambulances and four of the aging minibuses lined up at eight thirty out here. I had started waking up staff members at four in the morning. Then I served breakfast about an hour and a half early and the patients didn't even know that it was an hour and a half early—because they didn't know. And everything was routine. Good morning. How are you, Mrs. Whatever? And nice day, etc. Because most people couldn't understand anyway. So we just kept on going. At four o'clock I started waking people up to have them come in. I'd say, okay, I want you in at four thirty, I want you in at five. I want you in at six. As each person came in, I handed them a written

assignment of exactly what they should do. I called in anyone that would come, and then I assigned them, even if they were a housekeeping person and I needed them as a nursing person. We're so small here that everyone knows everyone else's job. So whoever came, I could assign whatever needed to be done. I know my people that well, so I knew which ones to give which kind of assignment with the least hassle.

We were chosen to go first because I was probably the most vocal of the homes and prepared to go first. We were all given one vacant wing in the Good Samaritan Hospital that was not used, and the administrator said, "Come in and set up your own mini-nursing home. Take the place, bring your staff, bring their charts, bring their medicines, and just set up your own mini-nursing home." The one little problem was that the hospital had us go through all the admission procedures, because they wanted a slice of the reimbursement. At the point when we chose to evacuate, we didn't know how much reimbursement we'd get, we're 70 percent medical assistance here. We didn't know if we'd lose it for all those days or if we'd be gone for days or weeks or indefinitely or lose our business. It was a real concern. But we put their safety above that possibility at that time. But when you are a small home, that's a big thing to put on the line. We had no official backing; we felt we were out on a limb. We didn't know if we'd get reimbursed or not.

Had you ever had any experience doing something like this?

Never. Just sort of instinct, good planning and good communication. It's incredible, though, the loyalty and respect the people had for me; they would do anything I said without question. And they were scared. Some were naturally more afraid than others, but they did whatever they were asked to do.

Were there any snags? Everything you said has been almost effortless, faultless, not effortless but perfectly running.

That's why I almost hesitate to tell my story, it sounds like I'm making it up because it was that good. The only slight thing was, when we were leaving, we had them all out and luckily I had one person in charge of crossing everyone's name off as they saw them get on the ambulances. Okay, they were all crossed off, except there was one name left. Everyone was in every room and

this man wasn't there. Here was a 93-year-old man, deaf and completely oblivious to anything, in his bathroom. And the last ambulance was leaving and I said, "Hey, hey, wait, there's a name here." Maybe he's gone. Maybe he wasn't crossed off the list but there's a name here. And he was in his bathroom.

Other than that, I just don't have anything bad to say. The hospital treated us royally. It's too bad I don't have a little bit of negative to make it sound better but—[*she laughs*]. One of the biggest things it did for me personally was, number one, the loyalty and respect that I felt I had from the staff, and secondly, it gave me a lot more confidence in knowing that if we ever had to evacuate, that fear of the unknown isn't as unknown and fearful anymore. Because we did have an actual evacuation, and even though nothing was immediately happening, we still now have a good idea how we would do it.

Your experience certainly speaks for itself, but I'd like to know how you do feel about nuclear energy.

I still have mixed emotions on it. I don't feel the public is informed enough to even take intelligent stands, and I'm wondering if this is on purpose. That's how I feel. The thing that kept hanging over me was that I felt negligent when this all happened. My first feelings were that I was negligent in not knowing more about nuclear accidents or possibilities. But I feel better today, knowing that *nobody* knew anything about nuclear accidents.

They were caught.

Not the governor, not anybody. So I take a little solace in that. Hey, I wasn't the only one that didn't know.

And it's been with us for a long time.

You'd think people should know. I felt there was no excuse that I'm this near and I don't know more about it.

Have you lived here all your life?

I'm from Anvill, the next town down the road. That was another thing. I've been here about 8½ years, and I've about hand-picked my staff, and there are people here that I've known since I was six years old. There's people I worked with when I was a nurse's aide, when I was a regular staff nurse. They are really my people, "my" people.

13.

Georgia Lookingbill, registered nurse. Hummelstown, January 8, 1980

Well, my name is Georgia Lookingbill. I live in Hummelstown, which is about seven miles from Three Mile Island. I am a housewife and mother of three children and wife to a physician. I am also a registered nurse, and I was working at the children's care center in Middletown, which is approximately 5½ miles away from Three Mile Island. That puts it not quite half a mile beyond the evacuation distance which the governor had designated. You could see the 5-mile limit out the front door, but we were 5½, so it was questionable throughout the period of Thursday, Friday, Saturday, and Sunday what was to be done with this facility. There are approximately fifty to sixty severely physically and mentally handicapped children here. Those children live here; it's their home; they have been committed by their natural families, and the residence is responsible for their care, and I was the nurse who was assigned to be on duty the evening shift (3:00 to 11:00 p.m.) the weekend of the accident.

Friday was when my husband and I as individuals decided that we would take our children out of the area. We really didn't feel any great degree of urgency to evacuate until Friday at noon when we heard that there was an unplanned release of radiation and a hydrogen bubble. I was at the medical center at the time, and it appeared to me that it was of great concern to the medical people, so when I came home—my husband came home shortly thereafter—we decided that that was the time we should move our own family. I knew I had to come back to the area because I had to go to work at the care center at three o'clock Saturday and Sunday. My husband, being a physician, had to be available in case there was an emergency that weekend at the medical center, which is two miles down the road.

You mean an emergency with the population?

Yes.

People would be coming in?

Physicians understood that they should be available.

Is there some law or something about that?

No, there's no law. But it's understood, I suppose. It's a question of honor that you should be available. Those who did make themselves unavailable had to pay the price afterwards in unspoken looks, glances, and talk—that kind of thing. After the fact, now that everything is okay again, it's like we

were the brave ones—we stayed—and what happened to you? You definitely had that pressure on you as a medical person throughout this entire accident. I'm sure my husband felt it over there and I know I felt it as the only R.N. that was scheduled to work the evening shift at the care center for the weekend. Of course no one is in fact indispensable, and I'm sure they would have found someone had I decided not to come back. We evacuated our three children and our pets to Philadelphia Friday evening, to my mother's home, and came back to Hershey again the following morning. The children stayed in Philadelphia until the following Tuesday. So they were there four days. My husband and I came back, and Saturday I went in to work at two o'clock. It was a weekend of very nerve-racking stress from a kind of situation which I have never had to cope with to that extent before. I have never felt myself so tight and just right there on the brink of blowing my cool at any minute, you know, particularly since I had to be the one in charge. I had approximately fifteen people who were nurse's aides that I had to be responsible for as well as these sixty kids. When I called the care center on Friday before we left town, I told them that I was going to Philadelphia and would be back to work by three o'clock Saturday; so that if they called me, they would know why they couldn't get any answer. I asked, "Are there any plans for evacuation at the time?" and they said, "Evacuate what? Oh, we didn't think about that. We really hadn't planned for that. We'll have to discuss that." It hadn't occurred to them that they might have to evacuate.

So while you evacuated to Philadelphia, they were discussing it?

They were discussing it. They continued to discuss it all weekend. Friday, Saturday, Sunday, which was really the height of it all.

The facility was waiting for the state emergency management people to say, "Yes, go." The government was waiting for Met Ed and NRC officials to say whether they should or shouldn't, who should go and who shouldn't go. At the facility the administrator and the assistant really didn't seem to know what to do. Let me just digress a minute to Saturday. I'll give you an example of how confusing this was. The Red Cross people kept coming into the care facility, and then the civil defense people were calling on the phone, and then other people from other emergency organizations were calling as well. Every phone was ringing every ten minutes; and the Red Cross would come in and say, "What are you still doing here? You should be out of here. Why are you still sitting here? You know we already evacuated the Veterans Administration Hospital in town."
And I am saying to myself, I wish I knew why I am still sitting here.

The level of tension was just so great with everyone, especially since most of the women who work there have families and kids of their own. Basically, they wanted to be with their own families. They did not want to be sitting not knowing what the heck was happening anywhere; and as the different shifts would change, as that weekend went on, they got less and less people coming in. That, as I understand it, is why they finally evacuated on Monday—because the people gradually had not come in. They had drifted away or gone, evacuated with their kids. They had held out, and their nerves finally just gave out and they said, "The heck with it. I'm getting out. That's better than sitting here and getting myself all stewed up over this." By Sunday night I think they thought by Monday there wasn't going to be enough personnel showing up to give adequate care, so they decided to move everyone. It was tough physically, too, because the kids still had to get care. Those kids need total care. I mean nobody over there walks; every one of them is in a wheelchair or is bedfast.

[*Georgia describes the particular hardship for one child who, already very handicapped, became so sick that she had to remain in the hospital to which she was evacuated.*]

You hear everybody saying, "Well, nobody died." No one was injured directly from the radiation, we hope, but some people were put through things that they will never recover from. And this little girl for sure was put through an experience that she would never recover from. Some of us have maybe suffered emotional trauma that we won't recover from, psychological trauma, and I think there were all types of casualties, not only radiation casualties, which are the only ones that seem to interest the government and utilities—direct radiation casualties.

And they don't even want to admit psychological trauma as a category for filing suit?

Well, neither does the NRC. That's still up for grabs, whether the NRC is going to admit it as evidence in the hearings on the restart of Unit One. It seems unfair that that's the way this whole evaluation of the accident could evolve, that it is a matter of cut-and-dried dollars and cents.

Radiation, strictly radiation.

Strictly radiation. Damaging health effects are certainly one effect, but they're far from all. That's why I decided to pursue it a little bit on my own and see if I was out of line in thinking that there was something important about that little girl's casualty from evacuation, or if I should just try and forget it. So I did call the governor's Three Mile Island emergency investigation committee, and the lady who was in charge of it took information similar to what I have spoken to you about and said that she would look into it and take it from there. That was two months ago, and I haven't heard anything from her, although I called her office three times and have never received a return phone call. I don't know whether she is just an awfully busy lady or whether they just dropped the ball or they didn't feel that it was worth investigating.

I've gone to a lot of conferences. I've listened to a lot of physicians speak out at radiology and health conferences. My husband attended the conferences and taped some. So I've listened to the experts. The radiologists and nuclear experts assure us that there is *no* problem when we are within our allowable "safe dosage" of radiation. But I have also heard Dr. Kepford's studies that he did during the accident, which would indicate that some things were not picked up by the government studies and by the Met Ed studies. I guess my own feelings would have to be that we got within safe allowable radiation dosage—because I couldn't stand it if it proved otherwise. I'm a person. My husband is a doctor, but he is also a person. I'm a nurse, but I'm a mother and I've got three kids sitting here. I'm not going to say, "Oh my God, they're not telling us the truth. We got more than our allowable dose. My kids are going to come down with leukemia." I couldn't live with that. So of course I'm going to accept it because I couldn't stand it otherwise, and it's too late to move out now. I still might move, depending on what happens in the future. I still might leave, at least for a while, while they clean up the containment building or if they release the krypton gas, because I'm not going to expose my family to any more.

Even though they say it's negligible?

No way! I'm not going to knowingly expose my kids to any more radioactivity than they have already gotten.

Any more of anything.

Period. They have too many years to live yet with radiation from high power lines, radiation from TV sets, radiation from medical treatment, radiation from the sun, and all the microwave ovens and everything else this high technological society is pushing down our throats. I'm not knowingly going to sit here 5½ to 7 miles from Three Mile Island and let them knowingly push any more down on us. But as far as what happened during the period of the accident, I guess I'm going to accept it. I'm going to think what they told us is that we got some, I'm sure we got some, but I really think that we got not enough to really lie awake at night worrying about it. Maybe it's a rationalization but it's one I've got to live with.

. . .

Since the accident, I have become active with this antinuclear group. All of a sudden

people think, God, she's nuts. That one is crazy. Really. They really think that you have a screw loose or something when you go out and protest.

Who, your neighbors?

Yes, mostly the ones who didn't evacuate; they think, oh, she was all wrapped up with this. They think that the antinuclear business is crazy.

Why? They think you are going to throw a bomb?

No, they think that everyone who gets all excited over this is overreacting. You've heard other people say this. If you're at all concerned about this, you're just overreacting to it. They've bought all the propaganda for so long that they really believe it.

I've gotten involved in a community group of citizens who are interested in doing something about this accident and being aware. It's a self-awareness to heighten our consciousness about the whole nuclear energy situation. So we went out and got 1,600 signatures from our township on a petition saying that "We, the concerned citizens of central Pennsylvania, never want the Three Mile Island facility to open as a nuclear facility." That's as strong a statement as you could possibly get, and in three weeks' time we pounded the pavements and stood on the street corners and in shopping centers and got over 1,600 signatures in Derry Township, in one little township. There are only 3,000 registered voters in this township, so it's a large proportion of the voting population.

On one weekend?

No, three weeks, including two weekends. We took these petitions to our supervisors. We had asked our township board of supervisors to pass a resolution before we got these signatures. A whole list of them that the other townships have passed—a list of demands, like we don't want the water dumped in the Susquehanna River; we don't want the krypton gas released; we want to be reimbursed for any ecological damages we might have had, etc. Well, Derry Township's board, which consists of six supervisors, unanimously, except one guy, voted to reject our resolutions. They considered our group rowdy and troublesome. They drafted their own resolution, which said that Three Mile Island Unit One should be opened immediately. They were the only township anywhere in this whole area who dared to pass a resolution encouraging Met Ed to reopen Unit One as soon as possible. Since it had a five-year good safety record, they felt that they should reopen it because we need that electricity. Well, we were just astounded. There were maybe sixty or seventy people at that meeting that night, the capacity that the room would hold, and everyone just stood up and

howled when they did this. So that's what urged us to conduct a door-to-door petition-signing campaign and show them that they were not representing the people in this township. How dare they! By the way, this resolution that they passed was drafted by three of the supervisors in a closed-doors, private session in Harrisburg on the afternoon previous to this public meeting.

What happened after the public meeting and all the signatures?

Well, we tallied up the signatures and made copies and went back to them with the signatures, and we said, "All right, here are the 1,600 signatures, and we would like you to revise your original resolution." You know, even *revise* it. We didn't ask them to adopt our resolution any more. "We know you're not going to do that. Please don't vote a resolution to ask them to open up that plant over there. Here's 1,600 people from this township who don't want it open," and they again said that we were emotional, excitable women—what are some of the other things they called us? I mean they were so derogatory and personal. It was unbelievable to the people who were there. They just voted again and they would not even consider reconsidering their original resolution. It stood on the line as it was.

The only thing they did as a reconciliatory act was that one of the commissioners called me one night, the night before the meeting when we went to ask them if they would reconsider. They knew we would be coming back and we had the press—TV, radio and everybody—there, and there was a big stink over this whole thing. He said, "Well, isn't there some way we can come to an understanding here? How about if we put a copy of your resolution in our office? We would attach a note to it saying that a few, some of the citizens, don't agree with the resolution that was passed by Derry Township's board of supervisors. We will make that available at the township office to anyone who comes in to read our resolution." I said, "What's the point of the resolution? A resolution is not worth the paper it's written on. How many people do you think are going to come into the Derry Township's supervisors' office to read your resolution and see that our resolution is lying there?"

. . .

Throughout this whole thing, I've lost a lot of naivete and idealistic thinking about how to get things done and who runs the show in government, even on the township level.

Finally, I really loved this area when we first moved here five years ago, but since March 28 last year I feel differently, I'm still here because my husband works at the medical center, and it's not easy to find a job somewhere else. He likes his work and his future is here, so I'm staying. I sure don't have the same feeling about it as I had before. I never will again.

14.

George Stauffer. Middletown,
June 6, 1979

What did you think when the accident happened?

Well, I really didn't think of nothing. In fact, I'm not afraid of anything, you know what I mean? Because actually I put my faith in the Man Upstairs.

It was pretty confusing for a while, though?

Oh yeah, it was confusing.

Did you just watch it happen?

I watched it happen; I walked around the town, and it was all just going on.

Didn't it bother you at all?

Didn't bother me at all.

Did you feel the government had it under control, or that it might have gotten a lot worse?

Well, where it got out of control was from the reporters. They confused the people, see? They made it worse than it was, see? Usually if a guy comes up and tells you, if you're in your house and you're in bed and you've got four or five children in there, and he says, "Well, your house is on fire!" What are you going to do? You're going to get so damn—and your house ain't even on fire! There you are! See? You're going to get so excitable! That's what happened with these damn news reporters.

Did you have the feeling that it could have gotten worse in reality?

No, no. Because there was this fellow from Utah, he made a duplicate of the plant over there on the island, and he somehow got down to a thing where he knew that they could turn it down and cool it off, see? That's what he maintained. And I think that's what they went by. I think he even came over here from Utah. I mean, if it was bad, why would the president of the United States come?

But then again, if it weren't bad, why would he come?

Well, he's a nuclear man himself. He was a nuclear what-cha-call-em in the navy. Engineer.

Did you turn out when he came?

Yeah, I seen him.

So things are pretty well back to normal now?

Oh, yes. Hell, guys who work in the plant didn't even move out of town. Not even their children. They stayed. And all the people that did move got compensated for it, you know. They got so much money.

Do you think the men in the plant know more about what happened?

Oh, no. They didn't know about it. Somebody made a booboo, I think, and forgot to turn the thing the way it should have been turned, and they turned it the wrong way.

I heard some kids were having bad dreams.

No, there was nothing in the paper about that. If it was, it would have been in the paper.

Last NRC public meeting, Middletown, March 19, 1980

Reginald Gotchy and John Collins, Middletown, March 19, 1980

Communities: Meeting, Listening, Protesting

During the first year following the accident, meetings held in communities around Three Mile Island gave citizens an opportunity to speak face-to-face with NRC and Met Ed officials as well as with their own elected representatives. These meetings were required by law, but after the anger shown at the dramatic meeting at the Liberty Fire Station No. 1 in Middletown on March 19, 1980, the NRC felt it advisable to discontinue further public meetings. Reginald Gotchy is the NRC administrator who ran the whole-body-count program in the TMI area.

Voice 1: The highest off-site readings that you ever had were at Kunkel School [*Kunkel School is located 5½ miles northwest of TMI. On March 28, 1979, a radiation level*

of 13 millirems per hour was measured over the school, the highest off-site reading to that time.] where my son goes, and you won't ever do it to him again.

Gotchy: Did we find anything in your son?

Voice 2: You wouldn't have told him if you had.

Gotchy: Yes we would.

Voice 3: No, no.

Voice 4: Why are you laughing all the time?

Gotchy: You'd laugh too—

Voice 4: You're an asshole. You won't ever come back here. You're a fucking asshole.

Voice 1: Your days are numbered. You hurt my kid. And there's nothing you can—

Voice 3: You don't give a damn.

Gotchy: You're wrong, I do care.

Voice 1: How much money do you make a year?

Gotchy: Does that make any difference?

Voice 1: I don't care if you make $2 or $2,000,000.

Gotchy: Ma'am—[*reaches out to touch woman's arm to calm her*]

Voice 1: You can't touch me! You hurt my children!

Gotchy: I haven't hurt your children.

Voice 4: You *cannot* tell me you haven't. You're not trying to keep them from getting hurt either.

Voice 3: And you sat up there and laughed the whole livelong night of this whole cottonpicking meeting.

Gotchy: I didn't know what else to do.

Voice 1: And then you got tired and you were going to go to sleep until we woke you up.

Gotchy: When people stood up there and lied, I didn't know what else to do but to laugh. Good grief, I wasn't laughing at you people. Some of those people are lying up there; you'd better believe it.

Voice 4: How about the people that are dying? The old people. People have bone problems. I had a miscarriage April 21. April 1 we got the wind. The wind came directly north. He [*referring to the child in her arms*] was throwing up long, slimy stuff that I'd never seen come out of a baby's mouth before. The calves were throwing up! In twenty years those farmers never had calves throw up!

Gotchy: My understanding was the state veterinarian went out and checked all those.

Voice 4: Oh, yeah, I don't trust the state, as I don't trust you.

Gotchy: We don't have any veterinarians.

Mrs. Reigle, a resident on Londonderry Township, ¼ mile from the plant, testified before The President's Commission on the Accident at Three Mile Island, May 19, 1979

I'd like to say, I love this country. I'm one of those minorities whose eyes still fill with tears when I hear "The Star-Spangled Banner." But I sit here in total loathing and disgust for the legislators, all parties, and I have worked very actively in political parties. I can't understand why human beings in a civilized country such as ours have a total disregard for other human beings. Why we even have to sit here and discuss closing a power plant that should have been almost an instant decision! I can't fathom that as a private citizen.

I've deliberated in what capacity I should speak. As a mother, who will worry till my death about the genes and chromosomes of my child, my grandchildren? As an angry victim, who has accumulated a library of 300 preventive medicine books, who eats health foods? I think it's a joke. It's an irony that I probably will be done in by something that I cannot taste, feel, or see. This is a laugh.

So I decided to come as a property owner. Because, unfortunate as it is, people's ears are in their pocketbooks. And legislators will hop on the economic issue before the health issue. I would like to propose a different aspect of the problem to the distinquished committee before me. Would you propose to the president, the federal government, Met Ed, whatever, to have some consideration for us in that quarter-mile perimeter?

The nightmare still continues for us. It's difficult to put into words how one feels. Feelings are abstract. I invite each and every one of you to live in my house. It's nicely furnished. I just housecleaned before the accident. See how ominous it feels to see these towers, experience the sirens, see them emit the smoke at night. They sneak it out in fire trucks at night, the radioactive waste. The trucks sneak over onto the island with their lights off at night to pick it up. And ungodly noises. These noises have been happening since they fired up Unit Two.

I have here a letter from Met Ed. I have called periodically every two or three weeks about these noises. Not because of the noises, but because of what they represented. I was told that they were generator shutdown. Now these noises were different. But they still gave the same reasoning. Some of them sound like thirteen supersonic jets. It's like Chinese torture, it's so piercing. You think that you're going to lose your mind. The letter here tells me it's fine, don't worry. It's a very well written letter, it's a public relations letter. But we've got to remember: communists aren't the only ones who use propaganda. This is a propaganda-type letter.

Now, just to tell you of some of the plight of some of us that live close to the island: I've had swollen lymph glands. I've had laryngitis, sore throat. Some people were bleeding from the colon. Iodine enters through the colon and settles in your thyroid. And for those who say this is psychosomatic, I invite you to meet my dog. I have a collie dog, and whenever anything is going on at the island, he becomes very frustrated. He paces, saliva comes out of his mouth. He's not going into seizure; he has done this several times. One time he woke me, it was Tuesday morning, 2:20. I looked out the window, and I saw smoke being emitted from below the cooling towers, not from the cooling towers themselves. This is now twice that these types of emissions have happened. It is not the same consistency as the smoke from the cooling towers, which is clear, sort of transparent. This was much denser, thicker, almost cottony. What it is, I don't know. It lasted twenty minutes. I telephoned the neighbor. I said, "Would you please look out the window?" I told her, "At this point I eat, drink and think Three Mile Island; maybe I'm hallucinating." So she verified this fact.

I telephoned Representative Reed's office the next morning. They've reassured me I'd receive an answer, but I've never received answers to any of this. As I said, come down and live in my house to appreciate what's going on.

[*On August 3 Mrs. Reigle's collie dog died of a cancerous tumor.*]

Richard Swartz, Middletown Council meeting, June 20, 1979

Ladies and gentlemen of Middletown, members of the Borough Council:

We didn't come here tonight to ask for better plans for evacuation, or seek the assurances from Metropolitan Edison or from our state government or our national government. Right here is why we came.

[*A man in the audience holds up a child.*]

How many watts is that kid worth? How many jobs is that kid worth? We're here because we feel endangered, and the next generation, and the next century, and their children. That's why we're here. Ladies and gentlemen, as long as there's faulty equipment operating in a nuclear power plant, as long as we have management and utility companies who care more for money than people, as long as there is the possibility of human error in the operation of nuclear power plants, considering Metropolitan Edison's past record and the fact that no one can any longer trust the people who control the nuclear situation in crisis events and in the day-to-day operation of these plants, I petition you tonight to not only slow down the reopening of Metropolitan Edison's Three Mile Island plant, but to close it down permanently.

A long time ago, some idiot had the idea of putting x-ray machines in shoe stores. They were dangerous. No one knew it at the time, or those who knew weren't doing anything about it. The people of Pennysylvania were the first to outlaw those things. They took a stand. They fought the battle. Tonight I ask the people of Middletown to begin that battle and once again have Pennsylvanians in the forefront of the war against nuclear insecurity in our own neighborhood. You know Ralph Nader, a great American, said that nuclear power plants are technology's Viet Nam. We have it right here, baby. It's not 25,000 miles away. It's 2½ miles away. Someone's going to die. Eventually there's going to be a disaster. You know it, if you don't shut them down. I don't want it to happen here. I can't look at these little kids sitting around here, the little one the man held up. Look at him. Do you want it to happen to him? It can't. That's why we're here. You know it's time that we all prepare to take this battle door to door, to the newspapers, the government, and to the gates of the Metropolitan Edison Three Mile Island plant if necessary.

[*Applause*]

Ladies and gentlemen, tonight I ask you to be patriots. For once, don't let them dictate to you. Don't listen to the big corporations. Don't listen to the big national government that can't, that doesn't touch you anymore. Ladies and gentlemen, be Americans. This is our town. This is our land. And these are our kids. Don't let them down.

*James Hurst, Middletown council
meeting, June 20, 1979*

I have lived in Middletown for thirty-four
years. Things are different in Middletown
and things will continue to be different, to
be wrong, until the cause of this difference is
gone, namely Three Mile Island. There is a
serious problem here. A threat to all of our
health, safety, and economic well-being.
Some people can't accept the fact that there
is a problem. They turn their back on it.
The problem is here, it's real and turning
backs will not solve it. I would like to
present you with a resolution, and I feel we
should have your action on this. We should
have your approval because if you don't
approve it, you're going to give them a license to kill us. That's what you're doing.
"The council of Middletown, Pennsylvania,
opposes the reopening of the nuclear reactor
known as TMI One until such time as all
investigatory commissions studying the
March 28, 1979, nuclear accident at TMI
Two have completed their investigations

and reported their findings and such
findings have been fully analyzed and
reviewed and all recommendations regarding improvement for the maximum safe
operation of TMI One have been fully
complied with."

*Steven Reed, state representative, Middle-
town council meeting, June 20, 1979*

I heard one member of the council say that if
he can receive assurances from the officials
of Met Ed and the NRC, he would consider
the opening of at least Unit One and maybe
Unit Two. I must warn you all, citizens and
collected officials alike, not to fall prey to
that type of folly. To believe once again people who have systematically misled us, mis-
represented their position, misstated and
distorted and warped the facts and withheld
the facts—something they are doing up to
and including this date—I cannot believe
that we could even give thought to placing
credibility in their continued assurances for

public safety after an accident happened
that was not supposed to happen in the first
place, according to them.

A combination of human error, lack of
training, basic design flaws, failure of safety
systems, failure of proper notification,
failure to provide information with regard to
public health and safety, failure to notify
your mayor and others about what was going on, each of those factors alone should
prove that they are not worthy of the trust
and confidence the NRC has placed in
them. Yet it appears, I'm sorry to say, ladies and gentlemen, it appears tonight that
there has already been a decision made
somewhere along the line at both the state
and federal levels, that Unit One in fact is
going to reopen. Therefore, the decision of
Unit One is just as important because it includes Unit Two, whether it says so or not
in your resolution. What you do sets a prec-
edent throughout this nation, maybe even
throughout this globe. It cannot be over-
dramatized—and I will conclude on
this—that the issue is more than just

whether or not Met Ed is going to be held accountable. The issue goes a little bit further into whether or not there shall be a penalty for those who placed into jeopardy our lives and our children's future health. I don't like the way they ran it before and you can bet, if you didn't like it before, you're not going to like it any better in the future. Business as usual in Three Mile Island. The real issue is, and I can't emphasize it enough, is whether or not the people with the vested powers and financial interest in this country and in this area, sitting on this island, are in fact the ones who run the government or whether government is capable and willing to have the guts to represent public interest against special interests.

Kari Light, Middletown council meeting, June 20, 1979

I live at 24 Ann Street in the first ward and I have my Ph.D. I don't have anything brilliant; I don't have anything documented, or anything political that I would like to share with you. But I would like you to know some of what this has meant to me personally and my relationship with this particular town. I have lived here literally since before I was born. My mother was pregnant here. And this has always been a safe, secure place for me. Like a lot of other people, when I was young and silly, I left town and I was away for awhile; but I came back because this is where I felt I belonged, where I felt safe, and where I felt secure. That is gone. That is important to me. That was a major loss. I work away from here, I work on the West Shore, and I used to feel really good when I'd be driving home. I'd be taking the Highspire Turnpike, and I'd be feeling good. Now I find any excuse I can not to come straight home. I no longer feel good getting back; I feel worse. That's important to me. Another very important thing to me is children. I work with children. Part of what I do is play therapy with children. And I love them. I enjoy them. There's hardly a child living that I can't feel joyful with, or at least that I couldn't feel joyful with. That also is gone. I can't look at children, play with children, enjoy children the way I could two or three months ago. I look at them and wonder what's going to happen to them. I wonder which ones of them are going to be able to produce children and which ones are not. I wonder which ones of them are going to have leukemia when they are older; I look at them and I grieve for them. They're not my children. I don't have children. And I'm grieving for your children, and you should be doing something about it.

I will never feel safe being pregnant in Middletown now. I can remember a time when women could be pregnant and feel good about it. I don't know a lot of women right now who are pregnant who are really comfortable. And I wouldn't want to have to go through that myself. That's another thing that I felt. Feelings about my own self and my own bearing and raising children here in Middletown. That's important to me.

Kari Light, Middletown council meeting, June 20, 1979

Walter Kreitz, Londonderry Township public meeting, August 1979

15.

Walter Kreitz, president of Metropolitan Edison, at a question-and-answer period at Londonderry Township public meeting, August 1979

Mr. Kreitz, I'm sure that you, as president of Metropolitan Edison Company, are aware that a lot of people in this area are angry with the company and unhappy about nuclear energy. Do you think this situation will continue to grow?

I don't see it as growing, I think a lot of it's education. It's important that people realize that they should know more about radiation. Radiation hasn't been invented. It's been with us ever since man has been on earth. I think it's just a matter of getting to know radiation, its relative effects, and just being more comfortable. It's a matter of how much radiation you want to tolerate, how much contamination you want to tolerate from other things. We're in this building, in this room tonight. There's people smoking and discharging gases into the atmosphere and so forth. I guess it's all relative. I'm sure none of that aids our health. Somehow we can get interested in becoming more knowledgeable. I think that could go a long way.

How you do this, I'm not sure. Like everything else, it's hard to get the American public excited, to talk to them, to learn things.

They seem excited over the catastrophic implication. Do you see yourself putting a new effort into educating the people to your point of view?

We're going to do whatever is possible to accomplish this, to provide this education and information to our customers, and to their children.

[Since this time, Walter Kreitz has stepped down from the presidency of Metropolitan Edison.]

53

16.

Nancy Prelesnik, Hershey,
March 2, 1980

I had never thought about having an abortion. I went to a Catholic nursing school, so it's something that was brought up and discussed in our theology and medical ethics classes. I guess once I got married, I figured I wouldn't have an abortion unless it was a life and death sort of situation—I would rather use birth control effectively.

It is a very important thing, having children and raising them. You try to create the best situation that you can, right from prenatal days on, and I did that. I did everything. I have had Lamaze births, and they were fine. I have two very healthy, extremely strong, cavity-free children—I mean it, my kids are healthy. They're superintelligent, right down the board. I think some of it is luck, and I think a lot of it is genetics, and also a certain portion of it is environmental. It's important for me to do the right things.

My youngest daughter was almost nine when I got pregnant this last time. For the last couple of years I haven't been thinking of getting pregnant. It was just the farthest thing from my mind. I had an IUD and it had been working fine, so I had no reason to feel that it wouldn't be fine until either one of us was sterilized. And I wasn't ready for that quite yet. I knew I was getting closer to thirty-five, and one of these days I would have to make that ultimate decision. I also was not ready to have an abortion. I found out I was pregnant somewhere around the first part of July. I only had a week to decide what to do before I would have been three months pregnant. That didn't leave me much time.

I was used to very free and liberal states, like California or Minnesota, and I was very taken aback when I realized how difficult it would be to get an abortion here. I did have a safe, good abortion, but the only physician in this area who would give me one was Dr. Tike. He's a courageous man. Back here if it's a therapeutic abortion, definitely therapeutic, you can get one in a hospital. They would not consider mine a therapeutic abortion, though I may have had good cause or reason. I had been exposed to radiation.

Everyone seemed to buy hook, line, and sinker everything the officials at Met Ed or the NRC said. They really didn't realize that what they're being told or what they're getting is not the real stuff. People are either busy or they don't care and that's it. They really bought the fact that not much was released and that there were no problems. During those months all pregnant women were being told the same things. There was no problem, no release; nothing that went on at Three Mile Island could classify you for a therapeutic abortion. The only thing would be the stress level. It would only be in stress that they would consider Three Mile Island affected a pregnancy. At the same time, there's no guarantee because there really is no guarantee in anything. I had my husband ask Dr. Sternglass on June 27 about chromosome testing. Dr. Sternglass said he felt it was definitely in order and would suggest that anyone living in the area who was even contemplating children should really have chromosome testing done. So, if we had decided to continue on with this pregnancy, I would definitely have had chromosome testing to rule out any genetic damage. That was all when I was three months pregnant and had to make a decision. You can't wait until you're six months pregnant. Around here, you don't know what's going to happen. There are continual releases; I didn't feel that I could go through nine or ten months worried about a continual release. Not just the radiation, but the stress. The stress is definitely a factor.

You're supposed to be happy through pregnancy, everything really matters. You can't think nice thoughts and you can't be without stress with everything that's in this lifestyle here—the food, the things you eat and drink. I try not to buy anything from Pennsylvania anymore. I always question things at the grocery stores, and they think you're crazy to want to know where you're getting your produce. I would not want to be a young person looking forward to my first baby.

I've felt slightly ostracized for having had an abortion. I'm the only person I've known that has had one and been outspoken about having an abortion and talking about it in relation to Three Mile Island. If I didn't have Three Mile Island to deal with—and the cat, the cat had leukemia. I was feeding the cat and giving the cat medication; we were breathing over the cat for three weeks, and I nursed it along until the test reports came back. The next day we took the cat in and had her put to sleep. I had been with the cat too much, it became a threat for me too. I couldn't handle having a baby that would either develop leukemia or be deformed or deficient in any way. I just didn't believe that I could have a child that would suffer like that. Had it been a different set of circumstances, I would have gone through with the pregnancy and then have had a sterilization. Now, I still wouldn't want to have a baby later. I still keep thinking of the nights when I was crying. I thought about it at the same time my baby would have been born, that was the night of the meeting at the church. I don't go around with it on my mind all the time, but it just doesn't go away. I still worry about my children.

If there is something strange happening to you, or if you really feel deeply, you always feel isolated. And then, all of a sudden, it's like a network. People who have gone through the same situation get to know each other and begin to see very well, very clearly what is happening. You continue to bump into pockets of people who don't know, who remain isolated, and they are fearful.

We feel like hostages. People are very concerned about the hostages in Iran, and nobody is concerned about us at all. When we evacuated during the accident, I thought I could empathize with what a refugee might feel like. I never thought I would feel like a refugee in my own country in peace time.

This accident has done a strange thing to our community and a lot of it is very good. You see how much one person can count; it's true, one person can make a difference. The personal qualities start coming out in people, people that have gone through this Godawful, horrible crap, this nightmare. The most negative obscene words couldn't even describe it. These people know it.

Nancy Prelesnik and Robert Arnold at a public meeting, February 26, 1980

Ernest Sternglass, fifth from left, with Japanese scientists, July 3, 1979

17.

Ernest Sternglass, Ph.D., radiation physicist, School of Medicine, University of Pittsburgh, made the following statement at a press conference at the Pennsylvania State Capitol. Harrisburg, July 3, 1979

The reason I'm here is that there is a very close connection between what happened to the people at Three Mile Island and in all other nuclear sites in the United States where releases have taken place and what is happening to the people of Hiroshima and Nagasaki over the decades following the war.

In fact, a book that I wrote in 1972 has now been translated into Japanese because what I had discovered then has now been admitted after many previously secret government documents have been released through the efforts of the *Washington Post* and the *New York Times,* linking very low levels of radiation to fallout from nuclear testing, something that I said would happen back in 1963.

The tragedy is that we have not wanted to learn because our government is determined to keep on building nuclear reactors and allowing them to have the same discharge limits that were used to allow nuclear bomb testing. At that time, 1969, I pointed out that the statistics throughout the United States showed that there were probably

some 500,000 children that died as a result of nuclear bomb testing since the atomic age began. With the latest statistics on total mortality, published by the U.S. Public Health Service, and looking at the decline of death rates before the bomb testing began, we see the decline halted during the time of nuclear testing, and it has now resumed for all ages. It is now possible to say that the total number of Americans who died as a result of bomb testing is close to one hundred times the number of people who died at Hiroshima, very close to 20 million people who died earlier than they would have if we had never dropped the bomb on Hiroshima and Nagasaki, and if we had never done the bomb testing in Nevada and in the Pacific, and Russia in Siberia, and England in Australia that has poisoned the atmosphere of the world.

More tragic is the fact that we are allowing the continuation of large discharges from nuclear reactors similar to the levels of strontium 90 that existed at the time of the height of nuclear bomb testing. According to the statistics gathered, not just by myself but by an organization called Another Mother for Peace, it is now clear that in California, Wisconsin, Pennsylvania, and Connecticut the strontium 90 levels near the nuclear plants started to rise again toward the values that existed at the height of the nuclear bomb testing. And at the same time the latest infant mortality data published by the U.S. Health Statistics Service in Washington shows that while infant mortality in the United States as a whole has been declining in the last year and has been doing so since the end of bomb testing around

1965, in New England, closest to the Millstone Reactor in Connecticut, cancer rates for January-February of this year have increased 100 percent. In Massachusetts, 27 percent. In Rhode Island, 14 percent. And in Maine, where a new reactor similar to the design at Three Mile Island started to leak, statistics show that infant deaths for January-February 1979 went up 114 percent as compared to last year.

A really devastating statistic that has come out within the last year indicates that Connecticut has now shown the least number of live-born children surviving to age five. In other words, many of them are born either defective or immature, and they die before they reach age five. Connecticut has the dirtiest nuclear reactor plant in the United States, Millstone I, which in 1975, according to the AEC's or the NRC's own figures, released the most radioactive gases of any plant in the United States, very close to 3 million curies per year. I've made an estimate based on the levels of cesium 137 and iodine found around Harrisburg and Three Mile Island, and there's a direct comparison between the two. There's roughly, within a factor of 2 or 3, as much radioactivity released at Millstone in a year as was released here at Three Mile Island within those few days.

From my own studies and those of Dr. Mancuso, Dr. Gofman, and Dr. Alice Stewart, I would estimate that the total cancer rates are probably something like 10 or 100 times greater, so that I would expect anything from a few hundred to a few thousand extra deaths in this area in the next twenty years as a result of the releases.

18.

Dr. Judith Johnsrud, Ph.D., is one of the founders of the Environmental Coalition on Nuclear Power, which was established in Pennsylvania and adjoining states in 1970 and serves as an umbrella organization for many local groups which are opposed to nuclear energy. State College, January 5 and 6, 1980

Those who despoil the environment have an unlimited number of opportunities to lose; they need to win only once. Those who would protect the environment must win every time. They get to lose only once. There's the problem. But the individuals in small groups, those without money and power *are* capable of winning, and winning repeatedly, if they have a few key things going for them. The most important of these key things is accurate information, early. Give people information and let them make up their minds, and they will know how to act. I haven't any use for professional community organizers. I think the American people are absolutely competent to organize themselves into an unlimited number and variety of groups, even without previous experience, *if* they've got an issue, if they've got accurate information, and if they've perceived an association with themselves —either a very positive one or a very negative one, as long as it has to do with something that matters in their lives. We've had a history of a dozen years, here in Pennsylvania, of successfully halting one nuclear project after another.

My own first activity against nuclear energy occurred in 1968 when I opposed (successfully) the Atoms-for-Peace Plowshare program in central Pennsylvania, which had planned to create chambers for the storage of natural gas by detonating more than 1000 nuclear bombs underground. In 1969-1970 I opposed the Demonstration Liquid Metal Fast Breeder Reactor proposed for northeastern Pennsylvania. When it was rejected here, this reactor was moved by the industry to Clinch River in Tennessee, where it is still a controversial issue. I was a founder of the Environmental Coalition on Nuclear Power in 1970, the Eastern Federation of Nuclear Opponents and Safe Energy Proponents in 1975, and in 1979 I became chairperson of the Nation Solar Lobby. In 1975 I organized opposition to "Energy Parks" in Pennsylvania—the national test case for Nuclear Energy Centers. They were totally rejected by the people of Pennsylvania. I've also been serving on the Pennsylvania Govern-

or's Energy Council Advisory Committee since 1975.

In the fall of 1976 Chem Nuclear came into Pennsylvania for a low-level commercial waste disposal site, and we got wind of their proposal. It was discussed at the Governor's Advisory Committee, and a number of us, maybe ten representatives from our coalition and various groups around the state, showed up at the meeting. The TV cameras were all there; it was on the evening news that night, and the project was simply flatly dropped because they knew from the very start they were going to run into major opposition, and they just didn't want to face it. I really have the sense that getting to the point early enough with reliable, official information is the key, and let people take it from there. They are competent. I respect these individual groups.

Interestingly, all attempts at putting together a national nuclear opposition haven't worked, because the groups themselves are on the whole philosophically dedicated to the concept of decentralization, not only of energy sources but of their efforts. They recognize the strength of community. They recognize the strength of small scale. And I think they recognize their limitations.

I did my dissertation on "Political Geography of the Nuclear Power Controversy: The Peaceful Atom in Pennsylvania." It's simply a geographic study of the ways in which political power has been exercised in this controversy. I looked at it from the point of view of government, the industry, and of the grass-roots citizen organizations. My point here is that out of these many small groups, there has grown an opposition to the nuclear power program that has developed into a nationwide movement, a challenge to the most powerful combinations of economic and political forces in the world. That's all we are challenging. Good Lord, if the nuclear industry gets polished off by 1985, assuming we don't have yet another major accident, it will be one of the most stupendous accomplishments in history.

Can you say something about the accident?

I don't know whether I'll be able to talk to you much about the accident. It was so painful.

They say it was the worst one. Was it?

The estimated release was 13 million curies of xenon 133.

What does that mean?

That number comes from an NRC internal memo dated April 12, from the head of the Environment Assessment Division. His name is Lake Barrett. Thirteen million curies of xenon, which is relatively short-lived and not the most hazardous of the isotopes, needs to be compared with the largest radiation that they calculated could happen in the design base accident when the plant

was licensed. Now the maximum dose to an individual that the utility calculated would result from an overall release of 88,000 curies of xenon 133 was 320 millirems. Yet the maximum dose that the NRC says anybody got from the Three Mile Island accident, with 13 million curies of xenon 133 released, was only 85 millirems. It raises a question in my mind.

What is a millirem?

A millirem is an expression of the dose received—it is a thousandth of a rem; 500 millirems is the maximum permissible annual dose to an individual in the general population. It can be alpha particles or beta or gamma rays. It's a very difficult calculation to make. You've got to know the isotopes, whether they are taken into the body as an inhalation dose or an ingestion dose.

So how did they arrive at the figure of 85 millirems per individual with 13 million curies released when they said that only 88,000 curies released would give on individual dose of 320 millirems?

We don't know. Dr. Kepford's calculation used NRC data and Met Ed's own calculational model for dispersion factors. It worked out to a very massive dose, and the NRC is simply ignoring those calculations, which show that it was a massive dose. I think outrageously so.

What did you do when the accident happened?

The real terror of the accident was knowing how large the distances would be at which major radiation effects would be deadly. had there been a breach in containment on March 28. Chauncey Kepford and I went to Washington during the accident to try to plead for evacuation. I left my home with one bag, with full knowledge of the magnitude of the physical damage and the economic and societal disruption that would follow a breach of containment. This is what I've been studying for years. I don't think that most of the people who left Harrisburg had much of a sense of how awful it would be, what would happen to water supplies, what the problem of contaminated refugee people would be. I don't think that most of them had a sense of fleeing with the likelihood of contamination of themselves. Where would they go, how would they be tested, detected? All of these things that are the reality of a breach-of-containment accident hadn't really ever been presented to the 144,000 to 150,000 people who fled the Harrisburg area. We understood, and there were a few others who did, and it induced an indescribable state of terror. I can't ever describe to anyone the feeling that people had, to leave their homes with the sense that they might not be able to return and that they would be caught in a massively disruptive society. Our distribution system, our life-support system, is so delicate—yet it never occurs to people what would happen if it were to break down. Do you know where the closest underground spring is where you could be sure of uncontaminated water?

It's interesting. If you read the Atomic Energy Act of 1954, as amended by subsection *i* of section 170 (1957)—the Price-Anderson Act—you will find that the NRC has the authority to withhold information on the severity of an accident from the public in their final report and during the course of the accident, in the event that it is deemed that the release of such information would be seriously detrimental to the national security of the United States. I confronted NRC Commissioner John Ahearne with this question: "Was section 170 put into effect during the accident?" He said, "No." And I suppose, as a government policy, it was not invoked formally, but I have a feeling as I think back over the news and over the change in the news that at some time around noon on Friday, as the real severity of that accident became known, that that decision was somehow either consciously or unconsciously implemented.

What happened when you went to Washington to plead for evacuation?

In the Price-Anderson Act there is a clause that the senators of the affected state and the congressmen of that congressional district were to be informed of the full magnitude; and the people that we saw had, I would say, a veil over their eyes, with the exception of one congressman. I had a sense that they knew but that they could not act. I was on a television program in D.C. with Senator Schweiker eight days after the accident. He had been at the plant on the second day of the accident during the initial stages of dumping the contaminated water into the river, and he described how he looked out of the window of the reactor and saw this water, the outflow from the pipes. He said, "What's that?" They said, "Oh, we're dumping some water in the river." He said, "Is it radioactive?" They said, "Yes." Schweiker was absolutely outraged. He had not been told. He had no idea of the degree of contamination. He was immensely angry. I'm very troubled at this. I'm very troubled at the degree to which the probable real doses of radiation for those close to that plant have been suppressed. The studies that would be necessary to assess the degree of damage are not going to be done. We don't keep population statistics or health data sufficiently for a population over the time period of the latency in order to know what the damage will be. And we aren't getting the data on miscarriages, spontaneous abortions, stillbirth. I'm not aware of any study since the accident that has looked at the incidence of respiratory diseases and death among the elderly, who would also be among the early-affected, along with the fetuses.

When Sternglass looked at infant mortality, he was ridiculed; and I have trouble with his figures because they are small-numbered statistics and they are highly variable, but I think they are indicative of the need for a much fuller and more careful analysis of data than we are getting or are ever going to get.

Many of the people who live in the vicinity of that plant have reported a set of symptoms that at the time of their reporting I think they didn't know were associated with radiation poisoning. The passage of the plume was very poorly monitored, especially in the first three days. We can show you data from the population dose-assessment report. The first three days were the worst. There are pathways for the plume in virtually every direction around the plant that would simply fall right between the monitors, so that the monitors wouldn't have picked up the plume at all or only marginally so. If you take a look at the data and the placement of those ground-level monitors, it's perfectly clear that there were none out in the areas where there are a lot of people: Lebanon, Lancaster, even north towards Hershey—there was virtually no monitoring; and toward Carlisle. There were several monitors toward Middletown.

In describing the exposures that the public received from this accident, the utility and the NRC use the term "low-level radiation," and it sounds rather innocent. What does the term really mean?

The fundamental point that one has to bear in mind is that any exposure to ionizing radiation may result in damage to genetic material. That damage may be the death of a cell, which is okay because you've got millions of dead cells. But it may damage a cell so that it reproduces defectively, and that's the initiation of the cancer. That can be at any level of exposure, no matter how small. It used to be believed until the early 1970s that there was a threshold level below which there would be no damage, or below which even if there were some damage, the cell-repair mechanisms operated. With the 1972 report of the National Academy of Sciences Committee on the Biological Effects of Ionizing Radiation [BEIR], they concluded that that wasn't really the case, despite the fact that we don't have adequate research at this extremely low level of radiation, below a tenth of a rem (100 millirems).

Is there a medium level?

Sure there is. When we talk of low-level radiation, we are talking about less than 5 rems, which is the worker dose per year, which is ten times what is permitted to a member of the general public. Edward Radford, who headed the BEIR committee, says that he thinks the dose to workers should be reduced to precisely the same as to the general population.

Why not?

Exactly. They are people. They reproduce. They are part of the gene pool. Karl Morgan explained to me that when the standards that allowed the higher dose to workers were set, it was within the context that there would be only a few workers in the industry.

There is a doctor, Dr. Alice Stewart, a British epidemiologist and pediatrician, who has recently established the sensitivity of the fetus to low levels of radiation; and she has written about the damage that can be done, particularly in the early trimester when fetal development is so rapid. A little bit of radiation at that point can cause a great many problems. She points out how everybody probably has a lot of cancerous and precancerous cells, but they don't develop if one has an active immunological system. If the immunological system isn't functioning properly, though, then the signals don't get through to the lymphatic system and the potential cancerous cell is allowed to multiply. Her feeling is that the immunological system has a very delicate balance, and impairment of it by very low levels of radiation—much, much lower than would give you observable blood damage—can be responsible for the problem.

You mentioned Dr. Sternglass. Can you say something about him?

Well, his doctorate is in radiation physics and it was from Cornell University. He was one of those with connections clear back to the development of the bomb. Here is a man whose family were refugees from Nazi Germany. He's sensitized certainly to the maltreatment of human beings by government, as well as by industries—the profit-motive people. He is an earnest scientist. He's very good in his own field of physics. He was at Westinghouse doing research on improving the imagery in x-rays, on equipment to minimize the dosage that would be received by the patient. From that he has gained, I think, extreme awareness of the sensitivity of the fetus, intrauterine, to the x-ray. He understood that connection as long ago as Alice Stewart, who did much of the pioneering work on the impact of the x-ray upon the fetus.

Sternglass was one of the people who publicized this whole relationship of fallout to cancer and infant mortality back in the 1950s. Ernest's article in *Esquire* in, I think, 1968, "The Death of All Children," pointed out what he believed to be 400,000 infant mortalities associated with fallout during a specific period. Subsequently, a more technical article was published in *The Bulletin of the Atomic Scientists* in 1968, and the AEC detailed John Gofman as head of the Biomedical Division of Lawrence Radiation Lab to refute him. John was doing a study of the worldwide impact of all sources of radiation in the environment, that is, all manmade sources: weapons, medical, and so on. He and Art Tamplin, who had formerly been with Rand Corporation, were detailed to refute Sternglass. What they came up with was 4,000 rather than 400,000. So there was a difference of two orders of magnitude; theirs was lower, but there *were* deaths that they would attribute to fallout.

You will find Ernest in the Congressional Hearings in 1959 and 1962 on the effects of radiation from atmospheric nuclear testing. He and Barry Commoner and, I think, Harold Rosenthal and Linus Pauling were the scientists who were responsible for the test-ban treaty.

Friday of the accident has been called "Black Friday" because of the unplanned release of radioactivity that day. What did you think when that happened? Where were you?

On Friday at precisely 10:00 A.M., I walked into a newspaper building at Hershey as a siren went off in a long, sustained warning. I glanced at the flag across the street, and it was headed directly away from the reactor; the wind was blowing from TMI directly toward Hershey at that time. I called a friend in Harrisburg whose husband worked for the transportation department, and she was simply frantic. She said that they were issuing an evacuation order there as well and that there was a very serious problem at the plant that morning. That was all he knew. I then talked to the news editor just as he was taking off the wire the news of the uncontrolled release on

Friday morning, and to me it meant there was a possibility that a core melt was in progress, but more important, that a steam reaction, or a metal-water reaction of some kind was happening too. I stayed long enough to do a videotape and I know they never used it, but I talked about what little bits and pieces people could do to protect themselves, and then I had to make the decision either to go back home or to continue to Philadelphia for a scheduled address. I decided that I better head home. When I came out of the building that morning, that heavy metallic odor was permeating the air.

Odor?

The taste that people talked about. Odor, taste as well. I have a very keen sense of smell.

I've never heard that. Nobody talked about the smell.

Yes, in fact, the night before a friend had called from Harrisburg. She'd been at the governor's mansion and she had described this metallic odor. She said it's like the smell of metal burning. I told her to get inside. These are real things. Reporters have told me that they smelled it; you know they don't dare say it to the editor, but they had.

And it was on that return trip that I had a sudden, very painful sore throat and a wave of nausea that I knew would be associated with a radiation exposure, although I was also willing to chalk it up to nerves. But the uncertainty of it—I had no way of telling *what* had happened to me. I had no way of

knowing whether particulate matter had also been released in addition to the gases, whether I was contaminated, whether my car was contaminated. I knew that I must not go back directly to my house, because I would not want to track any contamination in with me. And that was the question: How do you find out? Where do you go? To whom can you turn for detection?

I finally decided that the thing to do was to go to the Health Physics Department at the university here—the health physicist is a strong pronuclear person, but he's also careful. And I respect him. He took it very seriously. He kept his distance, and he sent me directly to start washing while he did a detection. They got a count that came off higher than the background, higher than we got subsequently on a Geiger counter, but I felt it was nothing, nothing to worry about. So that I felt much better about it.

At least you knew.

Yes, I knew, and I knew how to go about finding out.

Does that mean that most hospitals would have a detection unit like that?

I'm not sure. A hospital that does a lot of nuclear medicine might have one in order to trace some of the isotopes. I should think that they would have to have one, but I'm just not sure.

I bet a lot of other people don't know either.

Of course they don't. It's something most of us have never even thought about.

19.

Perce Dorwart, Etters, July 3, 1979

It's a beautiful valley, isn't it? But we could do without those towers. It wouldn't make it any uglier to remove them! But I'm in a nice position. My company has a few thousand shares of that stock, and we lost $20,000 quick when it happened, whoof! Well, that's no big thing. One of the fellows said, "Look, when it gets down to 8, I'm buying." It was down to 8½. He bought. He said, "When it goes to 11, I'm selling. It's up to 10¼. But most of us think it's managed, that it's not a valid market. One broker told me, "When it gets down to 6, don't wait till I call you, you call me!" It didn't go to 6. They were able to hold it. But the idea of who's going to pay for it—it's already paid for. The money's gone, see? Let's face it. They've lost half the value of the stock. It's quite a story.

It sounds like it all hinges on the money.

Well, sure. Listen, if there was any question in people's minds of which was more important, health or money, ha ha, well, Lenin might be right. He said: "Capitalism will commit suicide for profit." And I've always hoped that he was wrong. But when I see what goes on, I say "My God, maybe the man was right." When you think that human life means less than profits, it makes you wonder.

I'm one of those that has prospered in this culture and society. I have no complaints. But, brother, if you don't have a little good luck and some friends, well, the working people pay a price, I'll tell you. In a case like this one here, if there is a danger, the people in this area will pay the price.

Now some of our bureaus and agencies protect the people. For instance, you see a crop of alfalfa there. At one time we used dieldrin to protect it from the beetle. We used it a few years. Finally they found that this dieldrin didn't decompose; they found it in the milk. They knew it was dangerous. We weren't allowed to use it anymore. Well, this makes sense. We would have to say that in this the FDA is doing a good job. But

there wasn't billions involved. There's billions of dollars involved in the atomic thing. And what we thought was going to be the cheapest source of energy is now the most expensive.

And it's not all the corporation's fault. There's labor. I had some of the fellows who built it, the project manager and also the superintendent of steam fitters, live in one of my homes for two years. God, the money they spent and made! There just seemed to be no limit. You see, they wanted to do it quickly, and evidently no one ever questioned the labor costs of it, just gave them whatever they wanted. "We'll get this up," they said, "and we'll really make a mint." I think they built it as good as they knew how. But when I look at those towers, I don't think they knew how! I can't believe that you have to build things like that to make an atomic energy plant. They're horrible things. I just wonder how long it'll be till they say, "Gee, they were never necessary in the first place."

But it'll be interesting to see what develops. Listen, if you want to make money, bet it'll open.

20.

Henry and Nancy Gilbert have been raising exotic birds for ten years. On the evening of May 2, 1979, within two hours, 416 of their birds mysteriously died. Annville, March 3, 1980

Henry: Well, the birds were all out in this hothouse area. There was a room, which is 8 by 12, and where you came in there were two rows of cages. Where the plants are there were also big cages of breeders. The birds in all the rooms were dead; it made no difference which room it was. At first our theory was propane gas. We have this stove here, and if there was enough gas in here to kill all of our birds at such a rapid speed,

wouldn't the pilot lights here have caused the whole place to blow up? I don't know how much gas it would take, but this was my theory. But it's been running perfect ever since. We have birds out there in the same area, and we've lost only one bird since, and that we think was due to old age. The state people will of course try to blame it on the environment at the location. I think they probably tried to do this also with Mr. Hoover, indicating that conditions were poor. I'll give you some reports from one of Hallowell's men [*state agriculture department*]. He came out every few months, and at no time does he say it's dirty. The reports have little comments on them like "nice," "clean," and such.

Nancy: I'll say one thing for myself. My house might not look good, but my birds were clean, and nobody better ever tell me otherwise because I worked. And any of the neighbors, they know what my place used to look like and how clean my animals were.

They said, "How could you keep all of this up?" And I said, "I work, that's how I do it." Five hundred birds takes an awful lot of work. Doctor's Pet Center in Lancaster isn't gonna buy junk birds. We were really starting to build up the stock, just enough that we could start selling the birds off and start to show a little profit. It took ten years to do that. It takes a long time.

What was your first thought when walking in the door?

Nancy: Fear. Shock. Horror.

Henry: There was a tremendous discussion about Newcastle's disease. The whole pet industry has become superconscious of Newcastle's, and of course this was our first thought.

Does it strike rapidly like that?

Nancy: I guess not. If it comes over them, they should have signs of it.

64

Henry: No, it's not an instant thing.

Nancy: My neighbor had been up here. She always liked the animals. She came in just before we went fishing. She thought the birds were great and she just had to come in and see them all the time. She's really a bird nut. And they were perfectly healthy. In fact the macaw we had was talking and carrying on with her. They were perfectly healthy when we left; there wasn't a thing wrong with them.

What time did you leave?

Nancy: Around seven o'clock.

Seven in the morning?

Nancy: No, it was in the evening time, and we got back around nine o'clock. About a quarter to nine.

So you were gone for only two hours?

Nancy: That's right.

And when you got back, they were dead?

Nancy: Yeah, half of them were dead, and the rest of them were dying.

Sounds like you just missed a big cloud of something.

Henry: Yes, but the question is: What? What upsets me is with this tremendous fear of Newcastle's disease in the whole pet industry. In the morning when Hallowell's representative came out, he wanted to take with him six carcasses of birds, and the remainder of birds we were supposed to put in plastic bags and allow the trash man to take them with him. They put them in the back of those trucks that compact everything and burst everything out. He would take them to a dump and bury them under earth. Between here and the city dump I know of one big poultry house that he would go past. Now does this sould like accepted procedure? The man that came to pick them up doesn't have the slightest idea about diseases, he said, and he wants to load these birds in a trash truck and cart them off that way.

Nancy: If it was Newcastle's disease, we could have wiped out everybody.

Henry: By then the whole county would have been wiped out.

Sounds like they didn't think it was Newcastle's disease.

Henry: Before he even came in the door he had indicated to Nancy that he only wanted about six carcasses, so she could get rid of the rest.

Nancy: He shocked me half to death. I said, "What?" He said, "I only want six birds." I said, "You don't realize, I have five hundred dead birds in there. What are you doing? You want me to put them in the trash can? What happens if I had a very contagious disease here?"

I kept thinking that he thought I was out of my head or something. When he walked here he got the shock of his life. He was really stunned. He was so shocked, he just stood here with his mouth open for about three minutes, and finally said he had to call his boss, Dr. Maynard, and explain to him. He said, "This is Ken Miller, I'm at this lady's house, and you wouldn't believe all of these dead animals around here. So many of them." So that's when Dr. Maynard gave him the okay to put 'em in a garbage bag and take them along with him. They took the whole thing to the lab.

Henry: Out of courtesy they took them to incinerate them for us, which I think would be a proper thing to do.

Nancy: He said he was going to go through and pick out some specimens for testing, too. That was May 3, the next day.

Henry: They took all the birds in the morning time, and Ken Miller said they'll get in touch and let me know. I said I'll stay here by the phone because I wanted to know what was happening. I wouldn't even let the neighbors come in because they had a parakeet and I was afraid if I had a disease, it would kill off their bird.

Can a person carry a bird disease?

Henry: It's possible, but normally you would show signs of it yourself.

But you weren't feeling sick?

Nancy: Shocked and sick that way, but otherwise sick from the birds? No. Because the birds were not sick when they died. They were showing no signs of being sick before they got hit with what they got hit with.

So he called me that same day at four o'clock. I remember it distinctly. I'll remember it for the rest of my life, I guess. He says, "I have a report on your birds." Now I should have tape recorded what he said. I trusted him completely because I thought he was going to tell me the truth. I had no reason to distrust anyone. I didn't think they were gonna lie and carry on the way they're doing. So he told me over the phone that the birds had severe intestinal bleeding and they died in severe pain. He said they had their wings out and they were breathing real, real hard. He said the reason they were breathing like that was because they had severe pain in the gut. They were really suffering hard when they died.

Henry: Since this time we found that this man had no knowledge of any telephone conversation that he has ever had. He doesn't remember ever telling us anything on the telephone. There was even a question in my mind whether she [Nancy] had misunderstood. But we had a meeting with Mr. Hallowell about a month later, with all of the doctors present, regarding the telephone conversation. Dr. Maynard denies saying

some of the things I know he said to me on the phone. So he has a tremendous memory problem. Very convenient.

He denied making the call?

Nancy: He said he never called me, he said he never told anything to me.

Henry: He did eventually admit, "Yes, I did talk to her on the phone." But he denies any of these statements that we accuse him of saying.

Nancy: Now how in heck would I ever come up with something like that? I mean I just wrote down exactly what he told me so I wouldn't forget it because Henry was going to call me that night. I was nervous, yes, but I'm not one of those people who fall all over the place. After it's all over and done with, then I might, but other than that—why, I even repeated it to him so that I would get it right. That's what's so fantastic about it. I made sure that I got that proper. I said, "You mean to tell me that they were bleeding?" He said, 'Yes, from the intestines." He even repeated it to me, so I told him I couldn't have got his message wrong. And he told me he never called me that day or anything.

Henry: Another observation I made, when we had the meeting with Secretary Mr. Hallowell. One of the first things he said was "This is my meeting. It's going to be run the way I want to run it." That was basically his opening statement. For the whole meeting, the secretary was sitting up there, and you could watch his hand motions. A person would be talking and in the middle of a sentence he would stop talking. Other hand motion, then people would start talking. So this meeting that we had with him was all prearranged, everything was already organized.

Nancy: They were already in the meeting when we got there, they already had the meeting. They were already in there, and I'm sure he had told them what they could say and what they couldn't say, and it was already set up.

Henry: We asked, "Did you run any test for radiation poisoning?" Their observation was that they didn't feel it was necessary, they had no reason to suspect that radiation could kill them. They did not run any checks for radiation, that's what amazed me. We are approximately ten miles from Ground Zero. Again, I'm not saying it was radiation; I hope somebody can prove to me that it wasn't. I don't know what it was, but I was astonished to find out that they didn't, just out of curiosity, check for radiation.

How many people were there at the meeting?

Nancy: About ten veterinarians.

Henry: They made general references to what their various findings were, and it ended up they said they found absolutely nothing in the birds. Their autopsy report came back and there was absolutely *no* internal bleeding. No signs of anything. Yet there was a radio show where they had on Dr. Ingraham, Dr. Maynard's boss, and over the air this man said the birds had signs of blood in their lungs. This is again different from the intestines, as they originally said. Do you want to hear something interesting? I've got the broadcast on tape. He admits there was blood in their lungs.

I think it's a big coverup, and they don't know what they did. I truthfully think they got the birds up there and the doctor had a golf date that afternoon, so they didn't do a damn thing. I can't prove differently.

Nancy: Then he called me back and asked if I had used sprays. I said, "No, I don't use sprays because I'm diabetic and I can't use spray. I don't use it in the house, I can't use any chemical spray because I get sick from it."

Henry: They also initially tried to blame it on poison in the food itself, but we had about four different feeding programs so it would have been impossible.

Nancy: They took all food samples along. They told me it might be in the seed; it might have been a packet of bad seed or something.

Henry: Or the water.

Nancy: They weren't all watered the same day.

Henry: You may be interested in this document. This is the autopsy report from the Department of Agriculture. It's the Summerdale Laboratory report [*which reads in part*]:"Feed was checked for Warfarin content." Now, the Warfarin, as I understand it, is a poison for rats, and causes severe internal bleeding. Why would they have gone to the trouble of testing this feed for that if they had autopsied the birds and there was no internal bleeding? Why bother? Or am I looking at it the wrong way? They just want to waste their tax money running the tests? I received this autopsy report after our meeting with them.

Did you ever hear of anything else in the area that day or some days later?

Henry: One thing we did notice, from that day on there was a tremendous lack of wildlife in the area.

Nancy: Everyone noticed that.

Henry: Rabbits, pheasants, almost nonexistent. And now, we don't know, it could have just been a bad year for young being born.

Nancy: But this was sudden from May 2 on. They went just overnight. We used to go just around that curve and there would be rabbits everywhere. But the next day after this happened, it was like the world came to

an end. There was nothing there. It's still like that now, you're lucky if you see a rabbit on this mountain. The hunters are really complaining about it because there's no game.

Have people found corpses in the woods?

Nancy: I think people are afraid to go in the woods and look, really. They just put it out of their minds. But after Fred Williams got this on the air, on July 9, people were calling up to tell him they had been finding dead rabbits in their yard, dead baby bunnies or dead birds, all around the area.

Henry: But maybe these people just wanted the publicity too.

Nancy: Maybe they were just noticing it, and he'd called their attention to it. There were a lot of little birds lying around, but I think it was because there wasn't enough food for 'em. You know, when they spray, they kill off a lot of insects that are for the birds.

Henry: We have noticed a few other things since then. We have an incubator that we were running, and we were collecting birds from different people in the neighborhood, exotic pheasants and things like that that we were hatching out. We had a few birds remaining and knew they were good breeding birds for us. From the day, May 2, we have had absolutely no births on this property, not one bird has hatched; we cannot get our birds to go to nest.

Nancy: And the birds that survived—the twenty-five—had a strange reaction about three months after this happened. I don't know if it was just because the other birds had died around them, or what, but they weren't normal for quite a time. My birds are not wild; they don't jump around in the cage, and they don't bang themselves up against the wire and go crazy when somebody walks through because I had people coming in here buying birds right out of the cages, so they were used to people. Parakeets, they shouldn't be fluttering around and being scared or anything; but right after this happened, they came in a day or two days after, and you couldn't get near those cages. Those birds were trying to kill themselves. They were high strung. They were nervous. They weren't eating. I guess they were in shock. I fed them, and I had to leave them alone because they'd fly around, bang up against the wire and everything, and that was in no way normal for my animals to react that way. We would always be around them. We cleaned them all the time, and they could care less. I could hold their babies, and they wouldn't mind. But ever since that, it took them about three months to calm down, and they're still not right. We tried to breed them, and forget it; they just won't do it; the males are acting like the females, and the females are acting like they're males. I'm afraid to sacrifice one of

the birds to see if it's changed inside, because I'd have to send it out to the agriculture department, and they've pulled a good one on us already, and I don't know where else to send it.

Henry: One wonders at this point at the extent of the finding, whether we'd ever come up with anything. You'd have a test run for microscopic changes in the bird. I would assume this would be a very expensive operation.

On May 4 they finally came out and officially quarantined us with a piece of paper, and to date [March 3, 1980] we have not received an official notification that the quarantine has been lifted.

And traditional procedure is—

Henry: They must come out and remove the quarantine themselves. They don't seem to care about what they're doing. Are you familiar with the federal testing lab in Ames, Iowa? We were under the impression that they would send some of the animals to this federal testing lab to verify some of their findings, or, if they didn't have any findings, to get a second opinion. At the meeting we had with Hallowell two months later, one of the questions we asked was, "Why didn't you send some of the birds to Ames, Iowa?" First of all he indicated that all the birds, except for the six he wanted to work on, were immediately incinerated because he didn't want any carcasses lying around that could possibly have a contagious disease. He felt that his autopsies had brought up absolutely nothing, and therefore he felt it would have been a waste of time to send the organs from the various birds to federal testing because they wouldn't have been able to find anything either, and they would only run checks for the specific things that he indicated he wanted checked. They would not run massive autopsies to find out why the birds died.

So why didn't you send the birds to Ames?

Henry: Because a representative of the federal government who was a state man came out every couple of months and gave us a regular report that said in case of any massive bird die-offs, call this number.

Is that a state number?

Henry: Yes, and this is exactly what we did.

And their procedure is to do it at Summerdale Lab first, and then send it to Ames?

Nancy: We were under that impression, yes, and then Dr. Maynard called here one day saying they had them, and that there will be a report from Ames, Iowa, because they're going to send the specimens out there.

Plus, when my husband got back a week later, he told him the same thing. And yet when we had the meeting, he denied that he ever said anything.

Henry: I don't remember the exact date, but maybe two weeks after the bird die-off, I had called this Dr. Maynard on a Monday; I had received his autopsy report back, which told me absolutely nothing, and it didn't feel right to me, and I said, "Have you got the report back from Ames yet, and will I be receiving a copy of it?" He told me, "I have received an autopsy back from them. It is exactly the same thing; it is what you have, and therefore there is no reason for you to have a copy of it." Then at a later date he told me, "Well, I checked my records, and I made a mistake. I didn't send them to have a second opinion." So why on the telephone did he indicate that I had the report right here and it was the exact same thing that he had and there was no reason for me to receive a copy?

Nancy: You told me the Department of Agriculature spent 500 man-hours at Hoover's farm.

Yes, that's what Secretary Hallowell said.

Nancy: They didn't spend one blasted minute here. Just the length of time to pick the birds up and take them away, and they came back the next day and put a quarantine up, but as far as looking at the facility or anything like that, they did absolutely

nothing. They did have to put some time into the autopsy work itself in their laboratories, but that's all they've done.

And they kept saying they were going to send someone out with meters to check the air and maybe find something. I kept waiting and waiting, but nobody showed up.

What do you think of the March 28 accident?

Nancy: It scares you, it really does, and not for myself, but for the kids, when they're going to grow up and have children. The people that live right there, three miles from that nuclear thing, and now the ladies there are having babies, and they're being stillborn, and God, it makes you wonder. It scares you. They're not telling the truth, and now they're trying to push it on as heredity. I don't believe that crap because they lie so much. I think people are so dumb for falling for it; they just believe anything they tell them.

Henry: You just learn to have a tremendous—I don't want to use the word—hate, mistrust for public officials. If anything happens in the future, even if they blow all over the state, I'm supposed to notify them, but I don't feel that I want to.

. . .

WAHT Radio: Fred Williams Show, Lebanon, July 11, 1979

Dr. Ingraham: We absolutely knew about the Gilbert case, but did not consider that a major die-off. I think it's a matter of time, sir, where we decide whether this is a major die-off or not. Obviously we are very concerned with Mrs. Gilbert's case.

Fred Williams: Dr. Ingraham, it seems to me that your Department of Animal Industry did not become very interested in Mrs. Gilbert's case until we started this investigation.

Dr. Ingraham: That's not true, because we have had early on our—Dr. Maynard went out of his way to find out what happened on that property. He called her, trying to get her to think about what possibly could have done the damage because he did not find anything wrong with those birds. The live ones he got were absolutely normal. The dead ones showed very, very small, microscopic changes in the lungs, just a little bit of hemorrhage. It could have come from anything. Flying around, they could have caused it. Such a slight change that it had to be something physical happened to the birds. Humidity? Temperature? Some toxic fumes of some sort.

21.

Penrose Hallowell is the secretary of the Pennsylvania Department of Agriculture. Harrisburg, February 25, 1980

My family has been farming in Pennsylvania since William Penn's time; came over in 1680. My son now is on the home farm in Bucks County. Prior to being appointed secretary, for eight years I was director of the Farmers Home Administration, so I had administrative experience with the federal government. I had been director of the Land Bank and president of many farm organizations. My life has been devoted to producing, aiding agriculture in many ways.

Now they say about this area, Lancaster County in particular, that it is one of the richest farm lands in the world. Is that true?

Yes, it's true. Lancaster County, even though there is a great deal of tourist trade being built up, still produces more farm produce than any other county in the U. S. that does not use irrigation. We have about 40 to 50 inches of rainfall a year, which is sufficient to grow a great number of crops without irrigation.

What are the products that the whole area is most proud of?

Milk is our Number One item, but we have a lot of fruits and vegetables as well. The only commodity really Number One is mushrooms. We are in the top ten in many commodities, especially livestock, ice cream, eggs, cheeses, and tobacco for cigar leaf.

What impact did the accident have on the environmental situation you described, the farming and growing?

When the Three Mile Island accident occurred, the farmers were very concerned, because of the unique characteristic of a dairy cow, in that if a dairy cow picks up any trace of iodine, and we had iodine 131 coming out, it concentrates right in the milk. About the fourth day or so, traces of radioactive iodine were found in the milk. We were picking up samples all over the twenty-mile radius to see what potential there was, and of course the levels were very low even where they were found. But at the time farmers were wondering just like everybody else, the potential, if in fact we did have a big release of radioactivity, what would they do with their cattle? Should they leave them? Many farmers would very much resist leaving their animals; they are almost part of the family. We advised farmers to feed the animals only stored food, and not let them graze, as a precautionary measure. It was wintertime so the cattle

were not out on pasture yet and the barn had a good shield toward radioactivity. The cattle were relatively safe in the barns, having 70 to 80 percent of any radiation shielded by the roof and the hay over them. So the cattle would be relatively safe for a few days. A few owners did evacuate their livestock, but not too many.

Farmers are rather religious people, but also rather practical people and over the years have seen scares of one type or the other and recognize that the job of the news media is to publicize things and perhaps overstate them. So I don't know that they were as much concerned as the other groups of the population who were not as power oriented. In fact, during the last ten months quite a few of the farmers' associations have passed resolutions supporting the opening of Three Mile Island with the knowledge that proper safeguards would be taken before it is opened. But I think just to paraphrase some of the things they are saying, virtually any source of power has its risks. If they were mining coal, the miners would have to go down in the mines, where there are lung-disease problems; and people who live in areas where there are coal mines have the danger that their house may cave in or something. People mining oil have explosions and whatnot. And the record of atomic energy is better than any of the rest. I don't know that in this country there has been anyone killed in an accident involving a nuclear reactor. They don't exactly like the idea of having potential radioactivity but they are not afraid of it either, and that's the general statement. Our attitude has been not to state any policy as to whether it's safe or not. That's not for the Department of Agriculture to say. Whatever the governor says—of course he's speaking for the government, including me. We did not withhold any information that we found radioactivity in the milk. The highest level we found in the milk was 29 picocuries per liter.

You mean at the time of the accident 29 picocuries of iodine is what you found?

Yes, at a maximum.

And what is normal?

Anything below 14 is not detectable on the equipment used, and it's only recently that they can detect anything under 100. A picocurie to my understanding is one to the minus eleven power, which is one trillionth of a curie, which you can't see, hear, or feel. The standards are that if there were 1,200 in milk or air, then steps should be taken. It was very low, and about several years ago when the Chinese had the bomb and the fallout crossed over Pennsylvania, we had up to 480 picocuries per liter in the milk, so compared with that, this was very, very low levels. From 100 to 1,000 we advise pregnant women and small children not to drink the milk, and once it is over 1,000, we stop

the sale of it. These represent a very strict "action level." At the time of the accident FDA's action level was 12,000 picocuries per liter.

Now when you talk about that testing, was it immediately after the accident or was it for a prolonged period of time?

We started testing that day and are still testing now. We're down now to 6; that's all we're sampling, but you can see that since then they have all been low. Twenty-nine is the highest; then 13, then all less than 10. I thought there was one around 32, but maybe it was 29.

So now it's been almost a year since it happened. What in retrospect do you now think happened, not in the plant, but to the environment?

I think, assessing the information we have now, the government and everybody else did somewhat overreact and probably properly so, because we didn't know how bad it was going to be. We were concerned not about what had happened but what could happen, and as it appears now, we still don't know what could have happened. Some people say we could have had a meltdown in sixty minutes. Well, we can have a lot of things happen in sixty minutes, so I'm not sure that means anything, but it did raise a lot of uncertainty in the farming community. We've had several farmers who've had cattle problems that now think that radioactivity is part of it and we've tested them whenever these problems were called to our attention. One man had seven or eight animals that he said he'd lost, and first they were sort of rumored to be dead, but actually he only had three die with calving complications. But we tested them and took samples of all the various organs, the liver and everything else, and never found any evidence or any indication that radioactivity was a factor. This herd that had the problem had unsanitary conditions where his dry cows were, and they were getting an infection in the uterus, which is not unusual, but the unusual thing is that he had four or five cows in close proximity. As it turned out, both he and his wife worked off the farm, and they had undependable help. That's what they had. Our veterinarians identified an Infectious Bovine Rhinotracheitis (IBR) virus as the cause of his problems, and after a vaccination program began, his herd has cleared up. He is now satisfied that radiation was not the cause of his calving problems.

There was a situation where pet birds died at one time and we have run all kinds of tests and had to assume that the family was away at the time, and something got in the ventilation system, and they got asphyxiated in some way. The accident at TMI has raised the anticipation level, or whatever you want to call it, of farmers looking for or being on the alert for any kind of a problem that they can relate to radioactivity. But so far we have found absolutely no indication. And to the contrary, all the tests show that any level of anything anywhere was so low that it would not likely produce any problem.

Is there much of a history of this kind of thing happening here in the past? Have there been cases where a significant number of cattle have died or a number of birds suddenly died?

Yeah, in these large poultry places where there are a lot of animals confined in a small area. We have it all the time. If the electricity goes off or something in the ventilation system goes off, the birds die. That is not common, but it's not unusual in fact. Chickens are sort of stupid. If the temperature drops too much when they are small, they crowd in a corner so much that they kill themselves. If the temperature gets too high, they apparently can't perspire, so they do die. They are more susceptible than most animals.

As I mentioned earlier, we also have a responsibility for pesticides. We had one poultry flock where they had a disease, and a lot of poultry diseases are very contagious, wiping out 20,000 in a day. So if they get these diseases, they must clean out the house completely, and we go in and supervise a disinfectant. They put the chickens back in after keeping it empty for ten days or so, depending on the circumstances, and on occasion one or two mistakes have been made on what chemical has been used. In one case there is a suit involving a company that used a chemical which did in fact get into the food supply. It is the kind of thing we're normally really closely monitoring, to make sure that the animals are protected, or as important, the consumer who is going to eat the farm product.

I wanted to ask you about Clair Hoover, whom I assume you are describing. He said that when his cattle died, he took them to a state lab and also to the New Bolton Center Lab. The state came in and paid for the results and took them, and he didn't find out about that until he read it in the newspaper. He claims that he has not yet seen the full reports from the lab. Did that occur? Is that a normal thing to happen?

[*Tape recorder is turned off and later restarted.*] On the record I will say that we spent hundreds of man-hours going to his farm for weeks afterwards, testing cattle, helping him with the fresh cows, and trying to get the problem over. And I think partly because of our assistance and partly because of the fact that things were done right, the problem did disappear.

We were not testing everything for radioactivity, so we can't say definitely that there was no radioactivity there. That's what I suppose he wants the report to say. We can't say that, we can only say that we found no radioactivity, but we can't say definitely there is nothing there. The Department of Environmental Resources lab also conducted tests on tissue samples from Mrs. Hoover, and found no detectable levels of radiation. I guess one of the things the governor rightly did was to have us report facts, and we wouldn't try to air our conclusion as being pronuclear or antinuclear. I guess by now you realize that I'm sort of saying both sides of it. There are obviously advantages and disadvantages, but we are not here to say it was all good or it was all bad.

What inspired you to pay the bill for him?

We were doing it for everyone. The samples of the milk that we picked up, we paid for. It was a dollar and a half. And we did not charge anyone for the testing.

That in itself was not an unusual operation?

No, it was a normal operation.

In talking with him, he doesn't seem satisfied?

No. Although when I talk to him personally, he of course is rather friendly, and he says different things to different people.

At the time of the accident Hershey powdered a lot of the milk instead of using it directly for their chocolate products. Is that something you would recommend that they do?

We were in touch with them the day after it happened. I called in farm leaders and commercial people to give them the information we had. In fact, the morning that the news was released that the iodine was in the milk, I had a meeting here and told them exactly what it was. They were concerned more with the publicity danger than the actual danger. They didn't want to be identified as using milk from the TMI area. There were a few stores in Baltimore that were showing signs "We do not get any milk from Pennsylvania," sort of inferring that milk from Pennsylvania may have a problem. And just to avoid any possible statement that there was any problem with the milk going into their chocolates, they decided that they were going to keep it out, so they could honestly tell any reporters that no, there is none of that milk going into their product today. That was strictly their decision, I did not give them any advice on that.

. . .

I know that there is concern. I have talked to some of the people that are very opposed to any nuclear reactors, and they have given information that I have read. They say some things like there is this danger and there is that danger. I have seen some technically knowledgeable men generally refute that information. I believe the people that are doing the monitoring for the Pennsylvania Department of Environmental Resources and the Food and Drug Administration and the NRC have, as we have done, virtually left no stone unturned to try to detect any danger. They have told me there is no danger and I believe they are correct. The FDA was testing milk and food products in the area for iodine 131, cesium, and strontium 90 for several weeks following that accident.

It's really hard to tell, to get at the real source of radiation?

As I understand it when I have a tooth x-ray, I get something like 50 millirems of radiation. I would have received more radiation than a worker did at that plant that stayed there for three days during the accident when there were some emissions. That's how low the levels were. People who live in Denver, having less protection of the atmosphere from the radioactivity that comes from the sun or wherever, receive higher levels than a typical worker does in a year working in the Three Mile Island facilities. Again, I am not a technician in nuclear energy, and I have faith I guess in those that I have gotten to know personally that I think are very competent. All the advice I could get I sought, and all the advice I received indicated that the food supply is safe, and they were taking every precaution they can.

Did you ever think twice about the possibility of a nuclear accident, given the one in ten million chance of there being one?

Well, I had been aware of the concerns of nuclear power plants. First of all my home in Bucks County is close to Point Pleasant, which is the pumping station to a nuclear power plant in Montgomery County. It's going to go real close to my home. So I've been aware of those who are opposed to it. My religion is that of a Quaker, and the American Friends Service Committee and others have been concerned about all kinds of things. I've been involved in it from the input that I've heard from them, so I've maybe been more aware of the potential and the concern that some people have than others were previously to it. So that it wasn't that big a chance to me. People had been telling me that the danger was there, and of course I believed them and still do. The danger is there, we cannot avoid all kinds of risks. If we do, we will live a fairly dull life. And one without any power. Or go back to eating herbs and natural foods, which I guess I could do, but I'm not that afraid of anything that's going on in the environment right now.

Londonderry Township, with Middletown in the distance on the curve of the river, February 1980

22.

*Charlie Conley, farmer, Etters,
March 2, 1980*

Well, you wanted to know about this here plant. It gives me a lot of trouble. The first thing that started giving me trouble was the cattle. I lost three out of four. I got the one yet. It didn't kill him but I pretty near lost that one. What it does, it weakens the muscles, and it makes the bone brickle.

But this one you still have is starting to come back?

Yeah, he's coming back now. But it took a while. Weber's our veterinarian. It took him a while to find out what was going on. It weakens the muscles, and it causes the bones to break. It pulls the calcium out of the bone.

So they become very brittle.

Yeah, brickle. So the way he found now, he took one down to Eastern Lancaster to a laboratory, and he didn't give it any more medicine and it did good. They kept it down there for quite a while, then they killed it, and they checked all the bones, and you could see cracks in the bone. They had to use a microscope. Could see cracks in a lot of different places.

What does he figure is the cause of the cracks?

Well, brickle bones. You see it pulls, that fallout of the plant pulls the calcium out of the bone. And it weakens the muscles. The first place, they'll get down. I had one here all summer, last summer. Was it down when you were here?

Yes.

Well that one died on me after that. One Saturday morning, his heart conked out on him.

You just went out there one day and he was gone?

No. I heard him breathing real heavy. It was over at the pump there, and I went over and looked, and here he was, gasping for his breath, and I just stood there and watched him a little bit. He thrust his head out, and that was the end. I dealt with him all summer. Carrying water, feed. He ate. Had pills to give him and the veterinarian give him shots, but he never come out of it. He could walk on his knees on the front, and get his hind end up, but he'd just go around in circles. He could sometimes straighten one front leg out, but the other he couldn't straighten out.

What kind of treatment did you give him?

You see, what this fallout of the plant does is pull the selenium out of your feed. It pulls it out of our vegetables that we eat too. You see, selenium's a poison, but your system has to have it. So I went and bought a bag, 50 pounds of selenium, and I give him a spoonful of that in his feed. It seemed to strengthen him up some, but when they're so long down that way, that's the end.

Last spring one time it rained 3 inches in my water trough. Because it's south and it's a beveled trough, it might have rained more than 3 inches. And I let them big steers out, and they drink that water; and a day or so afterwards I let them out again, and, boy, they just don't like water. It gave them the diarrhea. So that took them off of feed for about a week.

Was that the white stuff [the "white fallout"] on top of the water?

No, that comes off of the roofs when it rains. Don't rain for a week or so, and then it rains and it comes off of the roof, and you catch that water, the first water is all white, like milk on top. You can't use it.

Did it used to be white like that?

No. And it ain't that way now since that plant's not in operation. Water's clear when it runs off. They wanted to tell us that it came from the airplane's flying around in the air and stuff, but it don't come from that, it comes from that plant.

You never had it analyzed?

Well, after the accident over there the plant wasn't in operation, and it didn't gather then. [*Describes other effects.*] My sow pigs never come in heat all winter long. It affects the breedings of animals. It's killed the trees around here. Another thing, on my garage, down here on the back side where the water run along the ground it killed all that grass, from that roof when it rains. Now over summer since it shut down there's fall grass that grew in there; but now it's all frozen ground. That won't take the winter, fall grass. So when spring comes, I won't have grass there again. It'll take a couple of years till that bluegrass comes back and grows together again, without the operation of that plant. It's got the nicest maple tree I had on the place out here pretty well killed.

Is that the one with the big hole in it?

One out here on the corner. Yeah. Another thing I noticed towards the fall was the pear tree up here on the hill, at my neighbor's. The leaves was brown on that tree long before fall. And in the fall I got the pears, and them pears on the side of that tree is only that big, and the other side they're nice.

They were small?

It gets the one side where it come in. But maybe next year, it might affect the other side, see, and I doubt if any leaves will come out on that side of that tree this spring. If that plant, I figure, is in operation for ten to fifteen years I don't think we'd grow much hay in this area. You'll grow your short crops like potatoes and vegetables and wheat and corn and oats, but the hay's a two-year crop. You sow it when you sow your wheat in the fall, and the next year you cut the wheat off. And the next year you make hay, you see, it's a two-year deal. So I doubt if we'd grow much hay if it was in operation a couple of years, ten or fifteen years.

What would happen at ten years that wouldn't happen before?

Well, you get enough of that there fallout in the ground, see, and what is happening, it was starting to grow into our hay already. It's what gave our fellows trouble with our milk cows. They got nervous in their front legs and shoulders. It falls to the ground long enough, then it grows into your hay, your feed that you feed them. Now milk around here had plenty of it in, but it was getting mixed with so much other milk away around that they figured it didn't hurt nobody.

You've learned that from the man testing the milk?

Yeah.

What did he tell you?

Well, he didn't tell me, but these fellows that have the dairy cattle, after the accident the place was shut down over there. Then they told them how much was in, but they said they didn't figure it could hurt anybody because it was milk picked up all over the country, far around, and all the milk was mixed together, see? They tested the milk every day.

For how long? Right after the accident?

They were doing it before the accident at the place every so often, but then when that happened, they tested it every day for quite a while.

How long have you been on the farm here, Charlie?. How old is it?

I don't know how old the farm is, but I came here in the spring of 1913 with my parents and been here ever since. My daddy bought the farm in 1912. I'm 74 now, and I was 8 then, so that's a good many years ago.

And you never had problems like this?

No, never had this trouble before, That TMI plant's caused us more trouble with animals than anything we had since we lived here. And I didn't finish it about the water. I got wise, and every time it rained after that, I washed. I took and cleaned that water trough out, before I watered the cows. See, it's out in the open, where it rains down there. Now my brother lives up here; he didn't have that trouble with his cattle because his water trough is inside where it doesn't rain in it; and another neighbor up here has running spring water, it's running all the time.

Have real estate values gone down in the area since the accident?

The valuations fell about half in the city of Goldsboro after that happened. You went down there, and Goldsboro looked like a ghost town. They really went out of there, and there's a couple that never came back. The Lutheran woman preacher never came back, and one of my second cousins never came back. I don't know if there's any more or not, but if they start that up again, there's a lot more gonna leave. They'll sell out for what they can get and leave. Cause that's how much they're scared of it. When they put that plant up they told people that they would generate electricity so cheap there that they wouldn't even need a meter to register. You know what it is now? I'm paying more for electricity now for one month than I paid for two months a year ago.

A year ago?

That's right, thirty-seven dollars for one month now, and a year ago it run in the high thirties for two months. You pay every month now. So that's how cheap they're generating electricity, and they want us to pay for that accident. It ain't our place to pay for it, but that's why they're all the time raising their rates. They want the money for that accident. That's the government and the stockholders' place to pay for that. Not us. Because we didn't tell 'em to build it, and if they don't know how to operate it, it ain't our fault. It's the company's fault.

That's right.

They have poor security over there. These fellows went in a boat and tested them out. Got in the plant and walked around, guards never stopped them. There was a fellow come from the other side of the river and drove across the bridge, got in there and was walking around, and that is what they got their guards for. Security. So that's how poor the security they got. They're not fit to operate the place. Well, I don't know if they're gonna give them any license to operate it anymore or not, but the thing of it was, if it had blew up, it would have been pretty bad because the other plant was already fueled for another year. They'd just fueled it up before that. That one was shut down when this other had the trouble. And the thing of it is, that Peach Bottom plant is too close to this plant. If that plant blows up, this one will blow up. If this one blows up, that one will blow up. They're too close together.

I blame the government a lot for it. They had no business to give them a license, especially to put it up in a populated area. Because if that blows up, it'll affect Harrisburg, New Cumberland, and Middletown, and all the other side.

Lancaster County didn't have as much trouble with the cattle as we have here because it was fair weather when it happened and it would go out over them higher and distribute much further around. They had some trouble with the cattle over on the other side there, but Metropolitan Edison—they're younger veterinarians and they pay them off, see, but they didn't pay Weber off. He's a spunky fellow. He ain't taking no bribe money to cover their mistakes up. But this one fellow hauled this calf that got down for me, and I couldn't get him up. They gather up them all, see, for cat and dog food. They take 'em in and kill them and cook them up. He said he's hauled a good many milk cows out down the other side of that power plant, down the other side of that aviary over there. They get down, they can't get up. So he figures that it's coming from the plant because he said before that was over there, he didn't haul any milk cows out of there. So they paid them *off*. They pay them off, and they want to put the electric bill way up for us to pay that yet.

I think it'll shorten the life of the people down too. That head doctor in the Hershey Medical Center said he ain't gonna know what effect this is gonna take on the people till three to five years. Then they'll start to get ailments from it. But what they *did* do was they ordered all the women out that was gonna have children, and the small youngsters. But what I did find out is different ones that's bothered a lot with rheumatism since that accident. My brother up here, he gets lumps on the back of his hands here, swells up, and he's got trouble with his feet. And Eddie Prowell up here, he's got trouble. He blames it on that plant. He didn't have it before that accident. And a fellow who lives down here at Pleasant Grove, a Ziegler boy, he was up here one day walking and limping. And I said what happened to him. He said rheumatism. He blames it on that. He said, when that happened, he said he could taste that in the air, in the mouth. And he had that trouble.

He's a young fellow?

He's not as old as me. I'd say he's in the fifties, up in the fifties pretty well. Yeah, they don't know what trouble it's gonna cause in people yet. But one doctor over here around Harrisburg said since this accident, he's got a lot more people with throat trouble. And the fellow that runs the eye place over here around New Cumberland has got a lot more people coming in with eye trouble, since that. So they don't know what effect it's gonna have on the people yet. But I know it has an effect on the animals because I had that experience.

Farm in Londonderry Township, July 4, 1979

23.

David Ingraham, V.M.D., Harrisburg, March 18, 1980

I am director of the Bureau of Animal Industry. Our basic charge is to eradicate certain diseases of livestock in the commonwealth, and these diseases that were designated for our work have to do with either public health concerns or they are devastating diseases if they get a handle on our livestock. So, basically, we are doing tests and eradicating diseases such as brucellosis, tuberculosis, anthrax, blackleg, and Johne's disease. The vast majority of our money and time is spent doing surveillance work for those particular diseases, conducting the appropriate tests and running a laboratory that can take livestock carcasses, find a cause of death or illness, and see if it is a disease that we should follow through with in our regulatory programs.

If there is something that you get in the lab that you don't feel you understand, do you send it to a federal lab or a bigger lab?

There are times when we will send specimens to the National Animal Disease Laboratory in Ames, Iowa, for additional testing if necessary, but our lab under this administration has been well supported and is very competent to conduct tests that many labs cannot do. So we have developed some very talented and trained people to staff our lab. We test over 1 million samples a year in that lab, including all the way from large carcasses to blood samples. It is a nationally recognized lab. It is recognized by the American Asociation of Veterinary Laboratory Diagnosticians, which established the standards for that kind of lab in the United States.

Now one thing that we wanted to ask about is the accident at Three Mile Island and the fear that's been unleashed. It is said that people are ready to blame anything which they do not understand on radiation. Have you noticed any effects that you could attribute to radioactivity, or effects of any sort that haven't occurred before?

From the monitoring of the environment around Three Mile Island, our tests did not show significant or more than usual doses of radioactive material. The doses that escaped at the time of TMI were not significant to even millirems. Some of the initial testing that had been done of course said that there was less than x number of millirems, but this had more to do with the sophistication of the equipment than the exact level. For instance, some of the early milk samples said that there was "40 mr or less" of measurable radiation, whereas if the tests had been done a few days later when the so-

phistication was put in place to measure down to 10 mr or less, it could easily be that the initial testing was less than 10 mr. The early testing was done under a lot of pressure to get reports out fast, and therefore they used the most rapid designation to get those results out over Saturday and Sunday. Yet later on when there was a little more time to keep running the other phases of that test, you could get it down close to the fact that, by gosh, there really wasn't much release at all, if any. So our statistics were pretty good around the monitoring sites that had been going on and around the ones that had been put in place immediately to get more testing going on. It showed that we did not have a contamination of the environment. In looking at our livestock populations around the facility, no vets in practice there were reporting any problems prior to or after the incident that could be attributed to radiation. Obviously vets were seeing medical problems ongoing, as you always have in any livestock area, and the kinds of problems were not problems that could not be explained. Things like abortions occur in normal cattle populations, and the incidences did not rise. Some of the farmers around that area found that their health problems were minimal before and after TMI. There is no substantiation that we had any kind of symptom that could be attributable to something vague like "low doses of radiation," or something mysterious.

We were talking to Dr. Weber, the main veterinarian on the whole west side of the river. He described some things with bones, an increase in brittleness in the bones, and implied that there might be a connection with the plant, but he admitted that he didn't know for certain. He also talked about lack of dilation with animals giving birth, how they always respond to hormone injections, but that they do not respond to hormones now.

The survey we did of some of the large farm operations showed that they were not having similar experiences. In other words, farmers that were in the business of making money, large dairy herds and commercially operated cattle farms, did not experience a problem with this, even though they were located well within the five-mile zone of TMI. In fact, when we did our survey after a farmer mentioned in a meeting that he was having a significant increase in deaths of his animals, we went out to see him. We went to see all farmers in the five-mile zone. This one farmer felt that he did have a significant increase in abortions and calf death and said it in a way that affiliated this problem with TMI, even though it occurred weeks later. We surveyed all farmers, because part of our responsibility is to know who has livestock within given areas, and we then made a farm-to-farm check of each individual who had some kind of livestock. Ninety-five per-

cent of them said that this year was better than any year they'd had or that there was no problem, no drop in milk production, no problems of Cesareans, no abortions to speak of. Weighing this statistically against a normal cattle population very far away from any kind of radiation will show that the incidence of disease problems was not higher in a five-mile zone around TMI. We did this within the past year.

What happened with that farmer? Is that Clair Hoover?

Yes, it is Hoover. What we did then was to find out why his cows were aborting and, through our veterinary lab in Summerdale and using the facilities of the University of Pennsylvania, we actually came up with a diagnosis of the virus which was causing the disease. We actually proved the virus, and the vets treated the animals for the disease, and the problem stopped. It was a direct cause that we identified, and therefore all kinds of incriminations that radiation did it were just not substantiated. It was a virus infection. With management and treatment the problem was stopped.

In our review in some of the farms where Dr. Weber called our attention to problems with bones, etcetera, we identified conditions very similar to rickets. Some of the animals would respond to calcium treatment, and this gets you into the business of nutrition of the animals. Were they actually being fed properly? Nobody else was seeing rickets problems right in the same area. It is very much contributed to by a lack of calcium in the diet and vitamin D sources, and a diagnosis made on a calf from that area showed definite signs of rickets, without describing how the animal got rickets. My point is that it is not a widespread problem in the area. Certainly Dr. Weber saw rickets in whatever number of animals he reports, not very many, restricted to a few small farms, and in fact he had some animals on treatment for another deficiency, selenium deficiency, which he treated for and did find some response. It is common on the East Coast to have selenium deficiencies in our soils, and farmers normally are supplementing the feed for selenium. Dilation problems would seem a strange condition to be related to a very minor (if any) dose that might have got out. It certainly seems quite specific and certainly hasn't been experienced by many places. I don't know if Dr. Weber stated how many cases he saw. But even in normal practice, particularly with younger female animals, difficulty at birth is not uncommon. So in all of our reviews of the histories involved and the personnel speaking to each one of these farmers reporting any kind of health problem, we found that in most of them the farmer had a reason why he thought this occurred, from management, wetness of the field, etcetera, and none of the incidences of disease therefore in the five-mile zone is out of line with any disease incidence in any other place in Pennsylvania. There is no change. There is no evidence that we could find that TMI caused any kind of significant, if even measurable, release. That doesn't mean that the potential wasn't there, but that the accident was managed to a degree that prohibited the release of these potentially harmful water and gases from contaminating the environment. So we did not feel that we had, based on our review of the whole area, found any evidence that low levels of radiation are causing any problems.

We heard another bizarre incident about some birds dying, a lot of birds all at once. The people thought it might be radiation because they felt that it couldn't be from normal things.

The Gilbert family called us the morning after the large die-off in their house, and we did secure birds for diagnostic work. You should realize that within an environment, the chances of radiation killing birds within a house and not killing them outside the house is just not logical. Secondly, it would take huge doses of radiation to have massive die-off within an hour or two, and a lot of other things are going to be affected besides a number of birds within a house. There are no diseases that will kill within an hour or two a mass of birds kept in separate places within a house, and kill them with no sign of anything. Therefore we felt and advised them that they should investigate things like temperature, humidity, gas leaks, and other physical problems that could have occurred. We were not given the opportunity, even though we interviewed the family here, to get back and attempt to identify the problem that might have occurred in the house. Of course this was some weeks later, and Mr. Gilbert felt that we probably couldn't ever find out what had changed within that couple of hours. We had therefore no way to give him a positive answer as to the reason for this sudden die-off.

You realize that we do see in the broiler industry, where they house maybe 50,000 birds in a single house, that if the electricity goes off and the fans don't work, those birds will start dying within fifteen to twenty minutes. With a high body temperature of birds running around and in close confinement, it is essential that the temperature and humidity is well controlled. Most of the broiler industry people have security and back-up electricity sources and alarm systems and are very much concerned with the physical problems involved with the close confinement with birds. You have farmers who will experience a 50,000 bird die-off within a couple of hours without this kind of monitoring, and there is not a physical lesion within the birds, they essentially drown. They just can't get any air, they start stacking at one end and essentially suffocate. And you open up these birds and there is not a sign of a problem.

Is this what happened to the Gilbert's birds?

There wasn't a sign of a problem in the Gilbert birds, and therefore it's very easy, particularly at this time, to think that something extraordinary must have happened. But the logic just isn't there. Really, you're talking some miles from TMI and nothing happened in between or to anybody else, and no birds outside the Gilbert's house were affected. If it were external radiation and getting through the roof of that house and getting into the interior, obviously the simplest thing, and marvelous for solving this problem, would have been for the Summerdale Lab to say, "Yes, x caused the death of these birds." We have no way to say that. We could easily bring something up and say that it was too hot in the house for these birds, but Mr. Gilbert has been raising birds for years and is certainly well aware as to how to handle pet birds, and he isn't able to discover either what happened. When you get to that position, they are sort of frustrated, and of course for us to tell them something that we aren't able to would be wrong also. We cannot find a reason; there is nothing pathologically wrong with these birds, nor did they have any sign of a disease. But if the humidity and temperature are high enough, they will die because they cannot respire the vapors out of their lungs; they are breathing in just as much vapor as they are breathing off, and they absolutely cannot get oxygen through their blood to their lungs. All you'll see is that they aren't breathing. It isn't a massive filling of the lungs with water, it is essentially coating the lungs with enough vapor that you can't get an exchange of oxygen. There would be no bleeding, no struggle. They just fall over. Here we have a situation where we are not able to identify that that's what happened. The owners aren't about to tell you what the temperature of the house was when they got back home. We weren't there. I think they honestly would like to know what killed their birds. It was a devastating thing to them. But it is not radiation—the logic is just not there.

We've heard a lot of talk about the Chinese bomb tests. Was that something that had a bad effect on the animal population? Do animals respond sooner than people?

Most animals are much more resistant to radiation exposure than humans. You will find in the West where they were doing A-bomb testing that there were minor changes in cattle, whereas some of the after-effects in people were significant. Of course you're talking about the fact that livestock don't stick around as long to show long-term effects, but basically the reasoning behind thinking that the total body exposure to radiation is going to be less effective in cattle and poultry is because of the fur coat and the feathers. They've got almost a barrier on particulate matter that would be tougher to penetrate than clothing, let's say.

Except if they eat it?

If they eat it, then you're into a similar exposure in numbers of millirems per body weight, but you're also talking larger animals. Therefore the total effect might be less because the total body exposure would be less. But it is pretty well documented that livestock and poultry are more resistant to radiation than humans.

We talked to a lady who lives right next to the plant and who has a lot of goats, Louise Hardison. She described a lot of trouble, but she also said that goats are the animals most sensitive to radiation. Have you ever heard anything like that?

I've never heard that. I don't know where she would have learned this. I'm not so sure I know of a study that was made to show one livestock more sensitive than another. Obviously the goat is a sensitive animal to many things, so I cannot back that statement up. I don't know where she got that information.

Are you familiar with her troubles?

Yes, we visited that premises. The things that she was finding wrong there were explainable in regard to normal incidence of problems in veterinary practice. I mean she was not experiencing things that don't happen normally. She might have an extra amount of problem on her place, but it wasn't something that we could lay to anything but management or nutrition or normal ocurrences in a given set of populations of goats. For instance, there aren't many goats around, but comparing her problems to her neighbor who has cattle, the cattle operation is fine. There are very, very many differences in the way that a farmer manages his farm and his livestock, and in veterinary experience you'll find that you'll need to go to some farms more often than others, for various reasons. It's a matter of variations in the physical environment around the farm, the quality of the animals, the nutritional aspects, management aspects, and other genetic factors that might influence susceptibility to disease or other conditions.

What is your response to the people's panic over equating whatever they are experiencing with radiation? Have you seen anything like that before? Are people a lot edgier as a result of this?

I feel that people *are* a lot edgier because of it. I think the potential for a serious impact on our farming community is there, particularly where TMI is located, because it is right upwind of one of the richest agricultural lands in the United States, Lancaster County. If we did have a significant accident that actually did release lethal doses of radiation, it could devastate a farming area and have a significant impact for many years on our livestock industry and agriculture industry.

Do you feel there is a possibility of that? A lot of people think it was pretty close and very touch-and-go; they are not even sure if the operators are competent to take on the kinds of risks that it implies.

I would hope that the regulatory agencies would be keen enough about the contributing factors in the operation of a nuclear plant that all plants would be supervised to the point where these concerns would be minimal. You have not only operator training and equipment failure that could plague the place, but also deliberate damage and problems, sabotage type things that could easily be a factor despite the millions of dollars spent to make sure safety was prime. The security of it is very much a concern of the future. The place is not open to sabotage because everybody involved is known to have security clearance, and it would be very difficult for anyone of unknown status to get in there.

Has your own monitoring capability been beefed up as a result of the accident?

The Bureau of Foods and Chemistry does their monitoring with the other agencies; we do not do any radiation monitoring here. Occasionally we have been instructed to continue to submit tissues to Radiation Health, Tom Gerusky's lab, if there is any evidence that we should check it out for radiation, but we don't do the testing ourselves. You should realize two things that I think were important in the diagnosis of radiation. One is that there are some very specific tissue cell changes when radiation has been exposed to cells, and therefore we used a diagnosis on slides, tissue slides, submitting them to a certified board pathologist for evidence of radiation damage to tissue cells. This is a supplement to running the tissues through a Geiger counter-type machine that actually would show emitters. We have, then, both the exposure of tissues and the carrying of emitters *in* the tissue versus the fact that tissue has been damaged by emitters, and we are looking for both. We do not rely on one or the other. So you can see where we feel our monitoring is

competent to pick up any sign that maybe there might have been radiation, and in all of our testing we have not found any signs.

So it's not really a problem?

It's not really a problem today! Now, that's what we are looking at, and the commonwealth is certainly getting us involved in the development of an emergency management plan for livestock and for events that might be of a similar nature, or worse, in the future.

We have no reason to cover up anything, either. We are certainly there for facts and to do what's appropriate, and so I think that many people would say that we have a vested interest in not telling the whole truth or something, but we actually are approaching this thing with the governor's point of view: "I want to know what's really going on" he told us, and this is the way in which we attacked the problem. So I think any agency you talk to in state government, you will find this same sort of attitude.

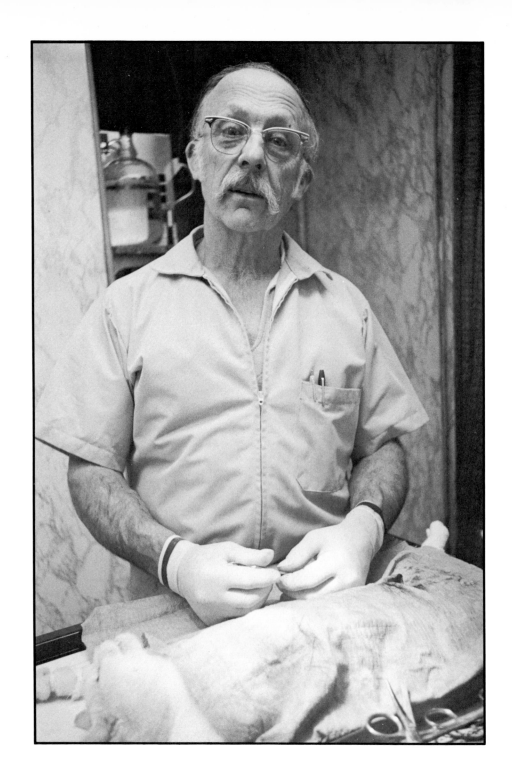

24.

Robert Weber, V.M.D., has been a practicing veterinarian in the valley opposite TMI for the past 37 years. Mechanicsburg, March 3, 1980

We started having a problem in that area about four years ago. In '76. From Smoke Dog Church to old 11, the old Susquehanna Trail. If you go down in there, you'll find there's two mountain ranges, the one that goes from Reeser's Summit and the one that comes up the other way, toward York. So in that area there's a valley, and that's where I experienced the problems.

What kind of problems?

Well, the problems we had were with the calves, particularly, and it happened that they were mostly steer calves, or bull calves. These particular animals would become prostrate, and before they became prostrate, they would become blind; many of them became blind. They walked with a stilted gait, with difficulty. So these animals exhibited a very serious deficiency. And at that time these people were recommended to feed five times the recommended amount of any balanced mineral of their choice. Some of them did it, and some of them didn't.

I wanted a balanced vitamin and mineral, with all the trace minerals and everything in it. And it looked like there was some selenium involvement; it looked like calcium phosphorus disturbances, that kind of thing. I would give them injections of those particular things, but to no avail. They kept on going downhill. So after about a year of this complaining to various people, Met Ed came to me and they wanted to know whether I would do some work on some of these animals we were having problems with.

People were approaching Met Ed?

Well, somebody was. They came to me and they said they would pay me to go take sam-

ples of these animals, blood samples or whatever I had. I said, well, better than that, we probably should submit a whole calf or two and something of that nature, which we did. And I have the reports, which I have never made public. Now, on those reports we had what was considered a very serious deficiency; and the animals that we removed from there improved. They began to see again, and they began to walk better, without medication. Now then, the ones that remained there. even those that I gave medication, it didn't seem to help too much, because eventually their bones would fracture. You'd have a fractured pelvis, fractured long bones, femurs particularly, the back legs. And then the ones we submitted for diagnosis had multiple fractures of all the bones, practically, in the body. They had multiple fractures of the rib bones, of the long bones, everything. So that's why they had pain walking. They especially had problems in the epiphyseal junction, which is the growth area between one end of the bone and the other. Of course, about the time that these reports came out, or near that time, this place blew up.

The accident?

Yeah. Whatever happened. It came apart. And so at the time that the accident happened we had, I would say, at least five calves in the area affected.

You mean affected immediately afterwards?

No. They had been previously affected, and they were still in the area. Hadn't died or hadn't been disposed of. But many of those people got very discouraged and just went out and shot them and that was the end of it. And other ones, a couple of them, they submitted them to a butcher, and they made calfburgers or whatever they wanted to make out of them. As long as they ate them themselves, it didn't matter whether they had inspection or not, so they didn't have inspection. They were killed and they were ate. Some of them. But I saw some of them killed, and there was so much evidence of water in the joints and multiple fractures that it'd make you sick to the stomach to eat them, I thought.

What would that mean, would it indicate water in the joints?

Well, just what the lab reports indicated, that there was a severe deficiency in the area.

Of what?

There was some imbalance. I figured it was an imbalance, and I told Met Ed that there was something had to be in the vapor that was coming out of the stacks that was spreading over the land that was neutralizing something that the animals needed. Or something that the ground needed to produce the correct nutrients so that the animals could survive. And so they said well, that was foolish for me to even think that because 90 percent of the time the air blew from the west, blew it across the river, instead of blowing it in this valley. I said all right, you can have your 90 percent of the time of the wind coming from the west and blowing it across the river, but when the wind is blowing across the river, it is rising in a real high altitude and being disseminated over a wide area. When it comes to this section, the 10 percent of the time, I said you can stand there and watch those towers, and the smoke comes out of them, or the vapor, or whatever comes out of them. It comes out and sinks right down over that valley. And disseminates immediately. And so it'd be a much heavier concentration there.

Well, the problem only went as far as old Route 11, the Trail. That's as far as it went, and immediately after the explosion, or whatever happened there, we had many sheep and goats that couldn't get up. Up to that time we didn't have problems with sheep and goats. Just mostly calves. The evidence of trouble came out in the swine and the sheep and the goats when this Three Mile Island thing came to a head. We were having stillbirths. Many. In sheep, goats, and pigs. Now that spread over about fifteen miles.

Both sides of the river?

Well, I don't know about the other side. I just know about this side. It spread as far as fifteen miles, where we would have one lamb be born alive and the other lamb would be stillborn. And the same way with goats, and four or five pigs would be born live, and the rest of the litter would be dead. The sow could not have these pigs. We had to do Cesarean in order to get these pigs out, because she would show no evidence that she would have other pigs in there, other than that she was sick. And so it would go two, three days till the farmer real- that there was something seriously wrong with her. By that time the pigs were so en- larged that there was no way of getting them out, other than by C-section. So then we did, I don't know how many, just loads of Cesarean sections on sows with stillborn pigs, say, after about June.

There were no more stillborn lambs and sheep because they mostly come in the springtime. So we didn't run into that. Now this year for about the past eight weeks, we're doing about two Cesareans a week on sheep and goats. Right now we have a dif- ferent situation. They're not dead in the uterus; they're not dead in the mother. The thing that's happening now is that we are getting animals ready to deliver their young, and they're not opening up. In other words they don't dilate. All the hormones that we used in the past to dilate an animal don't work. It does positively not work. We have the same constricted cervix after forty-eight hours as we had when we started.

What does that mean to you?

Well, it says it's a hormone imbalance.

But you can't correct it?

No. I can't correct it. I have been unable to correct it. I mean I've given them massive doses, and I've left the syringe and the bottle there and let them continue with the injec- tions; and finally, in frustration, I'll say, well, we didn't get anything yet. Don't wait till the sheep's dead or the lamb's dead. Bring it in, operate. So now we only wait twelve hours. If they don't open in twelve hours, open them. We don't fool around no more. We've had these kinds of things before, but we've never had it where the

hormones didn't work. I never did. Never ran into this.

What did Met Ed say when you explained how the other 10 percent of the fallout coming straight from the towers was more concentrated? Did they consider that?

They said there's nothing in there anyhow. They say there's nothing in that vapor. I said, well, I would like for you guys to go to the Department of Agriculture or someplace and prove to me and these people down here that there isn't anything in it. Have them come out here and do a survey and find out. Then the place came apart down there, and in the meantime the guy that I had contact with was fired. I didn't have any more con- tact with Met Ed from that time on. That was the end of that. That was the end of everything. I tried to contact him after that, and they said he was no longer with Met Ed and that was it.

And they never tried to get you and you never tried to get to Met Ed again?

No, they didn't try to get me and I didn't try to get them, because I didn't want them to fire me up.

Are you satisfied with the way the Depart- ment of Agriculture is handling these prob- lems?

Anything we've ever sent to the Department of Agriculture we haven't got any conclusive reports back. It all says, anything we sent up there, that it was nothing related to radiation. Well, I never said it *was* related to radiation, all I was interested in was *why*. But we get reports saying "no causative agent found," or "no causative bacteria was found to be the cause of death." Well, essen- tially, that don't tell you nothing.

Ordinarily we get good results, but it seems like we're not getting results when it comes to anything pertaining to Three Mile Island. The thing about it is we haven't had one of those animals ever since June of last year that went blind, arthritic, or broken bones. None. Since June. None.

Since it shut down?

Damn right. As I told you, if we moved one out of the area, it would recover.

How far out of the area would you move it?

Well, to Philadelphia. But how far out of the area can you get till you get to another nuclear plant?

Now Joe Conley went up by Chambers- burg and he called me Christmastime, and those cows that were pregnant down here, before he went up there, had calves after he went up there, and they didn't have any horns. They were born without horns.

But they were born out of the area.

Yes, but they were impregnated here. Now, the ones that were impregnated after he moved up there, he had one of them born the day after I talked to him, and that one had horns. That was born the end of De- cember or the beginning of January. So you see, they were only pregnant a very short time, if at all, before he left here. I asked him whether he was still on a good mineral program, and he said he was, and I said, well, I don't understand why you would have this problem if you're on a good min- eral program. And he said, well, that's the way it was.

You figure they'll start up that reactor again? The one that's okay?

Well, I hope they don't, until they get rid of the contaminants that they got in the other one. I don't see any sense in creating some- thing you don't know what to do with. You know, nuclear power might be all right, but why don't they finish the job before they get it going? In other words, they should have a way of doing something with the stuff in- stead of being caught there with a whole barrel full of it. That's my idea. But what are they doing with the stuff out of those other ones? Are they storing that right on the ground someplace and sometime they'll end up with the same thing as this? Yeah, now that's what I can't understand, why they create all that waste. They just never figure out what to do with it. I think that's only a half-done job.

25.

Louise Hardison and her husband live on a small farm overlooking the Susquehanna River and directly across from Three Mile Island, Londonderry Township, March 4, 1980

We're frightened, we're frightened. Most of my neighbors tried to sell their houses and run. Some of them are under psychiatric care from nervous breakdowns over nothing but Three Mile Island. Then they couldn't sell their houses, and the ones that did took a great financial loss. So it has devaluated my property; my produce and eggs and milk are not sellable like they were, my apart-ments are hard to rent. Yes, it did a lot of damage here. Why wouldn't it have? It affected everything here. Yet the president okays it and says we have to have it. But the Bible says that man will destroy himself, and he is doing a very good job of it. Isn't he? Look around. We're destroying our-selves. They had better learn to go back to nature, which is the herbs of the earth and the Indian remedies. They'd be a lot better off with candles and kerosene lights. They got along in those days very well. We're a spoiled generation.

Do you think it's possible to go back like that?

Well, I could try to go back; I don't know how I'd like it, but if that was a matter of life and death survival, yes, I could make it very easily.

. . .

I had a lot of death in my chickens. They seem to get a disease and they can't breathe.

What happens?

They just sit around dumpy and they wheeze. You can hear them rattling all over the chicken house, and they seem to be fighting for their breath and next thing you know they fall over.

How many chickens do you have and how many have died?

Oh, I lost dozens of chickens.

That way? And how many do you have?

Right now I may have 75 but I had around 125. I lost a lot of chickens.

Have you sent them to a lab or—

No. Took them over to the field. I don't have time to go to the lab.

Doesn't the lab come out and pick them up?

No. I sent dead goats out.

What lab did you send them to?

View of towers from Louise Hardison's farm, Londonderry Township, March 4, 1980

I don't know. TMI picked them up. TMI had someone come down here from Penn State and pick up one too. I never got an answer on that.

Most people don't deal with animals and birds. The farmer round here is the one dealing in that. What are we going to have? Barren land here in a few years? So you can't grow anything? And they say they didn't do anything to it.

It was a year ago, Louise, that the goats were birthing right during the accident?

Right after. They started two days after TMI. They said take all the pregnant women out of the area; well, the goat was the most sensitive. If I really would have wanted to start a riot, I should have loaded them on a trailer and taken them over to Hershey Arena with the rest of the pregnant women. But they were so close I couldn't bounce them around and I couldn't leave

myself. I stayed in the house most of the day, and I thought about all the animals that were over there hungry and thirsty and I couldn't stay any longer. But this is the result on my skin. A doctor has looked at it, and his comment was "Well, it's something. There was a lot of metal in the air that day." That was Doctor Leeser here in town. He did a TV series and he is very much against it.

Do you raise other animals besides goats and sheep?

I have cats, I've had two cats die this year. One of them just kind of came down with a leukemia thing and died. There's an old lady across the road in that trailer that has raised cats professionally for fifty years, and that old lady during TMI had two litters of Siamese born and for no reason they just up and died. Amelia Roberts. She's a good friend of mine and she's afraid to breed any

more cats because of what happened to the litters that she had. They just got to a certain age and boom—that was the end. Took them to the vet. She'll tell you. Couldn't find any answers.

Are you still raising rabbits?

I've had a litter of rabbits this year already. They were born dead, that was seven or eight days ago. Last year, after TMI, I had four litters born in a row. All dead. Every baby bunny was born dead. Some of them were deformed. That was strange; I never had trouble raising rabbits. Always had very good luck with rabbits.

How were they deformed?

Well, some of them didn't have all their legs, and the rest of them looked normal, just dead. Four litters in a row. I didn't get any rabbits to raise until late in the fall. None of the baby bunnies lived until then, so I had fall rabbits instead of spring rabbits. They died. And that's silly, too, because they get vitamins and they get molasses feed and everything plus their pellets, so if you give them everything they should have, and plenty of fresh feed and water, why should they all be dead? It hardly makes any sense, does it? Why did I have so many stillborn lambs last year? Why did I have a mother goat with four babies die in her? Why did I have three baby goats die after birth? They looked normal, they just—now I'm having this hemorrhage.

How long have you been here, Louise?

This is my home. I was born here. I lived in Michigan for thirty-four years but returned here in 1969; we live less than a mile from that plant, and I've been against TMI since the beginning. You might like to see this. It's a letter that I sent to the NRC last September.

"Sirs:

"This letter comes in response to your request for public comments. My name is Louise Hardison, and my husband and I have a 12½ acre goat farm. We raise goats, chickens, rabbits, sheep and we sell produce, milk, and eggs. Our property sits overlooking the Susquehanna River right in front of Three Mile Island. At the time of the TMI accident, we could not leave as we were warned, nor stay inside, as thirty-three baby goats were being born and animals have to be tended to. In the past we have never had any trouble selling our produce, and people came here for years to buy our goats' milk to drink and to make into cheese. Now nobody seems to want anything. We are full of anxiety and we worry about not selling our produce, milk, and eggs, and we're forced to sell seven milking goats because no one comes for the milk. To this day, some of our regular customers have not returned. [*Sept. 1, 1979*]

"We have two apartments above the house that we rent as a means of making our $500 a month house payment. One tenant came and told us that he could not live here, left immediately and came back a month later for his things. Upon trying to re-rent, the type of responsible professional clientele that we desire for tenants no longer wanted to rent this close to a plant and towers. Several neighbors have tried to sell, but have been unable to or have been offered ridiculously low prices, close to nothing. Our con-

cern is growing very deep over these devaluations.

"Of the damage to my own health, I do not know at this time, but the strain of not selling our produce or renting our property has taken a great toll on us. At the time of the accident, I had scratches on my left arm, not uncommon when working in a barn. My arm is still swollen and spongy in a four-inch area today. The doctor says there was a lot of metal in the air that day but still does not know what is beneath the skin on my arm.

"All these things taken into consideration, we feel that we will never get over this nightmare of Three Mile Island and wonder if life will ever resume the way it was.

"Sincerely, Louise Hardison"

Did you receive an answer?

No. It's the same as with the results of the tests on the animals. I never heard from them.

Do they still take samples of your goats' milk?

They still come around, but not so often. And I never get any reports. They're supposed to be published in the library, but the only testings they ever sent to me, I couldn't make any sense of at all. I turned it over to this Three Mile Island Alert group, and they couldn't read it either. We'll never get the answer and we'll never know the truth. It's nothing but beating around the mulberry bush about what's really going on. There's no answers.

Well, there are answers, I would think.

Are you going to dig them up? If there are answers, they're not going to tell us, or their employees. They don't dare. They don't dare.

I've owned this property since 1957 and moved back in '69. That's when they first started to build Three Mile Island. They came around and asked my opinion at that point, and I said the statement I have always made, "It's like living on a bomb." I felt that from the very beginning.

Had you had any experience before with nuclear power plants?

No, nothing direct. I just had this inward feeling that it was going to be not a good thing. And I just never liked it. But we had goats and sheep here then, because they

said they lived together so well. And everything was fine for the first couple of years. All of a sudden you couldn't breed anything. Well, 1970 and '71, '72 were fine. In '73 it started.

The plant began operating in '72?

Well, anyways, for three years after that I just couldn't get them to breed. I bought new billy goats; my God, they couldn't all have been sterile. It was impossible to have them all sterile. Then everything bred last year, and I don't know if any of them didn't take this year. They look, most of them, fairly pregnant.

You mean there might still be a problem?

Well, who knows what's coming out of them? This hemorrhaging is something they never had before. This is a new problem. Absolutely. And I don't know what's going to happen next. I have to be there, you know? I walked away from those kids, and they started hemorrhaging again, right from the navel cords. And when Ron Laughlin comes around—he's the one from the college, he does the testing—you know something's going on. They say there's nothing wrong, but there is.

Is that testing only since the accident, or is it ongoing?

They're always testing milk. They test the goats' milk because the goat is the most sensitive animal to radiation there is.

I didn't know that.

Oh, yes; I was told that by Ron Laughlin, that the goat was the most sensitive, and that radiation shows up most readily in goats' milk. And they test here regularly. Now, when that blew off here two weeks ago, they weren't here weekly, they were here every day to grab that milk. And one day they tested it twice. And Mr. Laughlin came in here, and I said, "Well, what are you finding? Is it safe?" I said, "I'm not drinking anything." And he said, "No, you can drink it. It's all right, we haven't found anything." So evidently there wasn't enough of it to show, but I didn't drink it for days. So there's a waste. You throw it down the sewer. Nobody else wanted it either. What do you do with it? I have a lot of waste here over that. What do you do with it? Who's going to buy it? Would you? So you raise all these things and you can't sell your produce.

26.

Jane Lee manages a dairy farm 3½ miles west of Three Mile Island. Since 1976 she has been personally documenting evidence of radical changes in plants and animals in the vicinity of TMI.

Our dairy farm is 159 acres and is located 3½ miles west of Three Mile Island. It has been in operation since 1752 and has continued in the same family from that time. Less than a mile behind the farm is an old dirt road that President Lincoln used to travel on in a horse and buggy. From my front porch you can see the towers of the Metropolitan Edison Three Mile Island Nuclear Generating Plant.

There is a growing concern among the farmers in our valley about their livestock and the continuing viability of the land. Since 1976 we have been puzzled by many physiological problems that have plagued the area. In 1976, four years after the Three Mile Island plant began operations, I decided it was time someone began monitoring and documenting the health events occurring in animals within the five-mile radius of this plant. The animals affected are: cows, horses, goats, sheep, pigs, cats, ducks, geese, guinea pigs, rabbits, and birds. The cats, rabbits, and guinea pigs appear to be the most vulnerable. The problems we are encountering are: increase in arthritis (enlarged leg joints); muscle deficiency (unable to walk or to sustain hind quarters); blindness at birth; and reproduction problems, such as lack of conception, cystic ovaries, premature births, abortions, mutations, hermaphroditism, still births, jammed birth-canal during delivery, lack of dilation during delivery despite hormone injections, extremes in size of newly born (very small or very large), litter indicating different fetal stages in one litter, increased Cesareans for sows (normal Cesareans used to be one per year—veterinarian Robert Weber of Mechancisburg has been performing one per week since January 1978), and increased Cesareans for goats and sheep (two per week since spring 1980; normally there is one per year).

These problems are not limited to one or two farmers; they involve a five-mile radius of Three Mile Island. Many of these farmers have been farming here for thirty-five to sixty years—most, if not all, of their active farming lives—and none of them have experienced these problems with *this kind of frequency* before 1976. (In 1972, Three Mile Island Unit One came on line). I have gone throughout the area cataloging animal health problems as best I could on my own time, at my own expense. I have prepared a report with depositions from the farmers involved. I am not a qualified scientist, and I am aware that my work lacks scientific credibility; but somebody must keep track of these events. I have sent my report to the governor of Pennsylvania and to my representatives, both state and federal; I have sent it to the NRC and to the president of the United States. But not one word, not one single word, has leaked out about what is going on with these animals. Still, as far as I am concerned, this is the key that is going to open the door. Because what is happening to the animals is going to happen to us—it's just going to take longer. The animals live in the environment; they are inhaling the isotopes that are close to the ground. Nature is revealing herself, as she always does. She is responding in the same manner in which she is treated. Those who are in a position to do something about it are not responding to the signals. Yet already many women have told me, "I cannot have any more children now." And women who are pregnant have told me they are weighing very seriously the abortion of their child. "I don't want to," they say, "but I don't want to bring a child into the world that might be deformed or genetically altered." This is a horrendous decision to place on a woman. It's a form of psychological terrorism. It's mental anguish. Met Ed should be sued for criminal negligence.

I think it is no longer a question of *if* we stop using nuclear energy—it is a question of *when* we stop using it. And if they don't back away from it soon, look for civil disobedience or maybe a revolution in this country—within two years. I have predicted to the Japanese scientists who came to study this whole area after the accident that it's going to take two years, but when it hits home what they have done to these people, and when the men really get involved in this issue, when they start seeing their children born with thyroid damage, respiratory problems, or developing leukemia, there isn't anything that's going to stop them. I'm afraid Marx said it better than anyone: "Take away everything a man has, take his job, his family, his home, so he has nowhere to turn, and push his back to the wall, and he's going to fight." Only this time the men won't be alone; the women are in this too. There is no other way, because Congress has abdicated its responsibilities.

Look at this from a government publication, drafted by the NRC, docket No. RM 50-2, enclosure B, page 91, dated April 30, 1975: "We have decided, consistent with the foregoing as an interim measure and until more suitable values or other criteria can be established, that $1,000 per total body man-rem and $1,000 per man-thyroid rem or such lesser values as may be demonstrated by the applicant to be suitable in a particular case shall be used in the required cost-benefit balances."

"Cost benefit" is the phrase to note here. They are weighing in dollars and cents the value of our lives. This document means that the NRC has decided that a nuclear plant needs to invest no more than $1,000 per rem of radiation exposure to an individual during a cleanup operation, or during any other kind of operation that will cause the public to receive radiation. And if it will cost more than this $1,000 per person to prevent an exposure of 1 rem, then they have agreed among themselves that they shall be permitted to just go ahead with the exposure. That is why they are venting krypton 85 into the atmosphere instead of freezing it and taking it away in containers. It costs far more to use the cryogenic method than to vent it.

Did you know that the elementary school kids are discussing the release of krypton on the bus? David came home yesterday and said, "Do you know what the kids are saying on the bus? 'I wonder who this affects most, the boys or the girls?' " Some of the parents have already moved their children out of the area. They aren't going to keep sending them to school in the Three Mile Island area.

Dr. Irwin D. J. Bross, who is the director of biostatistics at the Roosevelt Park Institute in Buffalo, New York, says venting should not be done at all, that the venting is a futile attempt to clean up a plant that can never be cleaned up. They'll go ahead and vent the krypton only to discover it is impossible to clean up because the amount of rems coming from the walls of the containment room above the water is 100 rems per hour. Five rems per *year* is the maximum dose allowed a worker in a plant! He also told me that the five-fold increase of hypothyroidism indicates that low-level radiation in the area of Three Mile Island is already high above what is allowable, and he feels there ought to be about 5,000 casualties attributable to the releases—not 5,000 people who are going to drop dead, mind you, but 5,000 people who have received chromosome damage. It will take ten to twenty years before such damage reveals itself. It's these low doses that do the damage, he told me. Extremely high levels of bombardment kill the cell outright, but the low levels damage it, breaking or just fracturing the chromosome. When a cell that has been damaged but not killed begins to divide, it will continue to multiply exactly the way it was damaged, and it will continue to multiply. When you get up to a billion of these cells that have reproduced, that's when you begin to develop problems. Dr. John Gofman says in his book *Shut-Down* that by the time one gram of cancerous cells forms into a mass you already have a billion damaged cells, and it takes about a gram of cancer to become detectable by x-ray.

There are a lot of forerunners in low-level radiation exposure, warnings two or three years ahead of the serious problems, that may indicate if you have been exposed to radiation; these include rheumatic fever, skin rashes (like eczema), allergies, pneumonia, respiratory problems, heart attacks, and premature aging. Now I don't want to go over the deep end and blame everything on radiation. Stress and psychological factors also have a great deal to do with general health. But radiation can be a hidden contributing factor, one which is hard to catch and hard to prove, but whenever you begin to see a large increase of diseases in small children, who don't have the same stress adults have, I think it indicates that something may be happening in the immunity system.

Our Congress, legislature, the public utilities, and regulatory agencies do not take low-level radiation seriously. But sooner or later they will have to come to terms with it, both morally *and* physically. The Heidelberg Report will bear me out in this. The

Heidelberg Report is a study done by a reputable group of physicists, biologists, chemists, doctors, botanists, cancer researchers, and veterinarians from the University of Heidelberg in Germany. It came out in May, 1978, and reveals the fraudulent methods used by the Atomic Energy Commission to alter their testing of radioactivity coming from a commercial nuclear power plant when those plants were first up for licensing. They routinely falsified their test samples by downgrading their radioactivity in order to establish that what a plant normally puts out into the environment is within "acceptable levels." So those "acceptable levels" that we have been living with all these years are, in fact, more dangerous than we were told.

We have already—Joan, Jerry, and I—reconciled ourselves to our own fate, and we have decided that we are not moving.

We're going to remain, if at all possible, in Etters. We've all had the metallic taste in our mouths, which nobody has been able to explain away yet, so I don't know how long it will take before the real facts come out about the amount of exposure we got from the accident. But I am sure it is much higher than we have been told. So where can we run? Jerry has lived on this farm all his life. I'm fifty-five years old, and I am not about to pack up and start trying to find some place to settle elsewhere. We were here long before the utility company. If anyone ought to move, it should be Met Ed. Not that their moving will undo any of the damage they have done. And even if they do move, that plant will remain. Did you realize there is no place on the whole eastern seaboard that is really safe? It is all honeycombed with nuclear power plants everywhere you go.

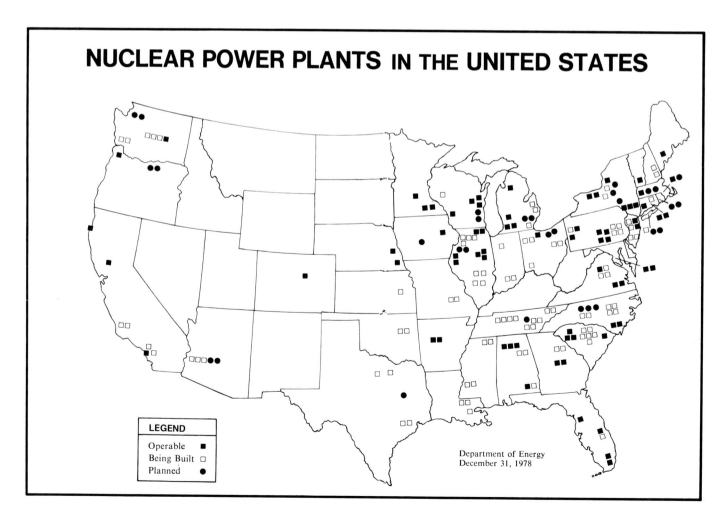

NUCLEAR POWER PLANTS IN THE UNITED STATES

LEGEND
Operable ■
Being Built □
Planned ●

Department of Energy
December 31, 1978

Robert Arnold, Londonderry Township public meeting, August 1979

27.

Robert Arnold, senior vice president of Met Ed in charge of cleanup, at a public meeting in the Bachmanville Church, where questions were asked by various citizens, February 26, 1980

If you look back historically to the development of nuclear energy within the United States, what is clear is that there was a public policy decision to utilize nuclear energy for commercial electric power. That was indicated by the legislation that was passed on the federal level, the Atomic Energy Act of the midfifties, and out of that really grew the technological basis for the commercialization of nuclear power. The General Public Utility Companies [GPU],

of which Metropolitan Edison is, of course, one of the subsidiaries, was involved with that development from the very early days. The first commercial nuclear power plant within our system was Oyster Creek Nuclear Station in New Jersey. The reason that we term it the first commercial one is that it was the first reaction power plant that was purchased by an electric utility company in competition with consideration of alternative methods of generation; that is, of coal and oil. And in the early sixties when they were taking bids for that station, doing an economic evaluation, it was the economics that clearly favored that the Oyster Creek facility be a nuclear facility. We were very careful at that time within the corporation, reviewing with the vendor and reviewing with the federal governemnt, whether the country was really ready to move forward with this and whether taking this initial step was a sound investment on the part of the company, because it was obviously a very fledgling industry at that time. The

GPU system continued to look at additional generating stations on a primarily economic evaluation on through the sixties, and Three Mile Island Unit One and Unit Two were initially selected as nuclear facilities based on the economic evaluation that we did. So we didn't get into nuclear power either suddenly or willy-nilly. We built within the company an in-house capability; we drew into the fold people that had backgrounds within the nuclear industry from other activity; many of the people we have involved with our nuclear power program are people who received training and experience through the navy's program. But the initial incentive, the overriding incentive in the sixties and on into the early seventies for generating power with nuclear energy was, in a word, the economics of it. And that's really proven out, even in retrospect. The operation of Three Mile Island Unit One for the 4½ years it was in service before the accident generated power at about $300 million less than it would have cost them if it had been generated with an oil facility and about $100 million less than if it had been generated over that period of time with a coal-fired facility. Up through the end of 1978, the economic analysis that we would do still came out with about 10 percent benefit to the use of nuclear energy.

When we look at Three Mile Island, post accident, it still remains clear to us that, number one, the country needs nuclear energy; I think that the situation in the Mideast provides a major pressure for it to come out this way. Since the accident, I think the statements of public officials, of elected officials, has been much clearer as to our need to utilize nuclear energy. On a national basis I think there is much more of a consensus as to what we need to do in the short term in order to meet our energy needs. That's not to say there are not those with contrary judgments; clearly there are. We certainly are with the group that thinks it's essential that the country utilize nuclear energy.

Clearly, from the accident we've learned a lot about things that we can do to improve the safety of the operation of nuclear power plants. I think we've learned the lesson very well and I think we've been very, very objective in reviewing what we have at Three Mile Island, what we have in the way of capabilities, in organization, and what changes we have to put into place in the way of plant design, training procedures, and people to be able to come to groups such as this and say, "We're confident we can operate Three Mile Island." Not guaranteeing you there won't be another TMI Two accident, but giving you the confidence that the probability of that is sufficiently low that it's worth the minimal risk that's involved.

Whether TMI One should be recovered and whether TMI Two should be cleaned up and, I think, eventually recovered as a nuclear facility gets down to what are in the best interests of the country as a whole and what are in the best interests of the customers of the GPU system. I think that those interests can only be served if we can give the kind of assurance to the people that live in the vicinity of that plant that they must have before it's appropriate for us to reopen those units. I know that I personally can vouch for the organization which I represent, that it is absolutely dedicated to providing that assurance.

Is there any decision made yet about what's going to happen to the water that's floating around over there in that building after it goes through Epicore [a system for filtering medium- and low-level contamination from water]?

The current situation is that we are required to hold it on site. And we can hold it on site more or less indefinitely. We only have to build some more storage or something for it. The water's being cleaned to extremely low levels of residual contamination, down in

the range of EPA drinking-water standards. I don't know what will be the ultimate way in which we work that out. In the short term we have a need to use water to clean and flush the systems, and we might as well use that water we've cleaned for that purpose.

It must be rather tempting to let it gradually into the river?

I don't think I've ever been faced with that temptation.

Maybe you haven't, but I know that it has come up several times, that just a little at a time wouldn't matter so much.

You know, I think—I don't know, you know, maybe I don't have any credibility in making these kinds of statements, and obviously—

Well, we read the newspapers; that's where we see this stuff, and I figure I could get an answer straight from the shoulder here.

Well, I'll give you my straight-from-the-shoulder answer. We've got absolutely no interest in doing anything that is not within the regulations, and is not within what people understand we're doing. Our incentive, our interest, is having people understand what we're doing and why we need to do it.

Talking about people understanding, I heard that there was a town forty-six miles northeast, Sunbury, that installed a radiation monitoring device in the town square as a result of the accident, and I'm wondering whether the company has been approached to install more monitoring devices in the towns, and what the response has been?

We have had inquiries from a number of municipalities, and monitoring devices fall into two general categories. One kind accumulates the history, provides data as to what has been the exposure at the point of that monitoring device; that's what I would call a passive device. The other type is read out on a real time basis, like your speedometer; you look at your meter and see what the current radiation level is. Devices of that type, that are sensitive down to the background levels and which show changes above background, are not that readily available. It's a matter of the state of the art. Most of those kinds of devices have been developed really for nuclear war considerations, where you're worried about very high exposure. They are available, though; we have ordered six of them, and we are looking at where to locate those six.

Bob, how stable is the plant now?

I think the plant is very stable presently.

You're not concerned with seals or valves going in the condition that you've got there?

Now there's part of the difficulty with the short answers. To me the stability of the

plant is in our ability to manage the continual removal of decay heat. A potentially serious problem would relate to a loss of the ability to remove the decay heat. That, I think, is very stable. If what you mean by "stable" is that releases from the plant will be maintained at the same low level they are now and that we won't see any excursion from that, that's not what I would mean by "stability." If that's the question that's being asked, there clearly are going to be events that take place there that are going to see some of the kind of perturbations and releases that we saw in the week of February eleventh.

Are you talking about gases into the atmosphere, or water, or what are you talking about?

Gases. Krypton is about the only radioactive gas there.

Is there anything else that will come out of that plant besides krypton now?

There is inside the containment building, in the atmosphere, a very small amount of particulate material, principally cesium; and probably there would be some strontium that would be airborne.

Strontium?

I'm sure it's at detectable levels in there.

90?

Strontium 90.

You scare me when you say that!

Well, I think the amount of strontium that's there and the kind of leakage we're talking about shouldn't be of concern. One of the benefits of a controlled venting is that the venting pathway will have filters in it that remove the particulate material; the minimum off-site releases, I expect, would occur with the controlled venting situation. If one were to go to any area and look for strontium 90 with sensitive enough instruments, you'll find it. And, certainly, that would be true of the air in the containment building. It's, again, part of the inventory we have within the world.

From a conversation between Robert Arnold and an unnamed resident after the public meeting at the Bachmanville Church

Mr. Arnold: I think that you have to realize that in the course of going into the atmosphere, the radiation is tremendously diluted from what it is close to the source.

Resident: But I saw in the Region 1 Logbook that it said "overexposure."

Mr. Arnold: What logbook?

Resident: Region 1 Logbook. Your handwritten logbook.

Mr. Arnold: But that overexposure referred, I'm sure, to one of the plant workers.

There was never a case of overexposure to the public.

Resident: Yes. To the total public.

Mr. Arnold: No.

Resident: Well, look on page 183.

Mr. Arnold: Of the Region 1—

Resident: Look at the radiological data.

Mr. Arnold: What do you mean by the radiological data? Their logbook itself, or what?

Resident: Yes. Your handwritten logbooks.

Mr. Arnold: From Region 1, though. Now you're talking about the log that Region 1 maintains—

Resident: Well, between the Met Ed facility, the Met Ed employees and the NRC employees. Locally. Here. What they maintain.

Mr. Arnold: You know, I'd really appreciate it if you'd give us a chance to sit down with you, with Jim Porter and Tom Potter, the people that have really done this work, and let us go over with you how we did the analyses, what kind of data we have and don't have.

Resident: It's not just your logbooks, it's even in the NRC's. I mean, they set an awful lot of the policy and the regs.

Mr. Arnold: But in terms of what we're actually—

Resident: And how many monitors were ineffective or were inoperable? And where were they placed? Even the plastic coverings that were on some of the dosimeters were preventing certain forms of radiation monitoring.

Mr. Arnold: Well, I'll bet you a chocolate sundae that page 183 is referring to the overexposures of our people that took the sampling on the thirtieth. Are you on? We have it on tape! We have it on tape!

Is it a bet?

Resident: I don't care. If he wants to bet, it suits me.

[*When the author checked the photocopies of the Region 1 Logbook in the Three Mile Island Nuclear Plant section of the Harrisburg Public Library, he found that page 183 of that book had been blanked out, leaving only the page number.*]

From a statement by Dr. Ernest Sternglass at a press conference at the Pennsylvania state capitol building, July 3, 1979.

I have seen the official announcement and I have seen the official letter by the Duquesne Light Company to Washington, to the Nuclear Regulatory Commission, submitting the new documents which will no longer make it necessary to monitor strontium 90, which is about twenty to thirty times as toxic as cesium 137. Strontium 90 will no longer need to be monitored, even though it costs a mere few thousand dollars for a billion-dollar plant to do it annually. It will not be monitored. It does not have to be monitored. And, in fact, as far as I have been able to tell, very few strontium 90 measurements have been carried out here, only a few isolated measurements; and none were recorded in detail in the official thick document that was issued by the health officials to try to allay the fears of the local people as to the levels of radiation that they have received.

28.

Virginia Southard was chairman of Citizens for a Safe Environment, the first group to question legally the operating license of Units One and Two. Philipsburg, January 11, and April 13, 1980

Judith Johnsrud told me you were like one of those canaries that miners wear on their hats when they go down into the mines. The birds are sensitive to dangerous fumes that the miner would not know about on his own until it was too late, so he keeps watching the canary to see how it is reacting. In your case this means a special sensitivity to radiation. How long have you been aware of this sensitivity in yourself?

The comparison with a canary is not exactly right because a canary's sensitivity to fumes is inborn and is due to its small size. I do not know that I was at first naturally more sensitive to radiation than anyone else. The sensitivity I now have was a cumulative thing. In my early twenties I had quite a few medical x-rays for a variety of reasons.

And then in my thirties when living in California I came down with an illness that was diagnosed as virus infection that damaged the sheath of the nerves, and it took me about three years to recover from it. It was during this illness that I discovered my sensitivity to radiation.

How did that take place?

While I was recovering, as part of my company's checking on my progress, I would be sent to the hospital and be given a chest x-ray among other things. Following the checkup, the symptoms of my illness were exacerbated. This happened several times. And I realized there had been nothing that happened to me to cause this setback except the exposure to the chest x-ray. So that's when I became aware of it; and at that time I also wondered if possibly the fallout that we were getting over Los Angeles from time to time from the bomb testing in Nevada might have contributed to the illness. The symptoms that I had were symptoms that I read later were the same ones that the soldiers had experienced during the testing.

What were those symptoms?

Very severe aching in the bones, along with weakness and nausea. It would also bring on a mental depression. I realized then that the depression was part of the reaction to the radiation, and it would go away as the other symptoms cleared up. I was curious to verify this; and I've asked about two dozen people that I have known in the years since, who've had medical x-rays, if they could ever in any way associate them with a

mental depression. They have all told me, yes, they had experienced depression following x-rays, but they had never made the connection because they didn't know it was connected. That's something that I have figured out on my own, and I think it's interesting that other people have experienced it as well.

Has this kind of knowledge gone very far medically among researchers in radiation?

None that I ever asked told me that they knew. But in a paper by Dr. Rosalie Bertell from Buffalo one of the things that she mentions as coming from people who have been exposed to radiation is a high rate of suicide. This would imply depression.

What year was this, when you were in California?

That was in 1955. The bomb testing went on during the fifties up into the very early sixties. And occasionally when the wind would shift in the test sites, it would carry the wind west, which was not the way it was supposed to go, and it would come out over the Los Angeles area. Los Angeles is set in a basin, so sometimes there were atmosphere conditions that would hold this over the city maybe for a day or two.

Have you ever received any medical opinion about your sensitivity to radiation?

I've been told by two people who have done some research on the health effects of radiation that there are those who are more sensitive to it. In my case, when there are releases of radiation, I have a sort of itching, prickly sensation on the skin.

What do you mean by "releases of radiation"?

Before the accident at Three Mile Island, from time to time they would have a number of unplanned releases, in addition to their regular, smaller planned releases. These plants always have unplanned accidental releases, they even work them into their dose assessment for the population living next to them. I moved to Harrisburg fifteen years before the accident, long before the plant went in. After the plant was built, I stayed because my job was here. Since I lived ten miles north of the plant, I assumed that the planned normal releases would not be great enough to cause me physical damage. But I really didn't know. Nevertheless I would have this slight irritation of the skin on days that, it turned out, there had been the larger accidental releases.

Also, once when I was working in Minneapolis in October of '79, I came home from work one evening and as I got out of the car, I experienced this burning, prickly sensation on my skin. And sure enough that evening on the news there had been an accident at the Prairie Island plant 25 miles south of Minneapolis, and they had had to release earlier that afternoon.

I wonder what it must be like living right next door to one of those plants?

Well, there is an eerie, peculiar feeling about the area around these plants, and I'm convinced that it has something to do with radiation. I'm speaking about the *normal* releases that come from an operating plant now as well as the unanticipated ones. I don't think it's psychological, I'd like to stress that. One day we went down to Middletown and to Londonderry Township; this was early in the organization of Three Mile Island Alert, and before the accident—about three years ago—we went down to go door-to-door to put out information about our meetings. Practically every house in that little borough had a big dog in it. They're German shepherds and other watchdogs. Almost every house had all the shades drawn—in the middle of a Sunday afternoon. It was almost like walking into a ghost town. People weren't out in the streets. Everything was shuttered and closed. I'm convinced the releases from those plants affect people, and I think it has something to do with the effects of radiation on their nervous system.

People don't know what they're getting. None of us know. I will bet you any money—for this is another thing that I have observed: there are periods of diarrhea and vomiting, and I'm convinced that this comes from the releases, whether they are announced as unplanned releases, or whether they are routine and unannounced. Whenever I hear that this vomiting and diarrhea are going around, I think, um hmm, I'll bet there was a release.

How did you respond to the accident and the large releases that came out? What effect did these have on you?

Well, I left town immediately, about ten thirty Wednesday morning of the accident, because I had learned about the accident by about 9:00 A.M. As soon as I learned that they were releasing radioactivity, which they were announcing on the radio, I left my office that morning, at about a quarter to ten; and as I was getting into my car, I experienced this tingling on my skin. On my car radio they were announcing that they had already been releasing radioactive iodine, in uncontrolled releases, for some hours. So as soon as I heard that I decided that I must leave town because I didn't want to be exposed any further. I made arrangements with my office; they gave me permission to take the rest of the day off as vacation time, and I immediately notified my family, stopped at my sister's to try to pick up my mother and bring her with me, but my sister did not want her to come with me. My mother was very old and we did not tell her what was happening. So I left, and as I was driving out of Harrisburg I experienced the rather strange metallic taste in the back of my throat. I remember having had the same taste in my mouth occasionally during the bomb testing in the '50s. I went north to Judy Johnsrud's and one of the first things I did when I got to Judy's was to gargle. Iodine is a particulate and if there was any sticking in my throat, I wanted to do something about getting it out. The first place it hits you is in the nasal and throat membranes. So I gargled immediately because I felt that if I could taste it, it might be in my throat.

I stayed clear of the Harrisburg area for ten days. Then I returned because we had a rally in Harrisburg the second Sunday after the accident, and I attended it. I regretted it later because they had a fairly good-size release that day, which was ten days after the accident. I stood out in the rain that day for about four hours. It was later that I found out about a rather large release that day. It made me feel short of breath and congested in my chest and generally feeling ill for several days. So I try to stay clear of there, although I do go down for a day or so every couple of weeks to see my family and for anything else that I have to do.

According to a lot of people, it's still quite dangerous, in terms of what is being released in the area, and it's not going to go down but possibly get worse as the cleanup proceeds.

My understanding from talking to Chauncey Kepford is that what will be coming out in the cleanup will be longer-lived radionuclides than what came out in the early releases. When they start to scrub down and clean the reactor there will be radioactive dust that will have things in it like strontium 90 and cesium 137.

Do you see that any steps are being made in improving ways of protecting people, ways of monitoring, ways of becoming aware of the amount of radiation in our environment?

I just read this morning that the state has ordered more equipment for monitoring, and I believe the Environmental Protection Agency is now going to be involved in doing more monitoring around the plant. They're also trying to include the citizens. This is to help, of course, with the credibility of the announced releases. So the public is involved in having some of these instruments.

That seems an improvement.

Indeed it is. If you're going to irradiate people, at least let them know it. Yet it's really sad that people have to be exposed to it and monitor their own irradiations. But it does give at least some sense of security; at least people know what's going on. I was talking with my niece yesterday in Sunbury, which

is forty-eight miles northeast of here up the Susquehanna, and they have in their town square there a radiation device that gives the readings each day. It was put in since the accident. The last time they announced a release my niece went down to the center of town to look at it, and she found no increased readings. The wind was going in the other direction at the time, and so none of the releases were being carried up there.

I heard you were in the hospital last fall. Do you care to talk about that?

On November 5 of last year they found I had a malignant tumor, and I had a mastectomy operation on November 27. I was lucky: I didn't have to have any chemotherapy or radiation treatments. They were able to remove the whole tumor and it's not likely to spread, the doctor told me. I cannot say what the cause of it was; who can? But I don't suppose the releases from Three Mile Island Unit One or Unit Two did me any good. I had lived there for all four of the years that that plant had been operating, so I'd have been around all those normal releases and also all the unplanned ones. I just loved Harrisburg. I thought I would spend the rest of my life there.

But both Chauncey [Kepford] and Sternglass told me, at the time of the accident, that releases would go on for a year or two years, and longer; as long as they tinker with that reactor they are going to have releases from it, they said, and they recommended I leave. So I have moved to central Pennsylvania. My reaction to all of this has been quite strong—on the Sunday of the accident I cried bitterly because of the people who could not leave Harrisburg. Now some members of my family—there were fifteen of us who left Harrisburg for Philipsburg—would get up and remove themselves from the room whenever we would start talking about it. They just couldn't handle it. I'm sure this happened with many other families, too, especially as they were trying to decide whether to leave Harrisburg or not. People were so traumatized—part of a family would want to go and part would want to stay. The terror would just immobilize and really damage people. I'm wondering if you have run into this in your interviews?

What do you mean exactly?

Well, it's like this. Months after the accident happened, in August, some movie people came out to interview me, and just as the interviewer was about to leave, a friend of mine who was over at the house came out onto the porch, and I introduced her. I said, "Maybe you would like to interview her?" He said, "I'd love to." I said, "Well, I don't know, do you want to talk to him?" And she

said, "Yes, I'll talk to him." So she sat down and started to tell him about the weekend, and she broke down and cried and cried, she could hardly stop crying. She was crying bitterly. This was months after it happened. That's what I mean about how deep the trauma was in people. My friend could hardly control herself, and yet she has not talked about this as I have; she does not want to talk about it. She doesn't want even to think about it. And there have been thousands of people like her who have been deeply damaged psychologically, because of the accident, and it may take them years—maybe they will never get out of it. I hope that this kind of data doesn't get lost, because it's very important. There are many people who have been traumatized and you may never get a chance to talk to them. So I was wondering if you were getting any of this, because I think it should be somewhere in the book that you are doing.

The following is an excerpt from a letter Virginia Southard wrote to the Centre Daily Times, *State College, Pennsylvania. It appeared on April 28, 1980.*

It has become increasingly evident that many people have lost the freedom to live in peace and security as a result of the accident at TMI. We have lost the right to stop this dangerous technology even though we have lived through a near catastrophic accident and even though we are now seeing evidence of thyroid damage and stillborn infants. The history of the Atomic Energy Commission and the present Nuclear Regulatory Commission is one of consistent coverup of their reprehensible practices and contempt for the rights and concerns of the people. Until the public takes political action to change the Atomic Energy Act of 1954, which mandates the promotion of nuclear power, to a mandate to promote public health and safety, they will continue to force whole areas to live in a state of potential emergency. This is not the way people should have to live in a democratic society.

It's about time we begin to hold particular people responsible for their actions. Perhaps the old-fashioned practice of "shunning" should be used against those who destroy the emotional and physical health of others while doing a job for the government or for profit. This would not be shunning for a religious reason but to set them apart because their behavior is unacceptable to our society.

[*Virginia was one of the first people in Harrisburg to evacuate the city on the morning of March 28. After the accident she moved to Philipsburg, in central Pennsylvania, where she lives now.*]

29.

Thomas Gerusky, director of the Bureau of Radiation Protection in the Department of Environmental Resources, Harrisburg, March 18, 1980

I began this job in 1961, about the same time the Russians decided to break the voluntary test-ban treaty, and all at once environmental radiation became a big problem. The federal government started giving us monies to expand our environmental programs to look at environmental levels of fallout. That slowly grew as the reactors came out, and it slowly changed from fallout to environmental monitoring around the reactors. Since 1969 we have

been the agency of the commonwealth responsible for all radiation protection activities, with the exception of nuclear reactors that are licensed by the federal government. We can't do anything in duplication of activities of the federal government. However, off-site stuff is not the responsibility of the federal government, and we have a contract with the Nuclear Regulatory Commission to do environmental monitoring around reactors.

So the NRC is responsible to the site boundary, and you take over from there?

Right. The NRC licenses the plant, but it has no authority about what happens if it goes beyond the plant. That's what made the accident situation so interesting, when NRC tried to come in and tell us what to do on Friday of the accident.

So the releases to the environment caused complications among the agencies?

Yes, but the release to the environment on Friday wasn't as great as they thought it was, and they were all mixed up. If there hadn't been a release to the environment, it wouldn't have been what they call it, "the most serious accident," because Fermi [a liquid metal fast breeder reactor near Detroit] had the meltdown [a partial fuel meltdown, in October 1966] and contained it.

Has this accident been categorized?

It was a class-9 accident, not in the true sense of the class-9 accident, but the NRC has defined it as a class-9 accident.

In what sense is it not a class-9 accident?

Off-site radiation levels were a lot lower than what is needed to really define a class-9 accident.

Then what made them define it as a class-9 accident?

Because they decided that it was a small-break type accident, which is also a class-9 accident.

What is a small break?

A small pipe break, which it really wasn't. There was loss of coolant in the accident, and normally in a loss-of-coolant accident you assume you got a pipe break, a small one or a big one. Well, it wasn't a pipe break, it was a valve stuck open, which caused it. In effect, it was the same thing: an opening to the containment and a loss of coolant. I believe the problem associated with the fuel and the melting of the cladding [a ceramic cover for fuel pellets] is the first time this has ever happened in a commercial plant. But there was no melting of fuel apparently, so it wasn't the classic case of a fuel-melt accident.

Then the classification of a class 9 is a little funny?

It's weird. And I think that it took a lot of ingenuity on the part of the commission to figure how to make it a class-9 accident.

Does that indicate that they wanted to make it a class 9?

I think it should be considered class 9 actually, because the potential was there for a real, real serious one, and much more than has happened in any other plant. A few minutes more and we could have been in a real, real solid class 9, so it was a semi-class-9 if you would call it that, bigger than a class 8 but smaller than a class 9; it was one of those things they hadn't really defined. I have nothing wrong with calling it a class 9. One of the problems is that the off-site exposure was such that they couldn't declare it an Extraordinary Nuclear Occurrence because the dose rates just weren't there. So people who are having to sue them for damages have to prove the damages.

Could you say something about the dose rates, what was released, or what you know was released? We heard that the monitors went off scale and that therefore nothing is really known about how much came out.

No, that's not true. The people who are saying that want everyone to believe that they received a lot more radiation exposure than they did; most of them are the anti-nuclear groups, people who don't want TMI One to start up again or people who don't want *any* reactors going. What went off scale was the stack monitor. The stack monitor was designed for routine releases, and it pegged when they started getting millions of curies of noble gases being released. I believe there was something like 13 million curies of noble gases that were released, that is, mainly xenon 133 and the short half-life gases, and 14 curies of iodine 131. These were calculated on the basis of measurements off site and on the basis of measurements of what is left. The 13 million

curies of noble gases are based upon measurements made by the DOE helicopter, in the plume, and by measurements off-site and by the thermoluminescent dosimeters that were off site, plus an estimate that at least half of the noble gases were released anyway. This incident indicated that if they could contain the other more toxic isotopes, then off-site exposure under even worse accident conditions would not necessarily require an evacuation of people; and for radiation exposure alone, the guideline would not even be approached on the need to evacuate. So when they're starting to think about what they are going to do about reactors in areas of high population density, the NRC is thinking of adding features which would in case of an accident allow the release of the noble gases but contain everything else, which would preclude the need to evacuate people.

But do I understand you to say that somehow the larger releases of the noble gases do not necessarily require an evacuation?

That's right. We had very bad weather conditions at the time. The stuff wasn't being dispersed into the atmosphere rapidly, it was staying around, floating around. We got maps of the plume, where the plume was and what the dose rates were at certain times, and it just meandered around the area. It never really dispersed until we got some high winds. Then they picked it up in upstate New York and Albany, some xenon.

Then was the weather the reason why it was decided to evacuate women and children, or was that decision jumping the gun? How would you classify that decision to evacuate?

I opposed the decision to evacuate pregnant women and small children. I opposed the decision on the basis of what I knew was being released from the plant and on what I expected to be released from the plant. Joe Hendrie, the chairman of the Nuclear Regulatory Commission, in conversation with the governor, recommended evacuation. What he said was that if his wife was pregnant and he had a small child in the area, he would move them out a few miles from the plant. He said that to the governor on the telephone. I was there and I just shook my head and said, "I don't agree that there is a need for it," but he said that the basis for it is that we don't know what is going to happen in the future. He said, "These releases may continue and they may get worse and I wouldn't want to take any chances, so I'd move *these* people who are particularly sensitive out." I said, "Okay, I can't argue on that point."

But on the basis of what we knew from the plant, most of the exposure had already occurred, and we didn't expect any additional serious exposures to occur. If you look at the plot of the exposure over time, of the

people in the vicinity of the plant, most of the exposure had occurred by that time, and it did happen to follow my sequence, not his. Actually exposures on Friday were less than what they were on Thursday, and it looked like this was the last time they would be releasing. The venting was over and the levels dropped down, though there were some small releases that occurred on Friday night and Saturday and Sunday.

But there was also the anxiety about the bubble?

Oh yes, the bubble was real, but the explosion problem was not real. The NRC knew it on Saturday, knew that it wasn't real, and they never told the public that there couldn't have been an explosion inside the reactor as a result of hydrogen and oxygen mixing. They had forgotten that there is hydrogen in there, and hydrogen is always put into a pressurized water reactor to prevent an explosion, to prevent oxygen from being formed from the radiolysis of water. If you put hydrogen in there, it stops the reaction; it reverses the reaction. There was hydrogen in there, there was a bubble of hydrogen in there, and they didn't consider that, and when they calculated it, they assumed no hydrogen was present and that it was at standard temperature and pressure. It wasn't at standard temperature and pressure, so there was no possibility ever of a hydrogen-oxygen explosion occurring inside the reactor vessel, but there was about 16 percent oxygen out there, so it was either a fast burn or an explosion, and it looked like a fast burn. That occurred on Wednesday.

They forgot *there was hydrogen?*

Well, in their request to their experts to evaluate the potential for oxygen generation, they didn't give them all the parameters. They did not tell them there was hydrogen already present and that it was under so many pounds of pressure, and both of those things would have precluded the oxygen from being formed. So Harold Denton finally said something at a congressional hearing when he was asked if there was ever a possibility of an explosion. He said no, but he never told the people that. The people, you know, that really shook them up with all the headlines in the papers, and here the president's trooping through on Sunday, and we're saying why don't they tell everybody? I don't know if they told the president! But some of the people in NRC, the top people in NRC, Vic Stello for example, had known; he had right away figured out that it couldn't be happening, he kept arguing, saying it couldn't happen, and Denton was saying, "Well, wait, wait, everybody else says it *can* happen." We had our nuclear engineer down at the site since Thursday, Bill Dornsythe, and he is a graduate nuclear engineer, and he was coming back saying it can't be; they are wrong, there just can't be

TMI Unit Two containment building, February 23, 1980

a possibility of explosion. By Friday and Saturday we were not allowed to talk to the press anymore. It was all taken over by Denton and the governor; we couldn't give out information to the press and we couldn't contradict then what NRC was saying.

It seems that people just don't know?

Have you read the report, the Rogovin Report? That's classic reading, that is fun reading. It reads like a novel. I found out some things from there that I didn't know had happened during the accident. That the governor's office had called up and told them to stop venting, things like that. I didn't know that. I think it was the most accurate presentation of the accident that occurred and easy to read. It's beautiful.

Has there been any effort that you know of to help people become more educated about radiation? There seems to be nothing but a welter of total confusion. How do you solve this?

I don't know how to solve it. I've tried. I was out Friday night at a meeting at Goldsboro and there were 200 or 300 people there. I tried to tell them that when you're dealing with the venting, krypton 85 does not get picked up very seriously in the body fluids. Radiation is radiation is radiation, a rem is a rem, and it doesn't make any difference what kind of radiation you're exposed to, you have the same effect. I said background radiation would have the same effect as the kind of radiation you're being exposed to as krypton 85, and they just wouldn't believe me. They said I was trying to cover something up, that all radiation is bad, and especially bad if it comes from Three Mile Island. I think the people in the area have an interesting reaction when you tell them that there are routine releases from Unit One into the river containing 1 percent of the maximum permissible concentration to the river. They say, "So, that's coming from Unit One." If you tell them that they are getting 100 millirems per year from medical x-rays in Pennsylvania, a typical critical organ exposure, they say, "So what?" You tell them you are going to have 1/10 of a microrem of radiation from a release at Three Mile Island or 2/10 of a millirem from all the krypton 85 if you stood right at the boundary, and they say that's bad. That's bad radiation. There is good radiation and there is bad radiation. People believe that everything that comes out of Three Mile Island is bad radiation, and everything else is good radiation. It's unbelievable. You can't tell them to stop taking dental x-rays every six months; they are unnecessary, but the dentists keep giving them. And the dentists tell the people to leave the area because of 2/10 of a millirem.

I don't understand. I can't get to people. We're *trying.* We're trying to write a White Paper. We're trying to put together something about radiation. We think that after all this time, with all the publicity—there's an article in the paper every day about Three Mile Island and about what the bio-

97

logical effects are—that they would finally understand. And they won't. There are some people who no matter what you say or what credentials you show will just not believe you, so you can forget about them, their minds are made up. You talk to the rest of the people. Boy, they were really mad at me for saying that on a television show a couple of weeks ago. "Are we one of those people? You just forget about us?" "I'm not forgetting about you, I'm here, aren't I? You know I'm trying to tell you, but I know it's not going to work." That's the point. So we are holding public meetings to try to answer any questions the public has on the subject of the cleanup of Unit Two, radiation exposure, anything anybody wants to ask we will answer. Mainly the press and the legislators and the local township officials ask questions, but very few questions concerning biological effects of radiation. Their minds are already made up. Take yesterday's editorial in the *Philadelphia Inquirer:* "It's a scientific fact that all radiation is harmful, no matter how small." It is *not* a scientific fact that all radiation is harmful, it is a scientific *theory* that all radiation is harmful. We have no proof that radiation goes down to zero. We assume that it does.

Goes down to zero?

That the effects are from zero and on. It's an assumption we've used ever since 1956, when I started graduate school, that all radiation is harmful; but it's not a scientific fact. They stated that and underlined it— "It's a scientific fact"—in their editorial. I think we are partially at fault, we in the business of protecting the public health. We've been working so hard on trying to reduce medical x-ray exposure and trying to keep down exposure of the public in the environs of nuclear power plants, to push as low as is reasonably achievable, that we have overkilled. When we say as a result of the accident there is going to be one additional cancer from the exposure that occurred at Three Mile Island—

Is that your feeling?

Yes, it's not going to be any more than that, if that. Everybody believes it is going to be them. We've got people in the area around Three Mile Island who have decided that they are not going to spend the money to send their kids to school because they are not going to live long enough. Because they are going to get cancer within twenty years, the kids are not going to live long enough to enjoy life; so they are going to take them out on a worldwide tour, spend their money on a worldwide tour so these kids can enjoy it while they are alive. I can't convince these people that they aren't going to die of radiation cancer. It's impossible to convince them. They hear the Ernie Sternglasses who come through, the Helen Caldecotts who come through, George Wald, Nobel

Prize winner, who was here. Dr. Ernie Sternglass said that all the babies on the East Coast are dying. He said there are a lot of increased infant mortalities and miscarriages and so forth. None of this has shown up in this area. "There are," he said, "animals dying all over the place." There aren't any animals dying all over the place any more than is normal. And where there are normal problems, the Department of Agriculture knows what those problems are and suggests ways to handle the problems. They are usually food problems.

We heard about some birds dying?

Oh, birds die all the time. There aren't any more animals dying now than there were pre-Three Mile Island or prestartup of Three Mile Island.

But this was some incredible number of birds, 500, that died very quickly.

It sure wasn't radiation. It was probably heat. There are a lot of things that could have caused it. Birds are very insensitive to radiation. The human being is the most sensitive creature, and we would have people dying if birds are going to die. There were no animals dying as a result of the accident. There couldn't be. The exposures were so small as to be insignificant.

There's a veterinarian who has been noticing—

Yes, I know. He said that it started since 1976, and now it's stopped, he's quoted as saying.

Which veterinarian are we talking about?

The vet down on the west side of the river, Dr. Weber. I've talked to our Dr. Ingraham, and he says that they have checked out all of those stories and none of those stories has anything to do with radiation. What is happening is what normally happens. Do you realize 7 percent of the births of calves result in death, across this country? Seven percent are born dead. That surprised me. If one is born dead in this area, they blame it on Three Mile Island. The other thing was the infant mortality.

That's Dr. Sternglass?

Yeah, well, Dr. Sternglass was completely wet on his numbers on infant mortality rates. They were cross-checked, not by us, but by a reporter for the *Patriot.* We also cross-checked but we didn't have to report it since the *Patriot* did. I don't know where he got his numbers from. I was lucky enough to be the first one to debate Dr. Sternglass back in 1961 on fallout. That was the first and last time. You can't win with Dr. Sternglass because every time he comes to a meeting he has a new number for you. "I found something brand new." You have no way of validating those numbers. Every time you study the Sternglass stuff, in retrospect he's wrong, but by the time you get to

him, he's got something new. You say, "You were wrong all this time." He says, "Well, that doesn't have anything to do with *this.* This is a brand new evidence we've just found, it's very important."

I've heard conflicting reports about Dr. Sternglass.

He has been completely wrong in every report that he has issued so far, as far as I know, including some in Pennsylvania which we commented on. He complained about people around Shippingport in the middle seventies. The governor created a commission to study his allegations, and they said there is no substance to the allegations, however that there was not enough monitoring data to say that there wasn't increased radiation in the environment. So they recommended a better environmental surveillance program. That report's available. It said Sternglass's data was wrong. It took a whole year, public hearings, and a lot of money to disprove him when it could have been easily done, but everybody got scared again. Then from that point he went on to something else, and he keeps going on to something else, and something else. He came through here and said that all the babies on the East Coast are going to die. Wow! He got carried away. He also called me an evil man, and because I didn't evacuate, I should be fired. He did that on the second day of the accident. I went home for about an hour about the third or fourth day and somebody had found it in the newspapers and I walked into my office and over my door was a sign, "The Evil Man," and they wouldn't let me take the darn thing down. Everytime I would take it down, somebody would put it back up. I just left it there. Because I wouldn't evacuate people during the accident.

Could I ask a few things about the cleanup? They say the water is intensely radioactive because it's the primary coolant and it's been sitting there seeping into the cement the way water does in a flooded basement. And this primary coolant water is now part of the cement itself and will not be able to be removed by scrubbing it off the walls. Is that true?

That's not the case. Inside the containment building is a liner of stainless steel, and so it is within the stainless steel liner; it's like a thermos bottle. There is a possibility of some seepage between the basement and the wall where the basement liner attaches to the containment liner. I doubt that they are going to have any serious problem in decontaminating it. Even if it did get into the concrete, all it takes is a jackhammer to get that little bit out, it's not going to go in very far.

Last Thursday, the thirteenth of March, they entered the chamber at nine o'clock in the morning.

Yes, I saw a picture this morning in the paper of me looking into the thing on Monday.

You were there?

I was there on Monday when they started manning it. It's a beautiful picture of me. They vented 47 millicuries of krypton. We were standing up at the vent where the krypton was coming out of the plant when they were venting and with survey instruments weren't able to detect it. They vent about 2 curies of krypton a day from the plant normally; it's just leaking and stuff, krypton is getting out, and this 47 millicuries of krypton over three days was infinitesimal. You couldn't even see any increase in radiation with a sensitive instrument at the release point.

Bob Arnold shocked some people at one meeting when he mentioned strontium and cesium as particulates that could come out into the atmosphere. He did say it would be so minute that—

It's gotta go through a whole bank of filters, and the chances of it getting out are awful slim. We will still be doing our monitoring in the environment to make sure it isn't getting out and to see what those levels are. Of course, there are strontium and cesium in the environment now, which makes it awful difficult to differentiate whether it came from a bomb test, an old, old, bomb test, or a year-old fission product.

But there are ways to do that. Have you ever considered using biological instruments to monitor radiation, like that flower in Japan, the spiderwort?

I really haven't thought about the flower in Japan. I don't know how sensitive that is, and I haven't really paid much attention to it.

Over there on the poster on your filing cabinet is the famous quotation from Albert Einstein, "The future of nuclear power must be decided in the town squares of America." Now I've been to a few meetings here, and it seems that the town square element, at least at the meetings, is certainly overwhelmingly opposed.

Yes. No question. Opposed to everything!

And they are also very frustrated. They seem to feel that they are not getting a fair shake according to that quotation, that that should be the case but there is no way, that the government will go ahead with its nuclear program in spite of what the people feel. And yet here it is on your wall.

What the people around here are concerned about is not nuclear power in general; they are concerned about Three Mile Island. I don't think they give a damn about Beaver Valley and Peach Bottom and the other reactors; they are concerned about Three Mile Island and Unit One starting up again, and any releases at all from Unit Two. If they knew that Three Mile Island wouldn't start up again, I think it would help a heck of a lot. We filed a brief with the commission's hearing board on the startup of Unit One, that the psychological effect of startup must be considered as part of the hearing. They have accepted that and have forwarded it to the commission asking that the commission approve it being included as part of the hearing. I'd like to see a referendum on startup of that unit. The problem is that you can't do it with people just within maybe three or four miles of the plant, because they'll all say no. It's obvious it'll be a no. You've got to have enough representation to get people who are both pro and con. I don't care one way or the other whether that plant starts up again, but I think it ought to be fair and I don't know how to do that. Maybe doing it with the four counties surrounding the plant. A heck of a lot of letters have come in from businessmen saying, "We want you to start Unit One up again, we need that power and we need it cheaper, or else we're going to shut down businesses," and then, "We believe it can be operated safely." I think Unit One probably can be operated safely. I think the chances of having another accident like Unit Two are very, very slim, but psychologically with that plant operating there and people knowing it, I don't know.

There are some people who are in desperate need of psychological help right now; it was obvious from the meeting on Friday night. And they're not getting it.

Some of them for their own personal health probably should leave the area if they could. There are some people that have really gone over the border. There was a lady there who believes she is being spied upon; she is worried about being killed by representatives from the industry because she's so anti-industry. She can't sleep at night; she's worried about people tailing her. That's a real serious psychological problem, and I don't think that's something that ought to be played with. But how many people are like that? How many people would be affected by a startup of Unit One, negatively, assuming no other accident occurs, and I think it would be a good idea to get a feeling of more of the residents in the area than just those that are vocal at the meetings. Whenever you go to a meeting about nuclear power, usually you get the antis attending. You expect it. Those who don't care don't go.

I would like to see something on the ballot for those reactors, especially for reactor Unit One. Unit Two I'm not even thinking about starting up again right now; I just can't imagine that unit starting up again within seven or eight or ten years. We'll worry about it when they say they want to.

You were talking about bringing new reactors and other forms of nuclear power in. Has that been affected by the trouble at Three Mile Island?

We may have a problem in Limerick because of population density. We may oppose that one. I doubt that we are going to see any more being built in the United States for the next few years. It depends upon whatever the president and Congress want to do, and how serious the energy problem is. We don't have many alternatives. We're hurting badly if we cut nuclear power off, so it depends upon how bad the energy situation gets as to whether they say we'll build more nuclear plants. With some additional money we can go coal. You can use solar on a small scale now, but it won't be major for twenty years. What I'm hoping for is the fusion proposal, hoping that that will do it in twenty years, to make electricity. Little hydrogen bombs going off, little tiny ones—beep, beep, beep, beep—you know, causing all that energy.

Lynn Ann Biesecker, fourth grade, Middletown, May 20, 1979

Children: Dreams, Memories, Stories

Maria H., third grade

I had a bad dream about TMI. I thought it was TMI in our house. I thought the oven was it. It started to smoke. Everybody died in our house.

Valerie I., third grade

The day after the accident at TMI, my friend was going to spend the night, but when my friend got to my house, my dumb sister said a lot of bad things and Chris— that's my friend—she started to cry, and she went home. That night I dreamed about TMI, and I dreamed that my father stopped at TMI to take a look after work. After he took a look he heard a sound. He turned around, and TMI exploded. And my father died. And then I woke up. I felt very bad because I thought we would have to leave all of my friends, and I would not like it at all if TMI really did explode and everybody died except me.

Charles A., fourth grade

I was kind of scared of the accident at TMI. They didn't really know what they were doing. They were drinking and smoking and playing cards. I felt that they were going crazy.

Mary S., third grade

One of the teachers, she said, "Quick, get away from the windows. Radiation attacks! Radiation attacks!" And my teacher, she lied. She lied so bad! It was my First Confession on Friday, and she lied about going home real early because of First Confession. But it wasn't. It was TMI.

Shirley T., third grade

I had a dream of TMI. I dreamed that somebody walked up to me and asked me to get in the thing to turn off the switch. And I said that I'd be glad to. I felt bad when the accident happened.

Robert B., fifth grade

Dear Mr. Robert Del Tredici,
Here are my reactions to the Three Mile Island Nuclear Accident. We weren't allowed to go outside because of radiation. We were all scared and I thought my throat was burning because of radiation. But I was just scared. I prayed to God for help and I felt a little better. But I was still scared because I didn't know what was going on and no one would tell me anything. These are my reactions to the accident.

Virginia I., fifth grade

I had no dreams, but I had a lot of feelings. Some of my feelings I would not be allowed to mention. I was very mad when we had to leave recess because of it but the part I really liked was staying home, do you know we had no school for 2½ weeks, and I am glad of that because our school is in the middle of Middletown. I was very, very scared too because my aunt lives in town too, and she has a two-year-old baby.

"Super Toilet" by Laura Bretz was written for a junior high school English class in Middletown.

They said it couldn't happen; it's impossible, but it did. On March 28, 1979, in the quiet little town of Middleburg, the people were sleeping. They knew nothing of the world-shattering news that was happening in their backyards. They woke. The children went to school, the parents went to their jobs. It was a day like any other day, except that *it* was there.

Around 10:00 A.M. the news of the incident came over the news media. The impossible happened. Super Toilet had overflowed. The mayor of Middleburg was furious. He had been told by the press what happened at Three Foot Island. The waste closet facility was operated by the General Waste Company. The mayor immediately tried to get in contact with Calder Brights, the president of Wet Ed and the main owner of TFI. The people of the surrounding area waited anxiously for news.

When they finally were told the details of the incident, they were horrified. A valve had failed. An operator hearing the alarms, and not realizing the potential dangers, misread the gauges and put the waste into the final flush cycle. Then it happened. A waste plant operator's nightmare. The giant commode went critical. In the days to come the tiny little town surrounding TFI would change forever. No longer would it be the quiet, almost unknown, rural area. It was now the symbol for antiflush groups throughout the world. No longer would these groups be laughed at and called radical. Now more and more people would listen and join the cause.

The president visited the plant and sent Darold Henton from the National Disposal Commission to calm the people. The pregnant women and preschool children were advised to evacuate. They left their homes not knowing if they could ever return. Darold Henton took charge of all the information given to the public. After ten days the people were allowed to return, but they had changed. From then on, they no longer trusted Wet Ed. They no longer felt safe in their own homes. They were haunted by the knowledge that so far they had survived the effects. How much gas had they received? No one knew. The people would wonder from then on if the sewer gas would have any future effects. They would worry for their children, for future generations to come.

Never again would this be the same beautiful, quiet countryside it once was. The future of the area is still unknown. Even now the plant is not in a cold flush, and no one knows when it will be. The utilities that own the plant want a rate increase, so the people will pay for the damages. These people are the same ones who lived in fear and were told to leave their homes, and whose lives were changed forever. Will the utilities win? They said it couldn't happen. It's impossible. But it did.

Kim L., fifth grade

My feelings about TMI are that I was upset when I found out we were being taken out of school that day. After I had gotten ready I had Reading with the rest of my group. I brust out in tears and tried to calm down. By the time I calmed down my father had come to get us. We went and left the state and went to Illinois to our aunt and uncle's house.

Paul F., third grade

My grandmother and I went to Hazelton with my mother and sister. We stayed here in Middletown and worked. All the time he had a funny taste in his mouth. And if it exploded, it would have gone a far distance. And we would have gotten it too. If it would have gone that far, we would not be able to take it. And my sister would be laughing at me when I was laughing at her.

Leslie S., fifth grade

In the middle of the nighttime I just get in bed and I start dreaming about how it'll come in and get us. You see, our door has a crack in the screen, and I dream like that stuff's coming in and trying to get us.

Children's Chant, Middletown

Two, four, six, eight,
Who do we appreciate?
TMI, TMI, Yaaay!

Two, four, six, eight,
Who made us irradiate?
TMI, TMI, Yaaay!

Gail Eby was a student last year at Feaser Junior High School in Middletown. Her physics teacher had been presenting a special unit on radiation the month before the accident. As part of the lesson, he described the grim death of Madame Curie. A week before the accident, Gail had this dream.

It was early morning and there was a girl lying in bed. She was just waking up. She had a little bit of sore throat, she thought, and maybe a fever. But she figured that she wouldn't tell her parents because today was supposed to be a family picnic; she got dressed and went into the bathroom and looked in the mirror to comb her hair, and she noticed these large blue lumps on her face. The large blue lumps, added to the sore throat and the fever, were symptoms of The Venus Disease. It was a virus that had been picked up by the space capsules when they'd gone to Venus, and it hadn't been killed on the return trip. It was spread all over the world, and there was no cure for it. It was very contagious, and it killed people with a horrible death. The way they treated it was by injecting a radioactive liquid into the bloodstream. It would kill the person they injected it into; but they would have to kill some people to save the rest. She was looking at the lumps on her face and wondering what she was going to do when suddenly I realized that the person looking in the mirror was me.

I walked into my mother's room and I started to tell her. And she started to cry, but I reminded her that once we'd gone to an astrologer who said I'd live to be an old woman, and reminded her that stars don't lie. So she stopped crying and dressed and got ready to drive me to the clinic, where they would give the radioactive shots that would kill the virus, but unfortunately also the person. When we got to the clinic, everything was all white. The whole place was white, and cold. But the nurse was very nice and even went as far as to ask me which arm I wanted the shot in. After I got the shot, they asked whether I would like to have a government funeral and just stay at the clinic. They would have my parents leave, and the government would pay for the funeral; or did I want a private funeral and to go home with my family and have them take care of me. She explained that the effects of the radiation would start after about an hour or so, and you could tell it was working when you started to get sleepy and didn't have any energy. Then one certain way to tell was if you lifted up your eyelid, there would be a large blue blotch on the back of the eye. I just laughed it off, and we drove home. At home I started to get sleepy and drowsy, and then I started to get nervous and anxious and began to doubt what the astrologer had told me. But everything else she had said had come true, so I thought this would too probably. But after a while I could not take the suspense; I had to find out for myself. So I walked into the bathroom and looked in the mirror; I pulled back my eyelids, and there were large blue blotches on the backs of the eyeballs. I walked into the kitchen where my mom was cooking and put my arms around her and kissed her, and she shed some tears, but didn't make any sounds, and I said, "Goodby," and she said, "Goodby," and I walked into the bedroom and laid down on the bed and drifted off to sleep and died.

Gail Eby, Middletown, January 10, 1980

Chuck Landi, Robert Kinsey, Rick Myers, and Rick Nelson, Middletown, January 3, 1980

30.

Prezence, new-wave rock group, Middletown, January 3, 1980

We're just starting out, it's been kinda hard for us to get ahead because of our own music.

We've got our own music, and no one's used to hearing it, so they don't want to hear it; they wanna hear someone else's music.

A lot of bands don't have that much material. You've got a lot of songs?

Eight songs out of twenty-eight are other people's. We do twenty of our own songs.

What are the titles of some of your own songs?

The Lady, Love Is a Design, When Your Love Goes Away, Little Sympathy, Guitar Player, You Don't Have Any Love, Evil-Hearted Woman, Comin' Down, Take It Away, Keep Me on Your Side, Backseat Boogie, Let Live Rock 'n' Roll, Look and See, The Base, Feeling Free, What a Surprise, Bass Drum Feed Out, Feel Like Coming Home, So Sad, Captain Coke, Want You Tonight, Downtown Baby, and Slow Down.

Have you written any lyrics about the accident at Three Mile Island?

One line.

But you guys write a lot of songs. You don't seem to have felt inspired.

Well, we don't want to give 'em any more publicity than they already have.

You know, if we start writing songs, like everyone is writing songs about it, and they're trying to cash in on it.

Yeah, we don't want to do that.

Do you think it has anything to do with not wanting to think about it anymore?

I don't really think about it, like till you say something like that, I really didn't think about it.

You said you weren't anti anything?

Yeah, we're not anti.

We're antidisco.

Why antidisco?

I don't know, I think it's just—

It's a ripoff.

Yeah, it's just somebody, one person can make a million dollars, just go into the studio and take an organ and a bass drum and just go boom boom boom, I mean it's all recorded there.

You can't do it live.

How many bands are there like this in Middletown?

What, like us? None.

Let me ask you a little bit about the accident. Were you guys all here when that occurred?

Yeah, we was supposed to play March 30, I think, yeah.

We was supposed to play that night.

It was like a Friday night, and it got cancelled 'cause of the TMI.

So, how did it hit you?

Oh, I freaked up, I thought we were gonna blow up man, I just thought, you know, I was over there working and like they said they wouldn't let nobody in and nobody out or something like that.

They weren't letting anybody out?

Nope, they weren't letting nobody in or out.

I haven't heard that before.

That's if they think we're contaminated.

But what happened to you that they wouldn't let you out?

Well, they didn't want me to go to the other side of the river, they just didn't.

Your employers?

Yeah, they just didn't want me to go back there because they didn't know what was going to happen, you know, they wanted me to stay there and find out further information.

I stayed for about three days, for about three days after it happened, and then they started saying about a big meltdown, you know, and it was supposed to happen, you know, so I took my chick, and we went down shore but we only stayed for about a day or two days, and then I heard on the radio that it was over, yeah, cleared up, so we came back, but it's still going on.

At first, I wasn't even worried about it.

Me neither, when they started leaving, man, I never even left.

I went down to me parents' house, and they were all crying and stuff.

But, the thing was, they were saying something about the radiation poisoning, and I had to get sick right at the same time, so I thought I had it, man, because I had every symptom of radiation.

What were the symptoms?

Nauseated, throwing up, eyes are red.

Like having the flu, just more.

Tired, man, washed out.

I don't know, our family didn't leave at all through the whole thing; we just kinda sat here and waited it out, which I think's kinda stupid and I don't know; I think if something hadda happened, people would've died; we all would've died 'cause we couldn't get out probably. I really didn't worry about it too much. At first, I did; it was kinda scary. You didn't know if you were gonna live through the night, and you'd be asleep and you'd think, am I gonna wake up in the morning?

I always heard that radiation, you know, you don't really feel it; it just kinda gets ya, and I figured I was just coming down with something sick, you know, like it happened Friday when everything broke loose, and Friday's when I got sick, you know. Friday night I just was throwing up and everything. I just was really weak and sick.

Had you been run down before that?

It just hit me all of a sudden.
It was really weird on TV, they were saying all the symptoms and stuff and they were saying basically just what I had.

How do you feel about it now. Do you feel that this is mostly over?

No, no, it's still leaking out; they just don't say anything.

Yeah, kryptonite or something.

Kryptonite, even Superman wouldn't have a chance.

I went for a swim a couple of days later.

In the river?

Yeah, I didn't think about it though. I was down below the plant too. Like, I was down there swimming and I was swimming by this thing, and all this water started coming out, and I said, "Oh no, that's right," and I hopped back out, yeah, I just didn't think about it when I was swimming, and then I saw all this water coming out.

Coming out of the plant?

Yeah, it comes off the outside of the island; it shoots out of this little pipe, and stuff comes out, and I was only about 200 feet from it, splashing and stuff.

Here comes radiation.

Yeah, I didn't know what was coming out.

I was trying to picture what it would be like if it really happened, if there really was a meltdown, to see what would happen, what people would do, where they would put all of us and stuff; I was just trying to picture what it would look like. Just picture a bunch of guys dead, and a bunch of empty houses, a bunch of people running through with cars, stealing and looting and all this, all that stuff. Then I thought it was just some kind of hoax to raise their prices on their electricity bill, trying to get the people to pay for it, that whole idea. That whole idea pissed me off, I'm glad I'm not hooked up to the plant. We don't have to pay that extra whatever they wanted us to pay.

Mickey Minnich, left of center in "Strength Training" t-shirt, January 11, 1980

31.

Mickey Minnich, football coach, vice principal, Steelton Highspire High School, January 4, 1980

Last year our team, the Steelton Rollers, were number one in the state. I've coached since about sixty-three. The record has been good, and I've really been successful. I like kids. We do a lot of good things with our kids. I'm a teacher, a counselor, and an assistant principal at Steelton High.

Are you getting any pressure because of your antinuclear activities?

Well, subtle things, like last year people thought I was wacky, going half crazy on this stuff. I'm a sane person, you know what I mean? It hasn't really seriously affected me except when I was gonna do it fulltime, and then they said, "Well, you're fired." Why can't I just be normal, work during the day and do this at night, they asked. No, sorry. People look at you, and they say "Well, you're normally a pretty solid guy, but what are you doing in this?"

There are a lot more concerned people now, and they're upset, but so many people think it doesn't exist. "Nothing to worry about." "Everything's under control." Blah blah this, blah blah that, and here it was even close to meltdown! Then you hear the Met Ed people. Something is haywire here. I say this is negligence. I say somebody is really shoddy here with the way they do things.

So I got actively involved. When you meet with people and talk with them and tell them about the answers you got, or that you didn't even get, then they start saying, "Look, this is not democratic, this is not fair, this is not American, we have to do something about this, how did we ever let this thing happen?"

You start looking at the whole thing; it's like a dream that finally pieces together, but anything you see in it, you know, it's crystal clear: this is wrong, this is morally wrong, it has no ethics to it. Then you go to public utilities hearings and you see Met Ed there and you begin to put in the typical corporate identities with them, and money being the top thing, not us, not human beings, we are expendable. You say, "Well, why didn't we know about these things before? Why didn't we have an evacuation plan?" And then we're wrong because we were ignorant.

You get these alpha emitters in you, could be in me or you; it's just there emitting, depending on what gene it hits, or when it hits; it could be now or in five years from now, ten, twenty—that fear of the unknown. It's like seeing a Frankenstein movie or walking a dark street or something. You're afraid of every corner, you walk in the middle of the street or close to the curb, so all those fears are conjured up now, and then you starting thinking of how a holocaust would be. Where have I been? It's like being born again but in a different sense, born again with nuclear power and what it's all about. It's like the title of that book on nuclear energy, *Poisoned Power.* You start reading *Brighter Than a Thousand Suns,* or *The New Tyranny* and all these books. All these things piece together, and everyone starts saying this is not safe enough just to generate electricity. Let us have input. Let us have a say; you're stopping us from our pursuit of happiness. Then you start thinking about the future generation and you start thinking about half-lives and things—they could be around for 25,000 years—and about waste. We have a big waste depository here, which is Three Mile Island. There's so much waste there, probably more than any place on the East Coast. Of course, nobody talks about that.

I'm really angry I'm even living here, I'd rather just get out. In fact, I was going to go to Arizona last year and just missed a job there, but then I'm glad I didn't go because they're building three nuclear power plants near Phoenix, and the West is not as clean as you would like to think it is. A lot of things are being uncovered out there right now, so I say, what the heck, I might as well stay in this contamination and try to fight it.

If they can't keep Three Mile Island shut down, then they'll never shut anything down, and they'll never make a stand against nuclear power. I tell you it has been very tough. We've been to all the Congress meetings; local people went to our state senator; we've had our people testify in Washington too. We went to the mill, did the circuit in trying to make people open their eyes and it's been tough. I think it shows that we're losing in a way. And I'm nervous about that. Our state legislature has done beans really—why don't they have an evacuation plan? Why don't they say you'll have it by—whatever? They keep giving out extension dates. They're losing money in here, investors, you know. I know people that picketed Wall Street; that was interesting. We had a group of people go up to Wall Street and picket the electrical firms and the heavy utilities. I thought that's really where the money is, that's where it is, but people laugh and look at us and say what are you, you haven't any power. There was a survey, and I think 65 percent of the people were against it, but that's what scares me. You could take a survey in a school and you might have 50 percent or 60 percent of the students for it. They don't know. You see the light, and they don't see it, and you wonder why they don't understand what's going on. I think it's a matter of education. There are different levels of awareness, and they affect certain people certain ways. There's a lot of people that are affected like me, and there's a lot of people that are very emotional about it. If they ever try to open it again, they're liable to have civil disobedience. There's a lot of radical people. I was telling someone in the cafeteria today, if they open I'm going to stand in front of whatever you have to stand in front of and chain my arm to whatever you have to chain it to. But it's embarrassing. You would lose your job. But I would go that far to do it.

A lot of people say this is just another cause type thing. "This guy here is a cause fighter." You have to deal with that. I don't know what it will take to wake people up. The invasion of Afghanistan, I guess. I wish you could smell it. I wish you could spray something in there that you could smell and it would be like chlorine. I tell you what, if that would have been chlorine on March 28, they would have evacuated everybody because you could smell it. It's irritating. People would be coughing, vomiting. I wish it would make you vomit.

32.

Robert Kapler is an investigative reporter for the Harrisburg Guide. *Using false I.D., Kapler applied for a job as a guard at TMI and was hired. Harrisburg, March 3, 1980*

What was your reason for originally coming to Harrisburg?

I came from the Philadelphia area to Harrisburg because the job offer with the *Guide* was my first professional fulltime job in journalism. I'd been doing investigations since I was in college—my first one was of the security force at Temple University—so this wasn't anything new to me. But the

accident was, well—like everyone else, I was scared. But I didn't know how serious it was, because I don't believe everything I read in the newspapers. I'm sure nobody else does either!

Can I quote you on that?

Sure! Everything I'm telling you you can quote. So—at the time of the accident I was kind of skeptical because I know the media. Then I came to Harrisburg—in November, 1979—and I started reading and talking to people. I've got all kinds of stuff in my files now: the *Philadelphia Inquirer* series on the accident, the report of the president's commission on the accident, the *Rolling Stone* story, and here's something I got from Chauncey Kepford, a *Washington Post* story on the Heidelberg Report, which was a study done of the Atomic Energy Commission by a group of scientists in Germany. Their report showed that all the assurances

by the AEC and the NRC are based on false assumptions, that the base line data from the original tests done by the AEC to determine if radiation gets into the food chain, into the atmosphere, and into everything else, were doctored, falsified.

Then, after you find out that we were thirty minutes away from a meltdown, you can believe anything! Did you see this thing in the paper the other day about the guy who caught his shirt on a circuit breaker at a nuclear plant in West Virginia? It shut down the entire plant. You start seeing all this and you've got to believe there is danger, I don't care what they tell you!

How long have you felt this way?

When I arrived in Harrisburg I wasn't pro-nuclear or anti-nuclear, or pro-TMI or anti-TMI, or anything. I was skeptical. I wanted to see for myself. Then I started talking to people who know about the situation, and

I found out there's a lot to be looked at and that it would be very, very foolish for anyone to take what the nuclear industry says at face value, especially Metropolitan Edison, which has proved time and time again how damn inept they are at controlling the damn situation over there at Three Mile Island. I don't know if they've even changed anything since I've been there. When I was there, anybody with half a wit could have walked right in.

How did you first get the idea to get yourself hired there?

Richard Halverson, the editor-in-chief of the *Guide*—my boss—it was his idea from the start. He'd tried to convince a former reporter to take it on, but the guy didn't want to do it. So he gave me the assignment. Everything he'd ascertained about the poor security system on the island he'd gotten from a couple of former guards there. He knew two of them who'd told him *anyone* could walk into Three Mile Island, get a job, and do whatever they wanted. Before I decided to try it, they talked to me and described all kinds of things that went on there: how the metal detectors don't work, how one guard had brought a cow bell through without anyone noticing; how some of the guards might have criminal records. They told me about all kinds of shoddy hiring practices, about the bad security, about the sexual antics that go on on the island. Now, you hear stuff like that and you've got to wonder what the hell's going on out there! All of that is what made me decide to go ahead with the project and that's how I ended up a security guard.

How would you characterize the people who work there?

Brainwashed.

Brainwashed? I often wonder: Do people really know what's happening, and is it just money that keeps them quiet, or—

Job security. You've got laborers out there making about nine dollars an hour. Do you know what they're doing? They're sitting around reading newspapers. They're maintenance men. They're supposed to sweep up, mop the floors. When I went to that place, when I got to Three Mile Island Unit Two, it looked like it was built in 1930! There was so much grime and dust and everything else on the floor, on all the equipment, on all the machinery, you would think the place was situated next to a coal mine or something like that. When I got there the NRC had just cracked down on Metropolitan Edison and said, "Look, you've got to clean this place up, it's a mess." And there were guys mopping the floors. Well, as soon as they got done mopping the floors—that lasted a couple of days—I'd walk by these guys sitting there reading newspapers! And I'd see this over and over again.

I caught one guy sitting next to one, possibly one, of the most radiating walls next to the containment building, this one area called Reactor Hatch One. It's a personnel area where the workers come in and put on their protective gear; it's a locker room. This guy's lying in the locker room, and the background radiation's like 300 millirems an hour, and this guy's lying in this locker room sleeping! You've got to question the intellect of somebody who would sleep in a place where he's going to be exposed to high levels of radiation.

There was another guy—you're supposed to be wearing protective plastic booties but instead of tucking his pants into his booties, he's got his pants draped *over* the booties and he's mopping the floors up with them. Now he's probably going to take that stuff home for his kids. He's going to drape his pants over a chair or something and he's going to have a little kid running about his house! Are there radiation safety controls there? Sure there are, but it all depends on the individual. The first thing they tell you when you get there is that *you* are responsible for your own radiation safety, which means, if you look between the lines, that you're responsible for my radiation safety, you're responsible for the next guy's radiation safety, and it's up to you to make sure that you don't screw up and release huge amounts of radiation in that environment. So what they're really saying when you go in there is, "Look we're going to give you all the ways of protecting yourself and protecting everybody else, but once we tell you it's up to you, you're on your own." But these guys out there just don't have it in their minds. They've got this idea that, well, if it's dangerous, Metropolitan Edison wouldn't have us out here.

When you walk in there, they're all smiles; and from the time that you walk in until the time you leave, it is their job to make you believe that nothing is going to happen to you. You will not become any sicker than anyone else in the world because you're working in a nuclear power plant. [*Robert pulls a pamphlet from his files.*] Now this is called *Radiation Protection Training* and every worker gets one of these. This really kills me. They've got a machine at Three Mile Island, and you step up to this machine—it's like a form-fitting mask—and you put it on, and it tells you whether or not you have the right bone structure to wear a respirator. That's all this machine does. This big, goddamned, thousand-dollars-plus machine, and that's all it does. I was completely amazed that they would have such a thing!

What would somebody look like who didn't have the right bone structure? Doesn't everybody have the right bone structure?

Well, some people have cheekbones too high, faces too fat or skinny, meaning air would be able to creep into the respirator.

Here's the first thing they tell you the second you walk in: "Each individual is responsible for his own radiation safety by following procedures complying with the radiation work permits and not exceeding dose limits." Now they go right into it—radioactivity simplified to the maximum—everything. "Radioactive material emits particles and/or rays in an attempt to reach a more stable condition." Well, that can mean anything. "Contamination is dispersed radioactive material in a location where it is not wanted." Now that could mean anything too. Then they go into the different units of measurement, the types of radiation, and explain it in very simplistic terms. Regarding biological effects, listen to this: "The affects of small quantities of radiation exposure over a long period of time are: increased chance of cancer, slightly increased chance of genetic mutations in future generations." Now, that's all they say about it. They don't give you another word of explanation. What kind of genetic mutations? What kind of diseases could you expect in future generations? How will this affect your ability to reproduce? There are so many different things they could tell you, but they don't. All they give is this one line! Then they spend more time talking about this particular aspect than they do telling you what the real dangers are. "In comparison, the risk of injury, sickness, or death related to work at a nuclear facility does not exceed the risk of injury, sickness, or death related to work in a occupation classified as safe—manufacturing, etc." Then they go on and this is where the great comparisons are made, "Fifty-rem whole-body exposure over a lifetime can possibly decrease the expected lifespan by one-half year." What does that mean? You're going to live to seventy, but if you were not working at a nuclear facility you would live to seventy and six months and all of a sudden drop dead? They don't tell you what's going to happen. You'll probably get cancer; they don't tell you that you can get about sixteen thousand blood diseases. There are so many things that could happen to you. All they say is, it's going to decrease your lifespan by half a year. Like all of a sudden you're going to drop dead one day and someone will say, "Oh, I can tell this boy worked at a radiation facility." Then they go on to compare this statistic with everything else. "Twenty-five percent overweight decreases the expected lifespan by approximately 3½ years of life." If you work at a nuclear facility, you're going to lose half a year—isn't that great? "Auto accidents"—now they're taking this thing beyond logic—"auto accidents decrease the expected lifespan by half a year." What do they mean? You drive an automobile, so all of a sudden, sure, they're talking an average, but because you drive a car, someday youre going to die, just drop dead, and they'll say, "Oh, this man's been driving a car,

I can tell!" Now comes the killer of them all. "Aircraft accidents decrease the expected lifespan by 1/20 of a year." Now what the hell does that mean? I don't know what it means.

Metropolitan Edison just sugarcoats the inherent risks of working at one of these places. By the time you get out, you think that everyone else in the community has just been a pawn in the hands of the media, that the people that are just so upset about TMI and Metropolitan Edison have just been reading newspapers too much and too long. And that's exactly the way I felt before I came here. But when you start reading all this material and you see that even though the media has been too eager to be the voice of the apocalypse and all this stuff, they were, in an offhand way, pretty much on base when they were talking about the dangers of this thing.

Well, how do you feel about your own closeness there to it?

When I found out that I could have been sitting next to a barrel that was emitting 4 rems of radiation an hour, I said, "That's it! Close the place down!" When I found out that two radioactive barrels had gone out to the Harrisburg incinerator by mistake, I said, "Close that place down! They don't know how to handle the stuff!"

Do the workers feel confident that their superiors will tell them the right things?

I had a guy tell me he's sometimes given a week to do a job that would take normally half an hour. Why? Paperwork. And confusion and just total bureaucratic red tape. Inefficiency. I've been told by other people that a guy—a very experienced, capable boilermaker—was sent to work on equipment in Unit Two, and he doesn't even know what the equipment does. He has no idea what the purpose of the equipment is. They just say, "Go out, check this," and they give him the work order, tell him what to fix, but he doesn't know what the hell the thing does. So he gets out there and he's fixing it! A women told me her husband was hired to be an electrician. This man had never been an electrician in his life and he's out there, one of the electricians. Now you've got to wonder what the hell's going on out there, if unqualified people and uninformed people are working on the very systems that could possibly kill thousands of people. So that's just a sampling of the comments I've heard. Par for the course for one of the subcontractors is "Hurry up and wait" and "just do the job and don't worry about what might or might not happen. Just do what you're told and everybody will make a lot of money." And that's why no-

body ever complains, because they're making an incredible amount of money out there.

Have you ever been back?

I was back one time. To get my whole-body monitoring done.

What was it like?

Of course, the supervisors were all very congenial. They were all very calm, very thankful, very nice to me. But the guards were staring me down, waiting for me to say something, for me to upset them, so they could tell me where to go. And the guard at the gate—see they really stress this perimeter security to the maximum. External security is unbelievable. If you walk in there, and you don't have the right color badge, or you're not supposed to be in there, they make a federal issue of it. I walked in, I wanted to get a temporary badge to be in there—once the story had broken—to get my whole-body count done, and the guard knew me, a guy I'd worked with, and he was one of the guys I'd kind of liked. He was funny. He wasn't really a macho man or anything. He wasn't out to slay all the women in the area and he just was a kind of nice guy. Well, he found out about this story and turned against me. I got up there, and he started calling me "Mr. Kapler" and pretending like he never knew me. Now I worked with the guy for a month, and he pretends he's never met me before in his life. I said, "Come on, all I want to do is get my whole-body count done and I'll be gone." And John Collins from the NRC drove up. He says, "Mr. Kapler, we have a problem here." I didn't have my ID with me. "This gentleman doesn't have any form of identification." I say, "Come on, you know who I am. You know exactly who I am! Just let me in. There's no big deal." He says, "You've got to sign a form, sir." He made a federal issue out of it. So it took me about twenty minutes to get in the place and they knew I wasn't in there to blow it up. When I was leaving, I had like an armed guard escort out—people in front of me, behind me, and every other way to make sure I didn't try jumping over the fence, I guess, or something. They were all standing in a line when I left. I backed my car up and they all stood at the south gate and just looked at me.

It just seemed to me they were protecting their little fort there. The place is separated as an island, and the people's minds are as if they were working on a real desert island somewhere and they had no contact with the outside world, because they are completely brainwashed. I don't care, I used to mince words and say, "Yes, they're aggressively instructed in the safety measures taken by them." I now call it "brainwash-

ing," because that's what it is. These people are brainwashed. From the day they walk in there, they are told that no harm will come to them by working at Three Mile Island, and they believe it. And why shouldn't they believe it? Nothing has ever happened; they can't see radiation floating in the air; it doesn't glow in the dark; they just can't see it. Now if they saw it, if their hands started dropping off, I'm sure things would be a lot different. But you just can't speed up the hands of time. They can't look down the road and see future generations, they can't look down the road and see any difficulties they might have—cancer, or anything else. So they don't worry about it. They just don't worry about it.

Once in a while these guys let on just a little bit that all is not right in Denmark. They let on some vague suspicion that things might not be the way they seem. But if you ever ask them directly, "Hey, what about this?" you'll never get a straight answer because they're afraid, afraid they'll—

Lose their jobs?

Yes, although if anybody questions anything out there, other people raise their eyebrows.

They've got the two containment buildings, right? There are these black streaks running down Unit One, and I kept saying, "What are those black streaks? I know that's not water. What is it, tar? What the hell is it?" Because I had been on the roof and I saw a dead pigeon lying at the base of one of these streaks. I thought maybe the damn thing had crashed up against it and was immediately overcome with a massive dose of radiation and died on the spot, giving out this black fluid. And I just kept saying to everybody, "What are those black streaks up there?" No matter who I said it to, I'd always get the same response: "Why? What do you want to know for?" "Well, I want to know what's going on. What are those black streaks?" "Oh, I don't know. Don't bother me about that." Nobody ever questions. And people who do question are ostracized by the rest of the group.

Well, now that you've finished your investigation of the island and are done writing your article—

No, we're not finished, we'll never be finished! We'll be finished when it's closed down.

[*Robert Kapler worked at the Three Mile Island plant unchallenged for one month from December 18, 1979 to January 18, 1980, then wrote a controversial account of the facility from an "insider's" point of view in the February 2 edition of the* Guide. *It was reprinted in the* Washington Post.]

33.

Brian F. McKay, Newberry Township police officer, March 15, 1980

As a police officer, I deal with all segments of the society which we live in. In a way you can see the decay of faith and trust in government, whether it's a small municipality, the state or federal governments, or big conglomerates. People just don't trust anybody today. I think most policemen enter a job to help somebody. It's not all television shoot-'em-up bang bang. Just like this incident with Three Mile Island. During that crucial period, a time when nobody knew what the hell was going on, Wednesday, Thursday, and then Friday, when it was finally announced to evacuate children under five and pregnant women from within

a five-mile area of Three Mile Island, there was fear and panic. One-for-all and forget everybody else! We could see the indecision. As a man who had been in the military, I could respond to an enemy that you could visibly see, or something that was taking place in front of you. To envision a nuclear meltdown, not being able to defend yourself properly against it, the piss-poor, I mean *really* poor, communication between the utility itself and state government, the poor communication from a state government to its county level and then from a county level down to its municipal level and finally to its own people, was atrocious. There was no way in hell that this area could ever have been evacuated in the proper amount of time if a meltdown had occurred. I remember the elaborate things that were supposed to be part of the grand plan: state policemen taking the interstate highways; and four lanes of traffic going north, east, and west; and tow trucks standing by at crucial areas

to pull people off the road; the food, gas, and so forth. When it happened, I was here at home, and my dad says, "Did you hear that on the radio? They had a nuclear accident down there in Middletown; they're asking all women who have children under five years of age or who are pregnant to evacuate the area immediately."

Does that mean you didn't hear about it until Friday?

This was the evacuation. I heard about the trouble earlier; everybody heard about the trouble. We were discussing it just the night before, Thursday night. I think I was working the daylight shift from seven in the morning to three in the afternoon. That evening Governor Thornburgh appeared on a television program on WITF, out of Hershey, with Chauncey Kepford. And here was the governor of Pennsylvania trying to remain cool, calm, and collected; and Chauncey was just blowing him out, telling him this is what can happen with a total nuclear meltdown—you'd have to do this, you'd have to evacuate these people, and here was the governor, newly elected to office, and he was the most uninformed. He inspired about as much confidence as a case of diarrhea. That was my feeling for the man. I became quite concerned at that point. There were no other government agencies available for the governor to fall back on. These people had been brainwashed over the years that nothing could go wrong.

What people?

The government. The Department of Environmental Resources, the Environmental Protection Agency at the state level.

Pennsylvania Emergency Management Agency?

They had this evacuation planned and all this other stuff. Sure I went through the flood of '72. I had ten feet of water in the bottom of my house in New Cumberland. I lived through the flood, I went through a war, and I worked around nuclear warheads when I was in the service in Italy. I went through the Chemical Biological Radiological Program that we had to go through and the intensive training. I could understand certain things about radiation. I knew what a dosimeter was. We were taught and trained basically about nuclear warfare, what a nuclear warhead would do. I knew what I had remembered from the service, and when they started talking about possible emissions and that if a meltdown would occur, radioactive particles would be thrown into the atmosphere, I became concerned. It would be just like being at Ground Zero, right at Ground Zero after a nuclear explosion. I knew all that ahead of time. Finally, somebody says, "Keep it under your hat, there's a problem down at TMI." I said, "Well I gathered that." They were saying there was a possibility of a meltdown like *The China Syndrome.*

Did you see the movie?

No. I didn't figure I had to since I lived through it. It just happened to be released in this area a week before the accident; that was what took the cake. I went to work Friday, and they said there was a possibility that an evacuation would have to occur, that the police would be responsible for maintaining law and order, evacuation routes, convoy routes to funnel the people out. The police would have to set up a plan to evacuate.

And you didn't have a plan ready?

We didn't have a plan ready. We didn't have anything, so we started to do things. We figured, when they told us where our evacuation point was for the municipality I work in, what the stages of evacuation would eventually be.

How many miles are you from the plant?

I'm sitting 2.2 miles from Ground Zero. That clump of trees blocks the view. When there's steam, you can see the steam.

Finally it came down, and they said, "Prepare to evacuate your families," and being as we were duly sworn peace officers of the commonwealth, it was a hell of a conflict of interest. My boy was only sixteen months old at the time of the accident, and he had been outside during those three days when there were radioactive emissions, and I was madder than hell. As a matter of fact, they were outside the day that it occurred. The chief informed us that we would be on one-hour call.

What's the penalty for splitting at a time like that in order to save your own? Is that like desertion?

No, it wouldn't be a form of desertion. If I was fully informed, I think I would have evacuated my family first. I'd have got them right the hell out.

And then you would have come back?

Well, I'm kind of duty-conscious. I figured that to maintain some resemblance of order, to prevent a panic like in *War of the Worlds* with the beings from outer space destroying the world, I felt that I would have to be present. So I would have got my family out, but I'd have returned to do my job, to more or less help my fellow man get out of the way. That's my job: protection of life and property. I wish the utilities would have the same priorities that I have to keep.

When did you get the word to get people moving?

That was Monday. We had people who were evacuating telling us where they were going on their own, or they were asking for our advice. My advice was: We have not received the official emergency evacuation plan, but if you feel uncomfortable with this situation due to the news media and the continuous coverage, if you feel more comfortable in leaving, then I would suggest that you do. It was an honest answer. I said that if you know all about the meltdown and the hydrogen bubble, then you know more than we do, because we haven't been told anything yet. The lines of communication were bad from every standpoint; it wasn't just one area. This was new. This was something that nobody had ever thought would happen!

Nobody was ready for it?

Nobody was, really. They could say they were, but where the hell would the decontamination centers be? What hospitals would treat as many people as were in this area if they were exposed to radiation, to combat the loss of white blood cells? What hospitals in the area would have anywhere from 100,000 to 500,000 pints of blood for

transfusion? There were no answers. There is no way in hell that it could have been prepared properly to deal with such a large contamination. I thought as a policeman thinks—the worst. The worst is going to happen, and if anything happens that's not as bad as what you expect, you're doing okay, the situation's getting better. In this case I was seriously thinking that if the meltdown occurred and there was a large amount of radiation or a terrific explosion and the area would be contaminated, the only thing I could think of that the state would do to protect the outlying or surviving areas would be to ring it with either the National Guard or law enforcement personnel like myself and say, "No, you can't leave!" That's the cordoning plan. It kind of reminded me of a film I saw when I was attending college, *The War Game.* I remember how the police had to destroy human beings that were so badly burned or so badly contaminated that they had no chance of living, how the police were issued sidearms and the area was cordoned off. Those that did have a chance to survive but were going to suffer were lying there on the streets, the police had to go by and destroy them—like euthanasia—putting them out of their misery.

If a meltdown had occurred, I don't even think the Pennsylvania National Guard could have got out in time to assist or to mobilize that quickly, because if I'm in the National Guard and I live in Middletown, Pennsylvania, I'm going to be worried about getting my family out instead of responding to the 28th Infantry Division or to whatever outfit. Who the hell knows what would have happened? But I was thinking the worst. It was just a quirk of fate that it didn't. It wasn't anybody's expertise or technology; it was just a quirk of fate.

From everything I read now, I'm totally disillusioned with the capability of a private utility to adequately inform and protect the public, because their motive is not safety—it's profit! Disillusioned with the government—they don't know what the hell they're doing either. I wasn't impressed when Jimmy Carter came here, to me it was just, "Okay, I'm going to show you that I'm here and everything is going to be all right." A symbolic gesture, like the commanding general seeing the boys in the front lines. Whooptee Doo! You're only going to be here five minutes, and then your ass is going to be back drinking some good scotch whiskey while everybody else is lying in the mud, wet, dirty, filthy, tired, and hungry.

We were fortunate that a lot of people did leave the area on their own. I think those people had the right foresight and put their personal and family safety as a priority, rather than trying to downplay the emergency as many government officials were doing.

It's basically like they're trying to tell you, "Look, we're experimenting with you.

You're the first guinea pigs, and then we're going to do the research after Three Mile Island." You read books by Gofman or *Everyone's Guide to Nuclear Power* and you hear how these eminent scientists who are Ph.D.'s in physics and genetics and everything else are telling you, "Look, low-level radiation does have an effect on the food chain and does have a definite effect on the body and the interaction of cancer, cystic fibrosis, leukemia, thyroid conditions, and other major diseases." My wife has a thyroid problem. Also, I had a German shepherd, and six months after the accident at Three Mile Island his body was riddled with cancer. I had to have him put to sleep. He was six years old.

What kind of cancer?

He had cancer of the throat, stomach, and liver. A good friend of mine is a veterinarian, and he opened the dog up to see what was wrong with him. He said there was no possible hope for the dog, adding that he couldn't understand how the dog lived as long as it did. From what I know now, there was a possibility that his exposure, or us living down here for that period of time while the reactor was functioning through the releases of radiation that no one really thought of or cared about, could have had an adverse affect on the dog's health.

. . .

My job is the protection of life and property and to protect everybody's constitutional rights. To make sure you don't commit any unlawful search or seizure, that if you have to exercise force that it is only that force which is necessary to overcome the resistance. These are rules of law that I live by every day as a policeman. But the unfortunate thing is, from this experience, it appears to me that the government is not interested in the protection of life and property or the protection of the individual rights of the citizens of this community. They are bypassing the basic human right to life, to be free from foreign oppressors or from foreign danger, or basically what is going on at Three Mile Island and their efforts to try and get the reactor restarted. They are not

looking at the whole picture of what my life is going to be twenty years from now. What about the baby that my wife is carrying? What is he or she going to have to face? If they go to restart it, I'm definitely going to move. I'm definitely going to move! I don't care what's happened to me, due to the fact that I'm thirty-four years of age. I've been through a war; I've been through a flood; a couple of times I probably shouldn't even have been here—you know, close calls—but I've got a full life! But I want my kid to have it better. If that means that I have to move another twenty or thirty miles away from here to ensure not to be exposed to continuous radiation, then I'll sell my home and move.

To me we are nothing but a giant test tube for the researchers for the Department of Energy, for the Environmental Protection Agency, for all the nuclear industry. The people at Three Mile Island for the next twenty years are going to be watched with health surveys and so forth. But I think that they should have been doing the research thirty years ago at the end of World War II, from the bombings of Hiroshima and Nagasaki, from the Bimini test grounds in the Pacific. Things like dumping the water in the Susquehanna River—people must realize now, it's just like in the books you read, that radioactivity has a tendency to linger a lot longer in the water than it does in the atmosphere. So if they are releasing it in the riverbed, it's the worst thing they can do. The whole drinking system for the city of Lancaster and further on down the river is all shot. They know it's there, but once that action takes place, there is no way that it can be reversed. How the hell are you going to clean the river up? It's not like removing a square yard of topsoil and putting it in a lead container and burying it out in the ground in concrete in Idaho. That's a river! It flows! That's a whole cycle! It's amazing to have a president say that "There is nothing wrong with nuclear power—we need it more than ever." I think he's full of shit, and you can quote me on that one.

If nuclear power is safe, I want them to put it along the Potomac and I want them to

put one in Plains, Georgia, and see how they like it. You see that 362-foot tower sitting there with the steam coming off and you wonder is that just condensation and evaporation, or is that the real stuff coming out? I think it's time that people take a long, serious, hard look at it. I have, and before the March 28 incident last year, I was ignorant and believed that nuclear power is safe.

The government, the utility, these atomic forums, these companies that do the studies, they're not thinking! They're thinking profit, money, and jobs. It's been proven that the nuclear industry does not employ more people. It puts more people out of work than it employs. Then you have eminent scientists that were working formerly for the Atomic Energy Commission coming out and saying, "Hey, man, radiation is bad news," and they were fired, they were cut off from research grants. "We don't want to hear from you anymore." But all these scientists that are pronuclear get the government grants for their pet projects, "Oh yeah, A-Number 1! The best thing that could ever happen."

You see through it now. It's a facade. There's no way. Now I'm going to do what I think is right. I'm going to fight any way I can as a representative, as a citizen to try to convince the local government, state government, or federal government that nuclear power is not the best way to go.

. . .

Here's a funny thing: I'm a police firearms instructor, and I'm certified by the state to teach municipal police officers in the academies the use of firearms. I'm also certified by the state to teach "lethal weapons training" for any company that employs private security forces. I teach Met Ed's security forces, and I do their annual qualifications with firearms. By the NRC's own regulations, the security force at Three Mile Island is supposed to be able to repel, now get this, *repel,* an attack by a dedicated group of terrorists armed with automatic weapons and explosives. But you could get into that place with a can opener. It's amazing! I do their annual qualifications, and here I am saying that!

113

34.

Arthur Haaf, Presbyterian clergy-man. Middletown, July 5, 1979

I stayed because that's my responsibility: to be of service. And I was not, and my wife, we're not fearful about anything.

That has to do with having faith, not being fearful?

True. "Be not anxious over tomorrow," is what Matthew is talking about.

Did that include the possibility that something truly fearful could happen?

There are no options if you have faith. You're not fearful. Period. It's not an "if" sort of thing.

Did many of your congregation come to you for advice during that time?

Didn't need any. Didn't need any. I've not counseled anybody. Nobody's uptight about it and no one has come to me. So a lot of this stuff that's being talked about is just kicked around. A lot of the protesters, naturally, are trying to look for information that backs up what they're trying to support.

Nothing changed me. When they interviewed me, they asked me if I was going to speak on Three Mile Island. I didn't speak on Three Mile Island; I preached on "Disciples of Salt and Light." That was April 1. But the next Sunday, let me see, [*looks in his record*] was the April 8. See, "The Disciples of Salt and Light." I didn't change a thing. Here's the topic. It comes from Matthew, and all I did was just use this whole. "Salt of the earth, and the light of the world." That's who we are. If you're Christ people, you can adjust and relate to adversities and everything else. It's appropriate because it includes any aspect of life. Because if you're a disciple, you do exactly what Jesus said.

You bear witness?

Right. It's easier said than done. The witness is the truth of the matter. There's a lot of people talk it, but you've got to live it. You know, it's like falling in love and being married. You can talk you're going to be a good husband, but if you're out six days a week, that's not good. Now, Palm Sunday followed. "He beheld the city and wept." That has nothing to do with Three Mile Island. It was all planned. All these were already in the design.

And you didn't find yourself speaking more about faith than you would have normally?

No. But one of the stresses is, Jesus always said, "Be not anxious." Being humans, anxieties are the things we deal with quite a lot. There are more tranquilizers being given to people than a lot of people realize. As a matter of fact a lot of people are living on that kind of lifestyle. That's their supportive strength, and so forth.

Take Matthew 6:30 in here, "Trust in Providence. If that is how God clothed the grass and the fields, which are there today and thrown in the furnace, see, today as to tomorrow, will He not much more look after you, you men of little faith?" See. So don't worry. Do not say, "What shall I eat, or what shall I, etcetera?" Now all right, let's look up the word "worry" here in my King James Concordance. It might not even give it under that. So take the word "fearful": here's all the places it is used, starting here in the Old Testament. Here's the word "fear," which is "emah." Now that would be if it's terror. Then "Fear and dread fell upon them." This is in Exodus. Then "trembling"; you're trembling because you're fearful. They would use the word "coff" (phonetic). Frightened. Terror. Now we're coming over into the New Testament. "God hath not given us the spirit of fear." You'll find that in Second Timothy, chapter 1, verse 7. Here "fear" is "phobos"; "phobos" is Greek.

That's where we get "phobia."

That's right. So all these are words that relate to fear.

Ah. A totally different meaning.

That's right. Here's "Fear not, fear not, fear not." Luke's telling that, on the resurrection. Revelations says, "Fear not, I am the last," and so on.

But you didn't find a great deal of fear among your congregation?

No.

So they were exempt.

No. Nobody's exempt. I don't know what you mean by "exempt."

Well, they didn't experience it, when most people did.

There is no exemption. It's just like sin. That's why I'm fulltime employed. There's no exemption. It's always going to be here, see?

. . .

Every day at ten thirty I go downtown. You see, my office has no windows in it. I don't know whether it's raining, snowing, or if it's all right, you understand? But when I go downtown, I'm out in the light. And also by doing that I can meet other people, and know what sin is like. You see, I don't stay in an ivory palace. I'm exposed to the good and the bad. With the bad, we just tell 'em to come and we'll clean 'em up if they want to.

Sort of like decontamination?

Ha! Listen, there's nobody contaminated around here. You know why? Everybody that wanted to got a read-out. They brought the machine in. What they should do is keep this machine in and have all these little children lie on it and find out how much they got from TV. That's serious.

So they had the machine here, and nobody had a high reading; everybody was zero. At my age it doesn't come through the grave. I'm sixty-one and twenty years from now it's not going to do anything to you. And being sterile has nothing to do with someone who's sixty-one, at least not with me. So I'd be in the grave. As a matter of fact, the radiation doesn't touch you there. Anyway, it doesn't touch your soul. And that's what's important, see?

35.

*John Collins, NRC deputy director
in Middletown, March 4, 1980*

I am the deputy director for the NRC support staff at Three Mile Island, and we are responsible for supervising the activities of Metropolitan Edison and the recovery operation of Unit Two. We're also responsible for overseeing the activities as part of the program for restart of Unit One. I've been here on the island since March 30 following the accident, and I guess I'll be here until the recovery program is over.

Do you live in the area?

Yes, I do. I live right here in Middletown. I'm originally based out of our Bethesda office in Maryland. My normal responsibility is chief of the Effluent Treatment System Branch in the office of Nuclear Reactor Regulation. I came up here with Harold Denton on the thirtieth of March, 1979, and assumed responsibility for the NRC staff here about June and have held that position since that time.

Often people who are frightened about what goes on there and who don't necessarily know what's involved say that the company is not competent to handle the operation down at the island. Is that even an issue for you?

The loss of public confidence in the utility came about as a result of misinformation immediately following the accident. I think that people's immediate reaction is that first of all the accident shouldn't have happened. They say it happened because management and the Met Ed people themselves were not competent to operate the plant. I can't totally subscribe to that kind of thinking, but on the other hand I can appreciate how some

members of the public can feel that. I think you have to recognize that the NRC does not indiscriminately go about handing licenses out to any utility without assuring itself that the utility has the competent people to manage the organization. There were significant findings, as have been reported in many of the studies that have been done, that the depth of talent within the organization was perhaps not as deep as it could have been. But that is not so much unique to Met Ed; that exists in many utilities or many organizations. And that does not say that the company itself is incompetent. There are many good, technically sound people in the Met Ed organization. I think that's been demonstrated. It's a matter now of trying to restore the confidence in the people that this organization can in fact proceed to carry forth the recovery program. Met Ed has some very dedicated people.

I wanted to ask you about those accidental releases of krypton 85 on January 12 and 13 [1980]. Is the plant stable?

Let me say, that I don't particularly care for the phrase "accidental releases." I would characterize them as "events," that it was an event. We have said from the day of the accident, even until now, there will be releases from the plant. The fact that you had that release had nothing whatsoever to do with the stability of the reactor. It was a sampling system that is used to collect samples out of the containment atmosphere on a routine basis. So it had nothing whatsoever to do with the stability of the reactor. The reactor has been very stable ever since we went on to what we refer to as natural circulation, which occurred on April 28. You have to recognize that in any operating plant, there's going to be small releases. These releases are very insignificant in terms of dose consequence to the public. Putting it in perspective, the particular incident that did occur amounted to approxi-

mately 4 curies of activity. A normal operating plant will continually release on a monthly basis about a thousand curies a month.

Certainly that small release did not in any way endanger the health and safety of the public. I think that the public must begin to recognize that you're going to have these small releases as part of the recovery program. There is no such thing as a zero-release plant. The public cannot grasp the concept that you're going to have releases from nuclear power plants.

If you go back and look at every environmental impact statement that the NRC has issued since 1971, we have always stated that there are normal releases from plants. We have quantized those releases, and if the public has not been aware of that, I guess there are two problems. One, we have not done our job in communicating that fully to the public; or the public is not taking advantage of reading the material that is presented to them and is available in the local documents room. It's never been a hidden fact. We have never tried to say that there was a zero-release plant. It's not the case. It's difficult in this area to do that because the people here have gone through a very traumatic experience. As I've said many times, in many talks I've given over the last year, that after an accident is not the time to tell people that the reactor—nuclear power—is safe. That's something we should have done years ago in building up an education program. I don't think it's too late. It just means that we have to work a little bit harder, and we're continually trying to do that.

A lot of farming people in the area are having problems with animals, and that seems to be consistent with the times of the releases.

I think that you can recognize that people who are not completely informed as to the potential health effect, both to themselves

and to other creatures, will latch on to blaming the accident on anything they can. I'm fully aware of this animal problem. I have discussed this with state officials and I would hope as a result of our discussions that they would develop some kind of a white paper, if you want to call it that, that discusses the problem and tries to make the public understand that there is no relationship between what they are seeing in animals and the releases. Because it just won't happen. At those very low-level releases, there is certainly no health effect on animals, but people have a tendency through their uncertainty about things to try to blame anything they can on the accident or releases from TMI. And I guess if I were in their position and not fully informed and not completely understanding what is going on, I would probably have the same reaction. But I can assure you that that is not the case, that there is no problem there, *it just does not exist.* It's a matter now to try to convince the people. It was of interest to me to find out that 7 percent of the calves born are born dead. I find that a very high figure, but that's—in general, 7 percent of them—that's statistically what it's been averaging.

There seems to be some kind of a general lack of information on a very basic level.

I think it's essential that those of us who are in this field, as regulators and state officials and utility operators and the press, try to educate the public as best we can to try to allay some of their concerns. We have to be careful we don't allow ourselves to get tied up in the emotions of the people. That doesn't mean that we should ignore them. I'm very sensitive to how the people feel. In fact, there isn't anybody in the NRC right now that has been here as long as I've been here, and I'm very, very aware of how the people feel. I try to do the best I can in listening to their concerns and transmitting their concerns to our people in Washington. I think that I have an obligation to not ignore.

The farther away you are from TMI, the less the problem is, and I think that a lot of people are reaching a point of complacency, thinking everything is okay and people are okay. Well, people are not okay up here. A lot of people have a sincere fear. It's not something they make up. It's a real fear. I've had people cry. I've listened to their emotions, and you know you can tell when people put something on. Now you have your intervenors and you have your activist group and certainly some of that is just, but they have always been against nuclear power for one reason or another, whether it's a lack of education or whether they just have a sincere dreaded fear of nuclear power. But I'm talking about the individual people who live in the community and in the surrounding communities. Many of these people are scared, and I think that the only thing that we can do is to go out and talk to

them, be as honest as we can, tell them what the information means.

The other thing is that the people hear bits and pieces of information, or the press does not convey accurately the information that is given to them, and I think they do a vital disservice to the public in doing that. For example, we have been for several months negotiating with the city of Lancaster and Met Ed on an agreement about discharging the waters from TMI. This was as a result of a lawsuit that the city of Lancaster brought against the NRC. We achieved an agreement, and in that agreement it said that no accident-generated water from Unit Two would be released from TMI for either a period of two years or until the NRC issued its environmental impact statement. Those were the primary conditions. The article came out in a Saturday paper from an AP story that said that the NRC agrees with the city of Lancaster that there shall be no more radioactive releases in liquid effluent from TMI. Well, that's not what the agreement said. We have continually had releases from TMI and we will continue to have releases from TMI. And as soon as I saw the article, I got hold of the newspapers and our own legal department and I told them, "Look, we have to correct this because if we don't correct it right away, then our credibility is going to go down." People are gonna find out we've had continuing releases. Well, naturally we're going to have continuing releases. The agreement never said that we're going to have no more releases. What I'm concerned about is that I don't want our credibility going down as a result of somebody in AP wanting to make a name for himself. That kind of reporting is bad. If the press wants to do us a service, report it the way we tell them. And I think the local media up here has been very, very good to us. At least to me they have been, anyway. But then, you know, I believe that we have to be honest. If the public doesn't have any confidence in what I say, who are they going to believe?

Now that we're just about a year away from the accident, it's been nicknamed the worst commercial accident in history. How bad really was it?

Certainly, in terms of what occurred, one has to characterize it by saying it was the worst nuclear accident that we have experienced. But if one puts it in its proper context—to classify the accident as a class-9 accident there are two conditions that have to be met. The first condition is that it must be a series of events that was not previously analyzed as part of the accident-sequence scenarios. Certainly within that context, you have to classify it as a class-9 accident, because it was not one of the accident scenarios. And then the second condition is the consequence of the accident. The consequence, of course, was more like a class-3 accident, in which the doses and the re-

leases, or the releases and the doses as a result of the releases, were rather inconsequential. I mean when you recognize that you did have a "serious" accident, the total dose to the public at the nearest site boundary was less than 100 millirems. That's a very small dose. I think the other thing is that people can characterize this as the most serious accident we ever had, but on the other hand, I don't think enough has been said about the more positive aspects of the accident, in that many of the systems that have been designed into these plants did indeed function. And they functioned as they were designed. You recognize that here you had a major release of radioactive material into the containment building and that activity still remains in there. It has not come out. The system was designed to do exactly that. We have continued to maintain the core in a very, very stable condition. The heat load today is not very much at all. Putting it in perspective, the amount of heat that remains in the core at the present time is equivalent to about eighteen hundred 100-watt bulbs. Now that's not very much heat. I mean, just picture yourself in a room with eighteen hundred 100-watt bulbs, and that's about the extent of your heat load and that heat load is decreasing every day.

We've always said that there's a probability of accidents. Nobody ever went around saying you're never going to have an accident. And I think we have fairly tried to characterize the consequences of these accidents. But maybe we didn't do enough to publicize and to educate people as to what these accidents are, what are the consequences of the accident, and to allay their concerns should they occur. Now, hindsight's better than foresight. It always is.

Let me ask just one more thing, because it came out in the paper and I've been wondering about it ever since. It said that the reactor came to within a half hour or an hour of a meltdown. Was that the case?

Oh, you mean the Rogovin Report. What the Rogovin Report was trying to say is that had certain actions not been initiated by the operators, you could have had a loss of water in the core and could have had a core meltdown in a period of thirty to sixty minutes. I think if you go back and read it very carefully, it didn't say per se that we were thirty minutes away from a core meltdown. It characterized it in such a way that had actions not been taken, had things not been done properly, within thirty to sixty minutes you could have had a core meltdown. I can postulate any kind of action you want to. I could "if" myself to death. If I didn't do this, if I didn't do that, we could have had it. That doesn't say we were that close to it. No, I don't believe that to be the case at all. That's my opinion. Now other people may have other opinions.

You know, people were very concerned

about an explosion, that the reactor was going to blow up. Well, when you really look at it, there you have a core sitting in a thick steel vessel, sitting inside a containment building that's concrete 3½ feet thick. I would have a hard time envisioning that thing blowing up and falling apart. I just can't envision that. Should you lose water, and we did lose water; should the core be uncovered for a period of time, part of the core was uncovered, not the whole core; there are systems that reestablish that water cover on the reactor. So the explosion was never a concern of mine. Having been here the evening of the hydrogen bubble problem, I was more concerned, and I know the staff people with us were, about the safety of the public because there was such a fear at that time that the thing was going to blow up, and people wanted to know if they should evacuate. Just consider trying to evacuate 200,000 people at one time. They probably would have killed themselves trying to get out. We were more afraid of that than the reactor itself. Most of us had confidence, I know I had a lot of confidence in our people who were managing the situation. And I've been in the business long enough to have a certain amount of confidence that these things were not going to occur. I think the public has to recognize, too, that the NRC people were trained. That's our jobs. On the other hand, we're

human beings. I have a family. I have children and I'm no hero; the last hero I met was a dead one. We cherish life as much as you or anybody else does. We just have a little more confidence in knowing what things can occur, so we don't have that same fear. I spent ten years at the National Reactor Testing Station in Idaho where we had at one time forty-eight reactors operating at one time. And I've been trained in emergency procedures and I've been involved in emergency situations, so I did not have the same type of fear. That doesn't mean I'm not scared, I can get scared just like the next guy does, but I was not scared that night from the standpoint of the reactor stability. I was scared about the public. I really was.

And that fear among the public is contagious?

It is. It gets back to the old thing about mob psychology. And that's dangerous. That's how the activist groups survive. You get somebody up there and you can build up the emotions of the people. You can instill either happiness or fear into them, depending on how you want to sway them. You know how people are when things occur; they want to grasp onto something, somebody, and they will reach out in total frustration and they'll believe things that if they were thinking rationally they would never do. But they're scared, so they're going to do it.

People in this area today, even when a fire siren goes off anymore, some of them are scared to death, as a result of the accident, the fire siren means something to them. It's going to take time to build up that confidence and make sure that the people are not fearful of it. I can appreciate how they feel; I live with them, day in and day out around the Middletown area. Very nice people. Very wonderful people. I've enjoyed the people very much. They've been very nice to me. But they do have a deep-seated fear in them. And it's just going to take time to work it out.

I guess the other thing that bothers me the most is that people will say they can't believe Met Ed. They can't believe the NRC. Now there's a new one says they don't believe the EPA, and they want to bring in another group to do the monitoring. You could bring in any group you want to, and eventually they're not going to believe them. 'Cause a certain number of people are only going to believe what they want to believe. They've made up their minds. They have made up their minds that there's radioactivity being released from that plant and that it's dangerous. So no matter what we say to them, they're not going to believe us. How many times have you heard people say, "I've got my mind made up. Don't confuse me with the facts." In many cases that's exactly what they've done.

36.

Willis Wolfe is a resident of New-berry Township, March 16, 1980

This area is referred to as Newberry Township. We're within a tenth of a mile or so of three miles from the towers, as the crow flies.

How long have you lived here?

My parents moved to Pennsylvania when I was four, from Kansas, and I've lived in this area ever since. My wife, too; she was born in Harrisburg. We've lived in this house for the past fifteen years.

You told me earlier that you built this house yourself. Are you a contractor?

No, when I built the house, I was working for the Railway Express Company. I just took a blank sheet of paper and started to draw up a plan and built this house while I was still working for the Express. When we bought the lot, it was just like a jungle. There had been trees dropped when the roads were made, and you couldn't even walk across the land it was so filled with undergrowth. We have an acre and we cleared every inch of that land ourselves, but it consumed two years of our lives to get the house. This is our home and we worked hard to get it. When we left, at the time of the accident, we didn't know if we'd ever be able to come back. We were told that if there was a meltdown, the place would be sealed off and nobody would be allowed in for a thousand years, and everything we left behind was gone forever. All our investment of time and money. Everything.

When did you leave?

We didn't leave until Sunday. We didn't realize that there was that much of a problem on Wednesday; and Thursday things seemed to stabilize. Then on Friday we had our CB scanner on and we were monitoring the police channel. They were telling the state police to get into action, and the police were to notify the TV stations and to tell the people to stay indoors, so we learned about that release even before the radio and TV stations found out. We could pick up communications between the state police cars, talking to each other, and they were being instructed to go into Middletown to Three Mile Island. They did not say why, but everything was being directed for them to converge in that area. This indicated to me a problem. After the worst had happened, at least we thought it was the worst had happened, then it started to leak out. By that time we realized if there was any contamination, which there already had been, we were already contaminated.

I keep hearing over and over that Met Ed doesn't want the public to have the truth,

that they feel people couldn't handle it and would not know what to do.

That is the thing that I resent most vehemently, that there are those who criticize the media for putting out false information. In retrospect, had it not been for the media, we would not have known about anything. They are the ones that helped to save us and inform us of the seriousness of the situation. So the press and the media should be commended rather than criticized, because they worked far above and beyond the tour of duty, you might say. "Keep the people in the dark; don't admit." That philosophy goes back to President Eisenhower's time, when they were making the atomic tests out in Utah. He said, "Don't tell the people," and that philosophy comes right on down. The NRC, the government agencies and bureaucracies involved with the nuclear industry are following that pattern: Don't admit to the people. Don't let them know. But there have been documents, information released.

I see you have quite a collection of clippings there.

Yes. Listen to this. Here's an article from the York *Daily Record*, on June 19, 1979, by Jim Hall: "You Can Move GPU Tells Us" is the headline. "'People who don't like the reopening of Three Mile Island Unit One later this year can move somewhere else,' the president of the company owning TMI said Monday.

"Herman Dieckamp of the General Public Utilities Corporation, parent company of the Metropolitan Edison Company, made the statement during a press conference apparently intended to launch a campaign to regain the public trust in Met Ed and TMI.

"Asked what the company would do if its campaign failed, Dieckamp said, 'If a given individual finds reopening TMI One unacceptable, then he has the freedom to move, to change something.' Dieckamp said he wouldn't know how to deal with civil disobedience, rumored to be planned for the reopening; but as for customers who refuse to pay the recent increase granted Met Ed by the Public Utility Commission, 'We will use the same course as before the accident.'

"Before the company dumps any of some 750,000 gallons of contaminated water in TMI into the Susquehanna River, Dieckamp promised, 'It will be as pure as most of the drinking water in this country. If it's necessary to convince the public, I'll drink a glass of it before it goes in the river,' he said.

"'I can understand why people are upset, why they feel let down, left in the lurch. I can understand local hostility, but the best approach is not for us just to go away, but to educate the public as best we can. A lot of the psychological impact on the public stems from unknowledge rather than what really happened.'

"'It's a serious matter,' Dieckamp said, but he contended the 'real seriousness of the matter is if the company goes bankrupt, you haven't saved the customer any money. The next service is going to get the same revenues. If we destroy the confidence of sources of capital, we won't find people willing to make available their money to serve the longterm needs of the customer.'"

This incident was recorded after the TMI accident and was published in the Harrisburg *Patriot*, Wednesday, April 18, 1979. "Harold Denton, director of the NRC's office of Nuclear Reactor Regulation said at a news conference at Middletown Bureau Hall that the increases in the iodine release rates 'seem to coincide' with the replacing of charcoal filters at the plant. 'When we looked into the status of the filter replacement activity, we found that twenty filters had been removed, but no replacements had been put in. So there was a potential for a bypass leakage through the filter space getting out without being filtered. All of the twenty filters have since been replaced, and, in the future, filters will be replaced as soon as old ones are removed. But the lack of filters has not been confirmed as a source of the iodine gas emissions.'"

Well, if they were put in there to filter the iodine, and they are not there, one can only conclude that the absence was somebody's negligence, or worse.

"Failure to replace the filters on a one-to-one basis 'was probably intentional' on the part of Metropolitan Edison Company. Denton said, 'Apparently they elected for some reason to remove the old filters, bag them, and box them and had not put any in up to about midnight Monday, which was April 16. Sometime during the night, as a result of our inquiries in this area and their efforts, they did replace filters in all the empty slots.'"

I think they did it because they felt they could do the job fastest that way. If the dampers on the seal were really rightly closed, both the inlet and output dampers, and if there was no leakage, it shouldn't really matter which way you do it. Sloppy.

There is considerable material in the *Field and Stream* December 1979 issue, but the part that impresses me more profoundly than anything else is the one relating to waste. Even without putting more nuclear power plants than those already scheduled into service, the United States alone would generate 1 billion cubic feet of radioactive waste during the next twenty years; enough to cover a four-lane coast-to-coast highway 1 foot deep. We still don't know where to put the poisons we've already generated, and some of it dates back to the manufacture of nuclear weapons in the 1940s. Now there is considerably more.

This article appeared in the *Evening News*, Harrisburg, Tuesday, March 4, 1980: "UPI dateline, Washington. The Environmental Action Foundation has accused the nuclear industry of using rigged statistics to show that nuclear-generated electricity is cheaper than power produced with coal. The foundation, citing a study by New York economist Charles Komonoff, said the Atomic Industrial Forum had excluded twelve of the fourteen costliest nuclear reactors as well as the two largest, most efficient coal-burning utilities from its most recent cost comparison. 'Nuclear power was actually 7 percent more expensive than coal power in 1978, not 34 percent cheaper, as asserted by the Atomic Industrial Form.' The bias shown by the Atomic Industrial Forum points up the nuclear industry's tendency to manipulate data to portray nuclear power in an unjustifiably favorable light. The forum, the main nuclear industry trade group, last May released a widely published survey of 1978 utility power costs. Komonoff's study, 'The Power Propaganda,' found the survey used costs of just thirty-nine of sixty commercial reactors. Among the twenty-one omitted were all but two of the fourteen costing the most to build, and six of the seven with the worst 1978 performance records. The average generating cost for the excluded reactors was 70 percent higher than the surveyed units, it said."

So they are selective in the information they want to put out to prove their points, and they regard the people as imbeciles. You don't have to go to college to see through that.

[*Willis's wife, Ruth*]: Watch your blood pressure now.

You know, they say that the pension funds are always invested in some way, and the State Employees Pension Fund has invested a lot in utilities. If Met Ed goes broke, then that investment will reduce the amount in the state's pension fund. They can't risk that loss, so when it comes to going to the capitol, they are all on the side of Met Ed to protect their pension fund. This is what we've been told.

How much money is involved?

I have no idea, but it's a lot, I would imagine. If you were at the meeting the other night at Goldsboro, then you heard me tell about this one.

Where's this from?

The Patriot, Harrisburg, June 21, 1979. "Washington Merry-Go-Round by Jack Anderson. We have uncovered evidence from the government's own files that makes it clear that atomic safety experts were worried about the possibility of hydrogen gas problems at Three Mile Island Nuclear Generating Station Unit Two a decade ago, even before the first concrete was poured for the cooling towers' foundation. It is also clear from the near-catastrophe last March

that the response and the expressed fears of the experts was a bureaucratic solution, one that looks good on paper but was proved wholly inadequate. Before a construction permit could be issued for the Three Mile Island plant, safety experts of the AEC (predecessor of the NRC) made a required evaluation of the design plans. Their report, dated September 5, 1969, was both candid and explicit. It reads: 'Hydrogen gas would be produced as a consequence of loss-of-coolant accident.' The report warned, 'We are currently reviewing the problem of hydrogen production and several methods for control of the hydrogen concentration for all reactors, and we have not yet established a method which will be acceptable.' Having posed the problem, while noting that they didn't have an answer to it, the safety officials almost incredibly decided it was okay to let things slide. It would be years before the plant would be in operation, so the AEC figured that something will turn up to solve the hydrogen gas problems."

Here's some more from the same article. "'Even the plant's emergency system, designed to render excess hydrogen harmless, was not hooked up,' the NRC's Dr. Roger Mattson told our asscciate Howard Rosenberg. 'The government had to fly planeloads of lead bricks in as shields before the emergency system of two hydrogen recombiners could be made operational. One of the two recombiners subsequently broke down.'"

They flew in these bricks during the accident?

Yeah, I picked that up on the CB radio. I was following these planes that were given clearance to land at the airport and then truck it over to the plant. I was listening to all of that on the scanner.

What were they saying?

They described them; said they were lead bricks and the highway patrol and state police were escorting the vehicles into the plant from the airport. Of course I could pick that up on the scanner. I knew what they were moving in but I didn't know why or what. Now it's out. The article goes on: "Incredible as it may seem, the NRC's advisory committee on reactor safeguards assured Congress in January of 1978 that hydrogen control was one of a number of inherent problems that had been resolved. But in the particular jargon of bureaucracy, 'resolved' in no way means the same as 'solved.' As a memo accompanying the NRC report explained, 'In some cases an item has been resolved in an administrative sense'; in other words, the problem has been resolved only on paper, not at the reactors where it counts. Footnote: Though the official explanation that the hydrogen problem popped out of a clear blue sky is dem-

onstrably spurious, federal officials can have no such excuse now, after Three Mile Island. Mattson assured us the problem is being reevaluated."

The other thing that makes me upset is the kind of testimony GPU and Met Ed are presenting to the Public Utility Commission to justify their astronomical expense, that they need rate increases; customers are expected to pay higher rates so that they can prove to the banks that they are viable—all that jargon.

Were you here before the nuclear plant was built?

Oh yeah.

Do you remember as it was going up your feeling about it and whether there was any concern among the community?

People were not aware, including myself. Had we known of the consequences, the potential, we wouldn't have moved here. We wouldn't have built here. We wouldn't be living here. They built it and did not reveal the truth. They did not tell what we now know. It was a deep dark secret. There was an Iron Curtain process; they talk about Russia, but we've got to be more scared of our own bureaucrats than we do of Russia. We know that Russia can't be trusted. We know that they are sneaky. We trusted our own country, but not any more. We can't trust our own politicians.

I first lost my temper over this at the krypton hearings, within the last two weeks. I asked them to tell me the density of krypton 85, and he had to stop and think: "Maybe three or four times heavier than air." Then I said, "What is the density of air?" and he didn't know. I said, "But you do admit that the krypton 85 is three to four times heavier than air?" He agreed. So I asked him, "How do you propose to keep the krypton suspended? If it's three times heavier than air, how do you keep it suspended so that it doesn't come back to earth?" "Well," he said, "the wind will take it away, and it will spread out and just disappear." I said, "It's gotta come back to some place, somewhere. It does not stay up indefinitely." He could not answer that. It's ridiculous.

What do you think the outcome of all this is going to be? Do you think the people have a chance of keeping it closed?

No, I think down there is a good example. They are sitting there letting the people get it off their chests. They know what they are going to do, and they are going to do it, come hell or high water. We don't count for anything really. Their minds are made up at that plant. The decision has been predetermined, and they are just letting us hold these meetings, get together and get it off our chest.

37.

Julius S. Kassovic teaches Folklore at Dickinson College in Carlisle, twenty-three miles west of Three Mile Island. He and his fellow researchers are preparing the results of their findings for publication. Carlisle, March 4, 1980

The Three Mile Island crisis was for all of us a nuclear nightmare; but for me it was also, in a perverse way, a folklorist's dream. As the crisis began playing itself out, I noticed the emergence of a tremendous amount of humor, from bad puns to elaborate jokes, that arose from the very problems that terrorized us. I had never before been in a situation of public crisis like this,

and in looking back on my own behavior during the situation I am frankly amazed. The Mr. Hyde in me, my social-scientist self, apparently emerged early, and stayed late. My everyday self, meek and mild mannered, apparently evacuated. I was overpowered by an irrational need to study the reactions of the people around me.

None of us had ever been disaster-researchers before. We did this project because this was an unprecedented situation, a crisis unlike any other. It was confusion that made people so upset—they didn't know what the effects of the accident would be. These people have gone through floods. They had hurricane Agnes here in 1972, and other before that; and almost all said they would rather go through another flood than this type of crisis. With a flood at least you can see the water coming up. You know what the danger is, and you know what you have to do. But with this, over and over again, in both unconscious, imagi-

native material and point blank outright, people said, "I'm afraid because I can't see it."

Was your research limited to Carlisle?

Yes. We worked in Carlisle because Carlisle is ours; we live here. We figured also that nobody ever studies the outskirts of a disaster, they always study the center area, the people who are really hit. This is why we wanted to study an area on the very edge of the crisis area, to find out what the difference is between living at Ground Zero and living at Ground Zero plus twenty miles.

Who made up this research team that you are referring to?

There were four of us: my wife, Melissa, and I, who are in Anthropology and Folklore; Lonna Malmsheimer in American Studies; and Dan Bechtel in Religion. We all agreed to go out and study our own specialties, so we made up a questionnaire that

123

reflected our interests and got about twenty-five students to work with us. I was interested in humor, Melissa was concerned with perceived threat to health, Professor Malmsheimer was interested in imaginative fantasy materials, and Professor Bechtel was interested in religious reactions and responses.

And what were some of the results of your research into the humor of it it?

Well, let me begin first by quoting humorist Max Eastman, who noted in his book *Enjoyment of Laughter* (1936) that "In everything that we do perceive as funny there is an element which, if we were serious and sufficiently sensitive, and sufficiently concerned, would be unpleasant." The jokes started out slowly, because information about the events at TMI came out only piecemeal, and nobody knew what was going on. The people only knew that *something* was going on, and it was growing more and more dangerous. And as they got the idea in Carlisle that it was growing more and more dangerous, right behind the events came the jokes. At the beginning it was just a small bundle of witticisms like "My you're radiant today" or "We'll never need nightlights again." Some of the jokes had a less optimistic outlook, like "My mind is in a meltdown, I just can't think about it," "Armageddon outta here," or "Do you know what the five-day forecast for Harrisburg is?"

No. What?

"Two days."

Any others?

"What melts on the ground and not in your hand?"

I don't know, what?

"Hershey, Pennsylvania."

Did these kinds of jokes keep on coming throughout the accident?

That's the interesting point because at the height of the crisis, when people could no longer tell the diference between the crazy caricatures they had built up in the jokes and what was becoming actually possible, they got scared and the jokes stopped. But not everyone stopped telling the jokes at the same time because people perceived the height of the crisis at different rates. So you had some people who were still telling jokes, which were being received coldly by people who couldn't tell them anymore, saying, "This is sick. I don't want to hear it. This is disgusting. How can you joke at a time like this?" These were the same people who had themselves been joking only a few hours earlier. With the hydrogen bubble scare, the jokes practically ceased. When the bubble began to go down, people were able to relax a little, and again they began to laugh at the jokes they couldn't laugh at before.

Of all the caricatures that you encountered, which were the craziest?

I'd say it would be the "flipper-baby" jokes. A flipper-baby is a congenitally deformed baby, one with little flipperlike arms. Let me caution you that these flipper-baby jokes never evoke laughter when I present my paper on this material; they're just too horrible. People do laugh, but as soon as they think about it, they catch themselves and say, "This is sick. This is horrible." And it *is* sick and horrible. That's the whole reason I was studying it—because people were upset and afraid, and they were using these jokes to allay their fears. As Freud once noted, "There is no doubt that the essence of humor is that one spares oneself the affects to which the situation would normally give rise, and dismisses the possibility of such expressions of emotion with a jest," or, as the local jokers during the crisis told me, "We have to tell jokes to break the tension, otherwise we'd go nuts!" So I was not surprised to find the prevailing style of expession during the TMI accident to be the "gallows humor." The flipper-baby jokes were the most abundant and complex jokes around the student community.

Can you give any examples of these jokes?

Okay, here are a few:
What's red and has a hundred flippers? Answer: The maternity ward in Harrisburg!

Just think about introducing your family to the boss someday, "This is my wife, and that's my kid over there in the aquarium."

Do you know what the flipper-baby soul-brother handshake is? Answer: Gimme one.

These jokes were told by students who, it is important to remember, are contemporaries of the tragic thalidomide babies, and many of them reported seeing television documentaries on them since childhood. Older people were generally disgusted with these jokes, and so were the students, on second thought, or if they told them to someone who knew a deformed person or had a deformed sibling. One cafeteria table was completely silenced by that kind of occurrence. It might seem strange to maintain that such gross caricatures of reality are a way of coping with reality, but the exaggeration is the point. People realized that it isn't *that* bad. Knowing that it's not *that* bad makes you feel better about your own situation—even when you still don't like it. Did you hear that right during the crisis, people in Middletown were putting up big sheets on their porches that read. "We survived TMI"? They really didn't know if they had survived it or not because they were still right in the middle of it; but they'd already put up "We survived." In a way that's what's going on with the jokes too. They're people's way of saying, 'I'm making it. I'm going to be all right." It's a macho kind of thing, you know; laugh in the face of adversity. You have to laugh, or else you'd cry.

You were saying earlier that Professor Malmsheimer was collecting "imaginative and fantasy materials." How is her research different from yours?

Professor Malmsheimer was interested in how people drew on past experiences, their cultural inventory, for clues on how to think about this crisis. One thing that she discovered was that people were singing songs at this time to themselves, unconsciously. They were humming or whistling melodies like "Waltzing Matilda" from the movie *On the Beach,* "Dust in the Wind," "Accidents Will Happen," or "Where Have All the Flowers Gone?" And I, for instance, found myself—and I could hardly believe it—but I was in the shower, (before Professor Malmsheimer even told me what she was doing), and I was singing in the shower, as people always do; and you know the song "Georgia on My Mind"? Well, I had substituted the word "fallout" for "Georgia," and I was singing away: "Fallout, fallout on my mind, fallout all day long." So I was doing the same thing everyone else was. This is one reaction people were connecting to, this type of thing in popular culture in the songs. She found that people were also thinking of the movies, like *On The Beach, Panic in the Year Zero, The Swarm,* and especially Japanese monster movies, where things were irradiated and grew huge. She was also collecting dreams.

Was there ever any doubt in your minds about staying in the area as you were doing the research?

We were ready to leave a number of times because we didn't know what was going on. And what happened to us was that, in a way, we sublimated our own fears and anxieties by studying the things that were going on all around us. In the same way people were getting rid of their anxieties by talking to us, we were working out ours by collecting and analyzing theirs. However, after about two months of interviewing, I couldn't stand it any more, and I finally got one of our coworkers and sat down with her and made here interview me. Because up to that point we had figured, well, we can't be interviewed because we're the ones who made it up. We're too contaminated by all of this other information, and anything we said would not be valid. But at that point I didn't care if it would be valid or not, I just wanted to get it off my chest. So I participated in our own project.

Was it a long interview?

Yes. I went forty-five minutes on the first question.

One final question. Have you discovered anything unique developing out of the singular quality of the Three Mile Island accident?

As you are growing up, you pass through a series of crises, your own personal crises and crises in a larger social context, ones that affect the entire nation. And it seems to us that the first major crisis that you go through when you're a teenager, when you're first really aware of what's going on in the world and can understand it, is a very important one because you fix on it; it becomes a reference point that provides you with a method for shaping current crises in terms of the past. For example, we noticed quite a difference between the way younger people and older people perceived the accident. The older people, who had successfully passed through the depression or Pearl Harbor and the war, had a fairly good feeling about what was going on here at TMI.

They felt things would work themselves out all right because they had already been through Pearl Harbor or the depression, and it had worked out all right then; and now this was another one. But the younger kids, who were going to school here, what crisis had they already gone through? Vietnam and Watergate—notorious debacles. So their impression of what was possible, of what might still happen here, was much worse; they had a greater distrust of the situation than the older people.

Now for many of the kids who went through TMI and stayed here, or even evacuated for that matter, this was their first major crisis, and it probably was a very important event in their lives. It may well be *the* crisis that they will refer back to. I found it interesting that the symbols we had formerly inherited to deal with our fears during this were the symbols of Hiroshima and the bomb, which are very unsettling images, and made it difficult for the people to accept what was happening to them. Those I talked to who knew there was going to be no explosion, who knew that everything was going to be all right consciously, unconsciously had dreams, thoughts, and daydreams about areas of devastation they wouldn't be able to return to for thirty years.

But now these symbols have been changed. It is from this event that we have gotten a new symbol for this type of disaster, for the commercial nuclear accident. Obviously it's the TMI cooling towers. The cooling tower is a powerful new symbol.

Afterword

I had to catch my breath when I caught sight of that first headline from Three Mile Island: "Nuke Leak Out of Control." Could it really be happening? The alarms and reports that followed, in and out of that whole week, left little room for doubt. Sudden confirmation from the synchronous release of *China Syndrome* tinged the air with surrealism and mixed this story out of Middletown with a million fantasies. As the worst of it and the best of it subsided, and the reactor was eased into a cold shutdown mode just this side of the abyss, the event faded from public view, superseded by fighting at gas pumps and trouble in Iran. But two images lingered after things calmed down, as they linger still: the vision of a vast and misty concrete tumor on an island in the Susquehanna and, all around the island, like a broken wreath of foam, the thousands of living souls who had been pulled toward the plant and locked into its orbit—the people of Three Mile Island. From the very start I had been eager to hear from these people, to read their faces, and to arrive at something approaching the truth of what they had been through. It seemed unaccountably important.

Historic events like this that affect the lives of so many sometimes condense themselves, in the mind's eye, into a single human countenance; and although I knew that such a face was here, I could not sense its contours forming in the coverage of the crisis. This troubled me. The news reports that followed, few would argue, had been remarkable. Hundreds of journalists from around the globe had converged upon the plant; this time there had clearly been the smell of blood. But what they found upon arrival had been maddeningly mysterious: a disaster with no bodies, an engineering crisis that baffled teams of engineers; emissions of invisible poisons that helicopters and ground monitors had trouble keeping track of, and required learning a new language before they could be reported in the press; and an unplanned evacuation that could at any moment be either cancelled or its radius extended to impossible parameters. Yet grave as these developments appeared, they were merely the advance guard to a more awesome, unthinkable prospect at the back of many minds: breach of containment. The reporters, honed on Watergate, asked hard questions, wrested facts from officials, stayed on the story till it peaked, then left. Their accounts dramatized the fear, the errors, core damage, the infernal mysteries of the releases, the disaster. But somehow in the excitement they had missed—the people.

In May, five weeks after the accident had been declared over, I took my first train to Middletown. I was nervous, but not in a rush. It was not news I was after; I was looking to enter into the record portraits of a people—and of a place—that would permit these people to speak out openly, in detail, to a world that had met them only once—in the dark, under conditions dense and alarming to the point of madness—and had then lost track of who they were. I was thinking more of Curtis and Atget than of Woodward and Bernstein.

The first answers I got to my questions on the street made me feel the accident had happened, not recently, but in some ancient time. When I asked more questions I found that hardly two people could agree about what in fact had taken place: the facts, the estimates based upon the facts, and the assessment of the impact of the estimates based upon the facts were all up for grabs. Plant workers were not allowed to discuss the accident with nonpersonnel; families were divided over it; and people who did not fight before were fighting one another now because of it.

I also quickly learned that this famous accident was far from over. Local media responded regularly with circumspect alarm to the staggered planned releases and the unplanned leaks. Tales of abnormalities among farm animals were in continuous circulation, and, close behind, reports of thyroid problems in newborn babies, and of a rising infant mortality rate that no one wanted to link with the event. On and off for ten days in January 1980 citizens of Goldsboro—using up to five separate radiation monitors—were getting incredibly high readings (200 millirems to 2 rems per hour) on the river bank near the plant that no one from the state, utility, or the NRC could explain. At town meetings held to discuss the venting of the krypton 85, the terrors of the early days started breaking out again and I watched a fierce and flinty anger that had been there all along growing stronger, taking on the scope of something monumental.

But whenever I left the area, nothing I had witnessed seemed to reach beyond a fifty-mile radius of the plant. Thinking back to when the accident occurred, I recalled how people hundreds of miles out had caught the sense of what was happening much more quickly than those living near the site, and had often been the first to tell them what was going on. But once the "transient" had passed, it became the people in the center who were full of terrifying news, while those outside the radius had gone back to living in an atmosphere of calm.

It dawned upon me early that the real wild card in the deck was the invisibility. Because the accident had left appearances intact, individuals seeking compensation or protection were burdened with having to prove that something was happening to them. Because the radionuclides and their impact went unseen, language models were needed to describe them; but officials who based analogies for low-level radiation on "airplane trips to Denver," "cars on the freeway," and "smoking cigarettes" were eyed with profound distrust by those who felt they should be hearing something altogether different. The crippled reactor was technically visible, but no human or mechanical eye could get close enough to see it. The mass evacuation it triggered had clearly left its mark on the finances and emotions of everyone involved, but afterwards many questioned how much of it was justified, and how much of it an overreaction? If it was a catastrophe, was it still with us, or was it over. The invisibility kept the question open and put protestors and defenders alike into a kind of netherworld, where perception was as much an issue as the facts, and where, like Alice's adventures in Wonderland, the play of the mind more often than not became the main event. An invisible disaster, this "nuclear shot heard 'round the world"—and once it quieted down and settled in, it could become as delicate and fleeting as a gilded butterfly.

Capturing this in photographs had been a challenge from the start. No Vietnam here, and no Minamata exactly either, and not a Watergate, although more than trace elements of these events were present. There was something extra here—something lambent, unnameable, and profound that would come through the information I was getting, but was not the information, that could become imperious and kaleidoscopic in a twinkling, then withdraw, leaving people furious and exhausted, but with little other trace upon the surfaces of everyday affairs.

I undertook to make this book because the moment in history that Three Mile Island represents brought keenly into focus my concerns for people, for the environment, and for the elusive workings of the human mind. I found out in the process that Three Mile Island is a disaster that behaves unlike any other, that it will be with us for a long time to come, and that it will get worse. Let the first year of the event and of what the people said and felt and looked like in it be entered into the record.

Robert Del Tredici
June 1980